The Synergy of Film and Music

Sight and Sound in Five Hollywood Films

Peter Rothbart

THE SCARECROW PRESS, INC.
Lanham • Toronto • Plymouth, UK
2013

Published by Scarecrow Press, Inc.
A wholly owned subsidiary of The Rowman & Littlefield Publishing Group, Inc.
4501 Forbes Boulevard, Suite 200, Lanham, Maryland 20706
www.rowman.com

10 Thornbury Road, Plymouth PL6 7PP, United Kingdom

British Library Cataloguing in Publication Information Available

Library of Congress Cataloging-in-Publication Data

Rothbart, Peter.
  The synergy of film and music : sight and sound in five Hollywood films / Peter Rothbart.
    p. cm.
  Includes bibliographical references and index.
  ISBN 978-0-8108-8758-9 (cloth : alk. paper) — ISBN 978-0-8108-8759-6 (pbk. : alk. paper) — ISBN
978-0-8108-8760-2 (ebook) 1. Motion picture music—United States—History and criticism. 2. Motion
pictures—Sound effects. I. Title.
  ML2075.R67 2013
  781.5'420973—dc23   2012033467

∞™ The paper used in this publication meets the minimum requirements of American
National Standard for Information Sciences—Permanence of Paper for Printed Library
Materials, ANSI/NISO Z39.48-1992.

Printed in the United States of America

For my parents, Jane and David, who gave me the tools,

For my wife, Linda, who gives me the reason,

For my son, Jason, who has surpassed my dreams,
and his wife, Debora, who showed him how,

For my granddaughter, Tia, who surprises us all

Contents

Acknowledgments

Many deep thanks to my wife, Linda, for her quiet and unwavering support and for knowing when to pull and when to push me; to my parents, Jane and David, who gave me the tools . . . all of them; to my son, Jason, who will surpass me and may already have; to Debora, who powers Jason and therefore us to new heights; to Tia, who does not yet know how much she inspires; and to my brothers, Jon and Larry, who provide constant love as well as cajolery.

Thanks also to Dean Art Ostrander, who displayed patience and confidence that allowed me to experiment and follow my instincts, though they did not follow the traditional academic path, and to Ithaca College for providing research and travel grants. Belated thanks to Stephen Landesman, my first real editor, who taught me that nobility and quality newspaper work can coexist.

Professional thanks to John Corigliano for generously loaning his score to *Altered States* to a naïve but enthusiastic doctoral student in search of a thesis topic; to Lenny Bernstein, who encouraged an insecure nineteen-year-old bassoonist playing *West Side Story* at Harvard to *go pro*; and to his friend and my teacher, Sandy Sharoff, who pushed me to release the music within.

And finally, thanks to the professionals at DreamWorks, the Library of Congress Music Division, the Columbia University Rare Books and Manuscripts Room, and JoAnn Kane Music Services, who so generously gave of their time and resources and thereby recognized the importance of educating the public about what they do.

COPYRIGHT PERMISSIONS

Introduction

The Synergy of Film and Music: Sight and Sound in Five Hollywood Films examines how music is used in general release movies to advance the plot, underscore character development, and enhance the action and drama onscreen. It is written to be an easy reading, informative, and nontechnical guide for anyone interested in gaining a deeper appreciation of film through an increased awareness of the role of music. I hope to illuminate the relationship between the multifarious elements of cinema: dialog, sound effects, drama, screenwriting, costuming, set design, editing, cinematography, and music. All of these elements combine to create a successful film.

I will avoid, as much as possible, a technical, historical, or theoretical approach so that the average filmgoer can more fully understand and appreciate the role and impact of film music, without getting too bogged down in esoteric theories, technical tricks, and historical anecdotes that can deflect the filmgoer from the experience of the film itself. After a few introductory chapters, I will do this by looking at the use of music in five select films.

As is the case with other film music analysts, I will explore the larger narrative and psychological themes of the film, especially when they are supported and revealed by the music. But I will use a much more *nuts-and-bolts* approach, focusing on musical and visual moments in detail, as would composers, sound designers, music editors, mixers, and directors as they collaborate to develop the film. By focusing on these details, I hope that the reader will more fully appreciate how the story line is supported (and enhanced) by the aesthetic, syntactic, stylistic, and technical decisions made by the composer, music editor, sound designer, and the director, among others.

Toward this end, the margins of each page of analysis contain timecode markings that the reader can use to correlate my text with exact moments, down to the second, within the film. This way, you may see and hear exactly what is under discussion at that moment. This will be demonstrated throughout the book by linking the timecodes in the book margins with the commercially available DVDs of the films. More on how to use this book will be discussed in a moment.

By describing what is happening aurally, and revealing its relationship to the visual image and all of its elements, including the screenplay, I hope to raise the readers'/viewers' awareness of all of these elements and their synergistic interactions so that they can then begin to interpret the film's intent and/or message and further deepen their filmic experience.

The descriptive nature of the five film analyses included here is designed to highlight the aural and visual activity, to bring them forward into your consciousness. I hope that this more organic or holistic approach to film music understanding will begin to rectify previous analytic approaches that Caryl Flinn describes as "limited by a number of methodological and conceptual problems. Most prominent among them is an aesthetic and formalist tendency that treats film music as a discrete, autonomous artefact. Scores are discussed outside of their cinematic context . . . this approach will often overlook how the score interacts with other facets of the cinema (concerns of narrative, editing, or genre, as well as the psychological, social and ideological factors of film consumption)."[1]

I will call attention to certain visual/musical events as they occur, sometimes with an explanation of how they relate to other musical or visual moments in the film, sometimes by just highlighting their presence. Certainly one aspect of filmgoing is the pleasure of the experience and perception itself, rather than the interpretation. I will try to strike a balance between the two, heightened perception and interpretation, in each of the ensuing chapters.

I have chosen five films with an eye and ear toward examining, in depth, the role and use of music in each film. Claudia Gorbman stated in her seminal work, *Unheard Melodies: Narrative Film Music*, that "although writers on film music frequently allude to specific parts of scores, exhaustive analyses of an entire score and its narrative functioning have been rare."[2] My intention is to, as Gorbman advocates for, account for virtually every musical cue in each film I've selected, discussing its placement, intention, and context in a linear fashion so that the reader can see how the music works with all of the elements of film to enhance and direct the narrative forward.

The Synergy of Film and Music: Sight and Sound in Five Hollywood Films, therefore, goes beyond past analytic adventures, extending and enhancing these intellectual endeavors by focusing on a few select films, examining them in great detail from beginning to end, so you can experience the continuity of a film's music rather than just a few highlighted moments. We can more fully appreciate the larger picture if we dissect the details and see how their construction and manifestation contributes to the film as a whole. We are exploring all of the cues in a few films, with the intention that, once having internalized this book, you will be able to extrapolate the ideas presented here to your own selected filmgoing experiences. By carefully choosing a few films to explore in their entirety, we can more fully grasp the influence of music on a film, any film.

The great film composer Max Steiner stated that "the toughest thing for a film composer to know is where to start, where to end; that is, how to place your music."[3] To a large extent, that is what this book is about. By examining a film linearly, from beginning to end, on its own merits rather than adopting a more comparative approach so often used in film analysis, I hope to get to the guts of Steiner's statement. I will specifically look at why the composer or director may have chosen to begin the music at a specific moment in the narrative, and why they ended it when they did. In the process, I will explore *why* music was used at a particular point, as well as *why* that specific style or genre of music was married to *that* sequence in the film. This way, *The Synergy of Film and Music: Sight and Sound in Five Hollywood Films* can empower you to literally read and listen to a film while you watch it; encouraging you toward an understanding of how the various elements of the film coalesce at a specific point to convey the narrative as intentioned by the film's creators.

This book, therefore, is written with certain readers in mind. For the film enthusiast, this book can be an introduction to how music is used in film, regardless of whether you read or are formally trained in music or not. For the professional, preprofessional, or anyone directly involved in the process of making films, this book can assist you in making more informed decisions regarding which music to use and when and why.

Finally, film and film music classes and discussion groups will find this a helpful preliminary or even supplementary text that can sensitize your ears and minds to recognize the importance of musical entrances and exits, musical techniques, and characteristics. This will later allow you to more fully focus on theoretical and philosophical strains of thought that form the basis of so much film theory and criticism.

NOTES

1. Caryl Flinn, *Strains of Utopia: Gender, Nostalgia, and Hollywood Film Music* (Princeton: Princeton University Press, 1992), 4.

2. Claudia Gorbman, *Unheard Melodies: Narrative Film Music* (Bloomington: Indiana University Press, 1987), 115–16.

3. Max Steiner, "Music Director," in *The Real Tinsel*, ed. Bernard Rosenberg and Harry Silverstein (London: Macmillan, 1970), 393.

How to Use This Book

The power of this book lies not only in its content but also in linking the written discussion on the page to the exact moment it is visualized onscreen. By using the timecode in the margins of each page, it is possible to link specific events in the film under discussion to the precise commentary in the text, down to the second.

The numbers in the margins of this book are timecodes from the commercially available DVDs listed below. The DVD timecode remains constant from player to player (and computer to computer), thus allowing the detailed discussion that is the heart of this book. I would suggest that you watch the film in its entirety first. Then, using your DVD controls, you can forward, rewind, slow, replay, and even stop-frame the scene under discussion, allowing you the full benefit of this book. Finally, enjoy the film in its entirety sometime in the future to fully appreciate the craftsmanship and artistry of its creative visionaries.

DVDS REFERENCED THROUGHOUT THIS BOOK

Altered States—Warner Bros., 11076, ISBN 0-7907-3912-7
American Beauty—DreamWorks, 85382, ISBN 0-7832-4123-2
Empire of the Sun—Warner Bros., 11753, ISBN 0-7907-6165-3
Psycho—Universal, 20251, ISBN 0-7832-2584-9
West Side Story—MGM Special Edition, Collector's Set, ISBN 0-7928-5501-9

The Many Roles of Music in Film

Music in a general release dramatic film serves many different functions. Good film music supports the story, and a skillfully composed musical cue can serve both technical and aesthetic functions. A great cue simultaneously serves many of the roles described below. A good film composer will use a variety of compositional tools and techniques, as well as an appropriate palette of orchestrational colors in support of the story. Anahid Kassabian is correct when she suggests that music in film serves three identifiable but by no means mutually exclusive roles: identification, mood, and commentary.[1] What follows is a brief but systematic approach to examining the role of musical cues in film within this context:

1. Establish time, place, and ethnic implications.

    A good film composer can set historical, geographical, and ethnic context for a film by incorporating stylistic characteristics of music of the era and locale into the score. In *The Year of Living Dangerously*, composer Maurice Jarre uses a Javanese gamelan and Javanese scales, rhythms, and textures to establish the nature of the Indonesian location for the film, as well as to set the overall exotic *tone* for the film (at least by contemporary Western standards of the times).

2. Establish tone/mood.

    Tone is a term used to describe the *psychological lens* through which we experience the film. It is the overall psychological atmosphere created by the look and sound of a film. For example, it can be described as dark, as is the case of the Batman series of films, overwhelmingly tragic, as in *Bram Stoker's Dracula*, or absurdly surrealistic, as heard in *Edward Scissorhands*.

3. Reveal psychological states of mind or implications.

    A good music cue is an aural extension of the visual realm. It can illuminate or intensify the thoughts and feelings of the onscreen characters in support of, or in spite of, their outward demeanor. Music is a powerful psychological force by itself. In film, a good film composer uses this power to create empathy in the viewer. It causes us to feel as the character feels. A classic example would be when a man declares his love to a woman, while simultaneously planning her demise. The music could be *played* either way. A consonant melody with broad gestures performed by strings would underscore his professions of love. But a harsh, dissonant drum figure or even pizzicato strings would reveal his evil thoughts, despite his outwardly loving words and gestures.

4. Reveal unseen or impending drama.

Music may indicate to the audience, but not the onscreen characters, that something is about to happen, or has happened, either on- or offscreen, or at another time. In the typical slasher film, it is the music as it intensifies, getting louder or faster or busier or more dissonant, that tells us that someone is about to lose his or her head before the actual event occurs.

5. Provide source music.

Music that is intended to be heard by the onscreen characters, as well as the viewer, is called *source music*. Film theorists tend to use the term *diegetic* and *nondiegetic* music in their analyses, referring to source and nonsource music respectively, but professionals in the film sound and music fields prefer the term *source music*. For example, in the famous cantina sequence in the original *Star Wars IV: A New Hope*, the bar band is physically onstage inside the cantina. We see them as we hear them. Everyone in the cantina can hear them (except perhaps some of the alien-looking patrons who may be earless). The band is part of the scene, along with the drinks and background chatter.

6. Provide transition or sonic glue music.

Music is one of the most effective means of linking contiguous scenes together, acting as *sonic glue*. It can smooth a transition or sharpen an edit point, depending upon whether the music seamlessly glides across the visual transition or is abruptly cut in synchronization with the edit. In the hands of a good composer (and music editor), music can be cut or written in a way that encourages the viewer to accept the nonlinear sequence of visual events or the sudden geographic displacements as the drama develops.

7. Provide intro or outro music.

Often called *credit music* if it occurs at the end of the film, intro and outro music brackets the film. It leads us into the visual experience of cinema and takes us back into the reality of the theater at the end of the film. Good intro or outro music elucidates many of the other roles indicated above, although too often, pop tunes only marginally related to the film are tagged on in the hope of increasing sales of either the film or the music (the intellectual property rights of which are often owned by the same parent company).

8. Supply musical sound effect.

Music is often synchronized in a way that complements or reinforces sound effects in the film. For example, the sound of someone falling to the floor may be musically incorporated into the score as a bass drum hit or a loud trombone outburst. In this case, it literally is a musical sound effect as the body hits the floor.

The process of linking a specific visual event to a short music gesture that somehow resembles the action (a sort of musical onomatopoeia) is often called *mickeymousing*. But unlike the musical sound that supports an extramusical sound effect, mickeymousing is usually humorous in intent and designed to be obvious—to call attention to itself. It *is* the sound effect, often actually replacing the sound effect itself, as is the case in many of the early *Betty Boop* cartoons.

NOTE

1. Anahid Kassabian, *Hearing Film: Tracking Identifications in Contemporary Hollywood Film Music* (New York: Routledge, 2001), 57.

A Word about Leitmotif

The leitmotif is the most common of musical devices used in support of a film's narrative. It serves many purposes. It is an aural code created by the composer to communicate with the audience. It provides continuity in a film and familiarity to the audience. According to Claudia Gorbman, "The thematic score provides a built-in unity of statement and variation, as well as a semiotic subsystem. The repetition, interaction, and variation of musical themes throughout a film contributes much to the clarity of its dramaturgy and to the clarity of its formal structures."[1] What she is saying is that the leitmotif can help unify, amplify, and clarify a film's story line and message, driving it home in a way not possible by any other means.

A leitmotif is a musical idea that becomes associated with a noun: a person, a place, a thing, or an idea, an emotional state or an activity. The quintessential example is the two-note pulsing in Steven Spielberg's film *Jaws*. While we clearly associate it with the approach of the great white shark, it also becomes associated with the human emotion, fear. This process of association, linking a recognizable musical gesture with a dramatic or psychological aspect of a film, is remarkably enduring and powerful. This is why in the irreverent spoof *Airplane*, we laugh during the opening sequence in which we see an airplane's tail fin emerge from the clouds as we hear a musical figure intentionally reminiscent of the opening *Jaws* theme. *Jaws* has become so familiar to the Western moviegoing public that it has become part of our culture's lore. Both the visual and aural elements are vital to the gag in *Airplane*, reinforced by our association of the shark leitmotif that has become stored in our individual and collective cultural memories. In *Settling the Score: Music and the Classical Hollywood Film*, Kate Kalinak correctly posits that "film music's power is derived largely from its ability to tap specific musical conventions that circulate throughout the culture."[2] Similarly, Anahid Kassabian indicates that "the relationship of any musical event to any particular meaning can only take place in a larger system of conventionally agreed on meanings. In other words, like any other language, music is acquired, learned in a specific socio-historical context that gives musical events the capacity to engage the listener in a process of meaning making."[3]

The use of an identifying musical idea that becomes loaded with extramusical significance is not new. The Romantic-era German composer Richard Wagner brought the concept of leitmotif to perhaps its highest form in his operas, carefully codifying musical themes with his characters and plotlines. Since many of the earliest American film composers were deeply steeped in the music of the Romantic era, having emigrated from Eastern Europe to the United States in the early twentieth century, it was inevitable that they would seize upon the use of leitmotif that proved so successful for Wagner, the nineteenth-century master of dramatic and musical form.

So the use of one or more leitmotifs in a film acts as a unifying force from a structural as well as dramatic perspective. The leitmotif becomes a sonic shorthand for that which it represents: a person, place, thing, action, or emotional state. In his *Film Score: The Art and Craft of Movie Music*, the well-respected film music composer Tony Thomas emphasizes that "once the leitmotif is linked to the action, emotional or physical entity, including either a person, place or thing, it can be liberated from the immediate synchronization between the aural and visual realms. Its own, independent aural appearance is sufficient to conjure up all the baggage that comes with the previously established association."[4] In other words, once an association between a musical idea and a person, place, thing, action, or emotional state is established, any reoccurrence of that musical idea will conjure up the relevant associations.

Each of the films examined in this book uses leitmotif in a slightly different way. But while leitmotif-based films dominate the contemporary general release film market, it is not the only approach to film scoring. Some films, such as *Laura*, use a primarily monothematic approach to music, reiterating one theme (which can be considered a singular leitmotif by itself) while presenting no other discernibly important themes. Others such as *The Year of Living Dangerously* use the music simply to set the mood, the atmosphere (in the industry called the *tone*) of a film, and intentionally avoid the use of recognizable themes entirely.

Still others use what is called a *composite score*, containing musical cues, usually entire pop songs, which on first listening bear no immediate thematic relation to each other. But the songs are often used specifically because they are pop songs, their *pop-ness* is the leitmotif, and can also serve to set the overall tone of the film. *The Graduate* is an excellent example of a composite score. Directors Quentin Tarantino and Spike Lee favor this approach as well.

And finally, all this is assuming that the director makes intelligent choices regarding music for a film. The danger in not understanding the importance of music in film is in using it to massage a poorly timed sequence or to cover an ill-conceived edit, or worse, simply to fill in some awkward silences in dialog. This draws us into the realm of deciding what is good or bad film music or more precisely what is good or bad *use* of music in film—something readers may be better able to decide for themselves after conscientiously following the discourse in this book.

NOTES

1. Claudia Gorbman, *Unheard Melodies: Narrative Film Music* (Bloomington, IN: Indiana University Press, 1987), 90–91.

2. Kathryn Kalinak, *Settling the Score: Music and the Classical Hollywood Film* (Madison, WI: University of Wisconsin Press, 1992), 15.

3. Anahid Kassabian, personal correspondence with the author, August 3, 2009.

4. Tony Thomas, *Film Score: The Art and Craft of Movie Music* (Burbank, CA: Riverwood Press, 1991), 67–68.

The Process of Music in Film

The process of creating music for film and the eventual marrying of the sound to the image is very much an individualized process that involves the collaboration and coordination of many people from disparate disciplines. Ultimately, the process is dictated by the work habits of, and the relationship between, the composer, music editor, various mixing and editing engineers, director, and producer. The process is often dictated by the time frame allowed by the production schedule and the economy of the production—how much money and resources can be allocated for each of the processes needed to produce the film.

In most cases, the composer is the last person to have major creative input into the film. While the composer may or may not have read the script and begun some musical sketches prior or during the filming, the real process of composing music for specific moments in the film only occurs after the film has been shot and edited. The composer may have the luxury of working from the final edited visual materials, called a *locked* picture, but more than likely, additionally cuts and edits will be made even after the composer has completed his work, often necessitating some recomposing, editing, or rerecording of the music. A successful film composer needs many talents, speed and flexibility being among the most important of them.

Once a composer has been hired by the director or producer, and the film has been shot and at least roughly edited, a *spotting session* is scheduled. During this session, usually attended by the composer, director and/or producer, music editor, dialog editor, and sound effects editor, the nature of the music to be composed and its specific placement in the film will be developed. The music editor takes notes to assist the composer, sometimes offering creative suggestions, sometimes adjudicating conflicting creative decisions among all the attending parties. The music editor may have already added *temp music* to the film. This is preexisting music that the director has requested to be temporarily cut into the rough edit for several reasons. It may aid the film editors in establishing the pacing or rhythmic flow of the editing, and therefore the film. It may help the director convey the stylistic characteristics he wishes the composer to evoke. One of the unfortunate hurdles the film composer often has is weaning the director away from the musical atmosphere created by the temp music and toward his own musical thoughts and ideas.

The music editor converts his notes from the spotting session into cue sheets, which contain specific timings and dialog or visual cues as well as summary notes from the spotting sessions. Along with a copy of the edited film, the composer uses these sheets to begin the process.

The actual process of composing music is unique to each composer. Some composers begin with a musical sketch, which they then orchestrate out into a larger, more complex work, either by themselves or with the help of a trusted orchestrator. The orchestrator is someone who understands the subtleties of orchestral colors and sounds, as well as the particular musical style and decisions of the composer. The music is then composed, cue by cue, and copied by a professional copying service in preparation for the recording session. The copying service prepares the parts for each of the musicians involved in the recording session.

The music supervisor will oversee and coordinate all aspects of the music preparation and recording process, in addition to securing the rights for any preexisting music that will be in the film. The music supervisor (occasionally referred to as the executive in charge of music) makes arrangements for the musicians and the location of the recording sessions.

Recording sessions are usually scheduled over a period of days in a recording studio capable of handling all of the orchestra's or ensemble's musical needs, as well as the unique needs of projecting the film as the music is being recorded.

Once the music is recorded and edited, it is delivered to the rerecording mixer who, along with the dialog and sound effects mixers, producers, and directors, will blend all of the sonic elements of the film together so that they are balanced against each other, all in service of promoting the narrative. Once the rerecording has been accomplished, the results are printed to the film or digital stock alongside the visual material. The film is finished, barring any additional changes necessitated by creative and marketing needs that arise from test screenings.

In most cases, the composer has limited creative control over how his music is mixed, edited, and married to the picture. For example, in *Altered States*, director Ken Russell recut and edited significant portions of John Corigliano's meticulously synchronized score such that at times, it is impossible to follow the written score while watching the film. Corigliano was not happy about this, but ultimately the director has final creative control.

In many cases, the composer does have total creative control over the soundtrack recording of the film. The soundtrack recording is the CD or download that is released separately from the film and contains only the music, as the composer intended it. The difference between the terms *score* and *soundtrack* is more than a semantic one. While the composer creates the music for both, the score is the musical recording (or printed score) of the entire film, and it may not represent the composer's true intentions. On the other hand, the soundtrack may not contain all of the cues in a film, but it will most likely contain those that the composer deems significant and truer to his ideas. It is unfortunate that the terms are so easily confused in the public's mind.

The Films Examined

Each of the films selected deals with the idea of leitmotif in a different way. In addition, several of the films allow us to look at other aspects of film sound, such as the relationship of the music to the other sonic elements, the use and significance of diegetic music, and the role of song lyrics. The five films chosen, *West Side Story, Psycho, Empire of the Sun, American Beauty*, and *Altered States*, have proven to be successful in conveying specific elements and concepts to my students in my Music and the Media class over the past thirty years.

Aside from its importance as a breakthrough musical film, having been adapted from a successful Broadway run, *West Side Story* presents a good introductory study of the use of leitmotif as a psychological force. Aside from the lyrics of the songs, the power and clarity of the leitmotifs make them easy to discern. They are easy to recognize whenever they emerge. The interrelatedness of musical themes is never so clear as when we realize that the *love* and *hate* leitmotifs are essentially different sides of the same coin of passion. Composer Leonard Bernstein constructs the core of both leitmotifs from the same musical notes only rearranged, musically commenting upon the duality of these powerful emotional states. It is passionate feeling, whether it is love or hate, that binds the gangs to each other and ultimately dooms the two lovers.

Psycho relies on leitmotif as an organizing function as well. It is perhaps among the most studied of film scores, the composer Bernard Herrmann being recognized as a major force in the film music field even while he was alive. His method of composition was unique at the time, the leitmotifs often not having a recognizable melody. Nonetheless, Herrmann successfully conjures up all of the same emotions and relationships as melody-driven themes through his use of rhythm, harmony, and orchestral color.

Empire of the Sun allows us to examine the larger idea of a film's sound design, which is the creative vision behind, and conceptual relationship between, all of the sonic elements in a film. While *Empire of the Sun* follows much of the same path as *West Side Story*, it affords us the additional opportunity to examine music's role in relation to the other sonic elements of film, dialog and sound effect. The umbrella term *sound effect* includes the normal, everyday sounds one would expect to accompany an onscreen action (such as footsteps) as well as hyperreal effects (such as explosions). These onscreen normal sounds may be recorded on location as the film is being shot (location sound), or they may be recreated in the more controlled environment of a Foley studio (Foley effects).

Identifying the leitmotifs and exploring their associated psychological implications for a boy growing into manhood in the middle of a war is valuable enough. But the underlying theme of the film, a boy's conflict between the fantasy of childhood and the realities of his emerging adulthood, find their most interesting manifestation in the aural battle between two of the three essential sonic elements in film, music and the sound effect. In this sense, *Empire of the Sun* allows us to expand the notion of leitmotif into the realm of sound design, acknowledging and examining its use and presence in the film as a narrative force.

American Beauty allows us to highlight leitmotif in a subtler surrounding. A wealth of leitmotifs exists in the film, most interrelated in terms of pitches, rhythm, and musical color. Most of the nondiegetic music is similar in sound and gesture, though a deeper listening reveals the subtle but essential differences between the different cues. Their constructed subtlety reflects the well-hidden emotions of the characters involved, as well as the bland sameness of their external existence. It encourages us to do as the sign on the desk says, *Look closer*, though we may extend that to include *Listen closer*.

American Beauty also affords us the opportunity to explore the role of diegetic music; music that emanates from within the scene itself (whether it is on- or offscreen). Diegetic, or source music, is music that is heard by the characters onscreen, just as they see their clothing, furniture, or wallpaper. We will find that careful selection of source music can fulfill many of the functions of a nondiegetic score.

Finally, *Altered States* affords us the opportunity to see how the idea of leitmotif is extended beyond the traditional building blocks of melody, harmony, and rhythm into the realm of musical color. The composer, John Corigliano, uses leitmotif in the traditional way, linking themes to emotional states or physical transformations. But the nature of his leitmotifs, their density, texture, and at first indefinable, unfamiliar sound and avant-garde musical techniques, remains to this day a model of the marriage between contemporary classical music and popular filmmaking.

West Side Story

HISTORICAL CONTEXT

The genesis for what would become the successful Broadway show *West Side Story* began in the 1940s, when American choreographer/director Jerome Robbins discussed the idea of a modern day *Romeo and Juliet* with composer/conductor Leonard Bernstein. They were not interested in creating a traditional musical, nor were they inclined to create opera. Along with Arthur Laurents, who eventually wrote the Broadway book for the show, Robbins and Bernstein wanted to create "a musical that tells the tragic story in musical-comedy terms, and avoid falling into the 'operatic trap.'"[1]

Earlier iterations of the script originally titled the work *East Side Story* and briefly, *Gangway!* and set the drama in the Lower East Side of New York at the dawn of the twentieth century. The early protagonists were the Jewish and Catholic gangs of New York and reflected the religious intolerance that pervaded the New York community. The time frame was set to coincide with Easter and Passover.

At Bernstein's suggestion, the locale was moved uptown to the midtown west side of Manhattan infamously known as Hell's Kitchen, and the antagonists were recast as first-generation Americans versus immigrant Puerto Ricans, two emerging and conflicting cultural groups that inhabited that area of Manhattan in the 1950s.

Early versions of the original Broadway script by Arthur Laurents were so riddled with the slang and scatological enunciations of New York's underbelly that it rendered the drama almost indecipherable. In addition, the central plot was scattered among several themes, one of which was the angst produced by the American-Soviet space race and its Cold War underpinnings and hysterias. The final script eventually removed all but a few slang phrases and scatological utterings. In the end, only a few, very oblique references to the space race finally made it to the Broadway stage and Hollywood production.

The Broadway show, which opened at the Winter Garden in 1957, was a resounding success from the beginning and broke many of the established Broadway paradigms. The film version, released in 1961, differed in several ways from its theatrical counterpart. While both retained their tragic endings (with the exception of *Carousel*, something unknown in a Broadway musical to that point), some songs were replaced; others were moved to different acts, altering the dramatic thrust of the narrative. But most of the conceptual aspects of the staging, dialog, lighting, and music carried over into Hollywood. This consistency between the two versions was no doubt due to the remarkable creative personalities that oversaw both productions.

Leonard Bernstein's legendary conducting debut in 1943, as a last-minute replacement for an ailing Bruno Walter with the New York Philharmonic, firmly established him as one of the first native-born American conductors to successfully lead a major American orchestra. Bernstein defied categorization, however. He was a master in the classical interpretation of music, yet he was often the life of a party, improvising on the piano in a variety of pop and jazz styles. As the theatrical young conductor of the New York Philharmonic Orchestra, he resurrected contemporary interest in the symphonies of Gustav Mahler, and his trendsetting Young People's Concerts were broadcast on the emerging medium called television, making classical music accessible to an entirely new generation of American children (and adults).

His gritty, hard-hitting score for the 1954 film *On the Waterfront*, in which Bernstein developed many of his ideas that later found fruition in *West Side Story*, was an earlier film success, and he had already collaborated with choreographer Jerome Robbins on the ballet *Fancy Free*, which evolved into the Broadway show *On the Town*. In short, Bernstein's effusive personality and creative spirit refused to be bound by traditions and artificial barriers. His collaboration with lyricist Stephen Sondheim, choreographer/director Jerome Robbins, screenwriter Ernest Lehman, and director Robert Wise reflected his enthusiasm for new artistic directions that simultaneously built upon and transcended the work of his predecessors.

Jerome Robbins, a multitalented perfectionist, originally conceived the idea of *West Side Story* as a modern adaptation of Shakespeare's *Romeo and Juliet*, and he both choreographed and directed the Broadway incarnation. Robbins began his professional dance career on Broadway and moved to soloist with George Balanchine's American Ballet Theatre. He danced in and choreographed the ballet *Fancy Free* and its Broadway version, *On the Town*, his first collaboration with Bernstein. In short order he choreographed the dance sequences in Rodgers and Hammerstein's *The King and I* and George Abbott's *Pajama Game*, among many other productions.

It was Robbins who initiated what would become *West Side Story*. He conceived of the production as an *integrated musical*, a term used to describe a work in which all of the elements contribute seamlessly to the natural flow of time in the narrative. Movement becomes dance and music, while speech becomes lyric, all contributing to promote the organic flow of the work. As lyricist Stephen Sondheim described it, "There are certain kinds of shows which are presentational. You just get out there and sing the song. But that's not *West Side Story*. It's supposed to be an integrated musical. It's supposed to be full of action. It's supposed to carry you forward in some way."[2]

Previous to the show *Oklahoma!*, which opened in 1943, Broadway musicals were more of a series of song-and-dance numbers draped on a story line that may or may not have been topically relevant or historically accurate. But if *Oklahoma!* opened the door to the integrated musical and topical relevance on Broadway, *West Side Story*, as conceived by Jerome Robbins, forever made Broadway a microcosm of the contemporary world, warts and all. Robbins's influence defined the integration of all of the elements of a production. As described by Rita Moreno (*West Side Story*'s Anita onscreen), "What he [Robbins] did was so unusual, that he choreographed for character. He choreographed the way a writer writes."[3] Arthur Laurents, author of the Broadway show's book (the Broadway equivalent of Hollywood's screenplay), explained that "he would not choreograph a dance as a dance, he had to know what the dancing was about."[4] Robbins conceived of the full experience of *West Side Story*, recognizing the importance of seamlessly integrating all of the show's elements to achieve its power, message, and relevance.

When the filming for *West Side Story* began, both Robbins and Robert Wise shared directorial responsibilities, though Robbins's perfectionism caused the production to run overbudget and behind schedule. He was relieved of his directorial responsibilities, although his screen credit as both director and choreographer remain.

Overwhelmed by the amount of music and lyrics to be produced, Bernstein approached an upcoming young talent to help him with the lyrics. Stephen Sondheim took over most of the lyric-writing responsibilities and was credited with the lyrics, while Bernstein was credited with the music. Sondheim produced song lyrics that only hinted at his future success in expanding the dramatic song form for which he is internationally renowned to this day. *West Side Story* was Sondheim's first Broadway production. A protégé of Oscar Hammerstein II, Sondheim was initially hesitant to accept Bernstein's offer as lyricist since he had been trained as both a composer and lyricist. But at the behest of his mentor, Sondheim accepted the role as lyricist only.

Sondheim's approach to lyric and songwriting proved to be an excellent match for the integrated musical, a form he would later expand and perfect as his career as a composer and lyricist developed. In an interview with Mark Eden Horowitz, he explained his perspective: "I'm essentially a playwright in song, and I'm not asking them [actors] to sing songs, I'm asking them to play scenes."[5]

Robert Wise was already well into his career as a director and producer, having directed the thinly veiled antiwar film, *The Day the Earth Stood Still*, among many others. He was no stranger to Hollywood's heavyweight, creative forces, having been nominated for an Academy Award for his film editing on *Citizen Kane* and serving as an editor on *The Magnificent Ambersons*, on which he also shared some uncredited directorial responsibilities. Wise, along with Robbins, carefully preserved the vital elements of *West Side Story*'s Broadway production and deftly adapted much of the staging to conform to the unique requirements of the camera.

Ernest Lehman was brought on board to *West Side Story* to adapt Arthur Laurents's Broadway book to the Hollywood screenplay format. With the exception of Stephen Sondheim, Lehman, like the others, was already an experienced Hollywood creator, having written for the films *Sabrina*, *The King and I*, and Alfred Hitchcock's *North by Northwest*. In his adaptation of the Broadway book for *West Side Story*, Lehman understood that the music, lyric, and dance was of paramount importance in moving the narrative forward, and he wisely downplayed the dialog and kept it to a minimum.

In *West Side Story*, we see and hear how a clearly defined leitmotif becomes an essential unifying device, linking not just scenes or characters to each other but fleshing out the underlying themes of the film: the duality of love and hate as a manifestation of passion, the alienation caused by hate and anger, and the unification that is love.

Bernstein's now-iconic three-note theme represents both love and hate, depending upon the order of the notes within the theme. Love moves from a dissonant to consonant sound; hate, just the opposite. But they are both of the same sonic material, the same notes, reordered. Tony and Maria momentarily enjoy the rapture of love, even while surrounded by hate.

But the strength of *West Side Story* is not just in the music itself. Rather, it is in the unifying of all of the disparate elements that makes it such a powerful film, presenting its powerful message. The complementary interaction between the script, set design, costuming, lighting, choreography, staging, music, and lyric creates a synergy that is the essence of the new Hollywood musical as well as the contemporary Broadway spectacle. *West Side Story* was not the first Broadway show to find new ways to integrate all the creative elements. But it is among the best and remains so. Over fifty years after its Broadway opening and screen debut, the cinematic version remains as relevant as ever, its synergistic creative and technical achievements a model of the power of creative expression.

THE FILM

West Side Story is a good film to begin illustrating the role of music in film, not because it is a musical, but because it is so rich in examples of the elements that make a film score great. The leitmotifs illuminate the archetypal story underlying the plot. The score uses a variety of traditional film music techniques, such as mickeymousing and counterpointing the drama. But more importantly, the film and score collaborate to provide a rich and fertile ground for examining all of the roles music can serve in film. The songs, while musically significant by themselves, are not crucial to our discussion of music in dramatic film. A more extensive examination of the lyrics and formal structure of the songs is better left to a discussion of musical theater and musicals. We will be concerned with certain aspects of the lyrics and song structure in *West Side Story* only as they relate to the visual elements in the film.

Chapter 1: Overture/Main Title

The opening to *West Side Story* provides a minimum of visual material, focusing our attentions on the musical overture. We are treated to a static, abstract image of the New York skyline seen from offshore, south of Manhattan, very much the image of Manhattan as if seen from the torch of the Statue of Liberty. This image remains motionless for the duration of the cue. Only the lighting of the singular image leaves us with any sense of progression.

By definition, an overture is a compilation of significant musical themes and melodies, a collage of most if not all of the songs and musical motifs from the entire film, or in the case of theater, the musical. The overture's declarative opening statement introduces us to one of the film's two defining leitmotifs. For the moment, we hear only the *hate* leitmotif, a three-note sequence that moves from a consonant musical interval to a dissonant one.

This arrangement of consonance to dissonance is crucial to our understanding of Bernstein's use of the love/hate dualism that is the source of the story line. The *Maria* or *love* leitmotif, as we shall see later, contains the same musical intervals as the *hate* leitmotif, but in reverse order. They move from dissonance to consonance, musically representing Tony and Maria's coming together from seemingly disparate cultures. Remember our discussion from the chapter on leitmotif. By having the *love* leitmotif and the *hate* leitmotif both derived from the same basic musical materials, Bernstein musically manifests the duality of the love/hate relationship so essential to the story line of *West Side Story* as well as Shakespeare's *Romeo and Juliet*, upon which *West Side Story* is founded. The two leitmotifs consist of the same material, yet rearranged to evoke the opposite emotions. The emotions love and hate, the yin/yang manifestation of passion, is embodied in this duality. Passion, whether love or hate, is the common denominator that binds.

Chapter 2: Prologue

Upon the conclusion of the overture, the camera flies in toward Manhattan from above, now accompanied by the distant sounds of the city—remote,

removed, leaving us feeling alone and alienated from the vibrancy of the city. **[00:05:00]**
The opening musical motif is a solitary, monophonic whistling of the *hate*
leitmotif, as we fly above the concrete jungle that is New York in the 1950s.
A responding whistle answers the solo whistle, the call-and-response from **[00:05:15]**
the natives within.

The notion of the city as a jungle (an image popularized in the 1950 film
The Asphalt Jungle, directed by John Huston, from the book of the same
name by W. R. Burnett) is reinforced by a series of short drum riffs, coun- **[00:05:32]**
terpointing and yet responding to the whistles, indicating communication
among the natives. Neither the whistles nor the drums give any regular sense
of meter; there is no steady, constant beat, just lonely, forlorn calls from
anonymous heathens emanating from indistinct locations below. The three-
way counterpoint, two distinct whistlers and the drummer, communicate with
each other until a lonely horn enters as the camera draws us down into the
canyons of Manhattan.

The camera zooms into a nondescript city playground, into the Jets, a **[00:06:24]**
1950s-looking cool teenage gang, snapping their fingers in rhythmic unison. It is compound duple meter, but Bernstein disguises the beat, offsetting
the trumpets and strings by an eighth note from the percussion, lower reeds,
and violins so that the aural conflict between the orchestra and the gang is
apparent. Aside from the coloristic effect, this causes confusion when the
listener tries to find the beat. Bernstein further disguises the compound
duple nature of the time signature by ending triple-based phrases with a
duple figure. This constant duple versus triple rhythmic battle reflects the
underlying emotional turmoil of the gang members and in fact the entire
story line. This gang is offbeat, deranged, and not normal; their existence
is as skewed as the music.

The Jets command the playground, they saunter as a loosely connected
yet cohesive unit, erupting into short, understated dance gestures and combinations that emerge from their jaunts, very much in the *cool jazz* style of
the 1950s and early 1960s. Yet, no melody or dance combination emerges
for any length of time. The Jets' life is a disjointed, disconnected existence,
nihilism interrupted by a wayward handball. The music synchronizes with **[00:06:43]**
the gang member named Action catching the ball. But what follows sonically is of more significance. As the handball player chasing the ball enters **[00:06:46]**
the frame, we are confronted by silence. Throughout *West Side Story*, moments of confrontation are suddenly silent, a poignant counterpointing of the
drama and underlying emotions, which successfully heightens the moment of
confrontation. It is a very *loud* silence, from which emotions and eventually
music bursts forth.

This is an important stylistic characteristic of Bernstein's score. Other
composers of dramatic film will more often than not heighten confrontational
dramatic moments with carefully synchronized and scored climactic musical
moments. Neither approach is correct or incorrect, simply different solutions
to the same artistic problem. They are compositional decisions that reflect
stylistic preferences often made in conjunction with directors and producers
during preproduction and spotting sessions.

After strutting through the playground, surveying their turf, the Jets interrupt a one-on-one basketball game, forcing the two players to relinquish the ball to them. The Jets begin an impromptu and chaotic game of basketball among themselves. The music takes on a playful air, with a more consonant flavor, and a longer, more coherent melody that even begins to resemble normal musical phrasing, until the ball is returned to its rightful owners. The gang continues to swagger their way through the neighborhood to the returning accompaniment of the playful music. The gang reinforces the disjointed lightness of the music with the occasional dance movement and combination, all coolly accomplished.

[00:08:22] Another and more significant point of silence and confrontation occurs as the Jets' dance is interrupted by a chance meeting with Bernardo, the Puerto Rican commander of the rival gang, the Sharks. We hear the trombones starkly articulate the *hate* motif. War drums and a snakelike rattle combine with a woodwind figure to heighten the emotional discontent underlying the scene.

[00:09:53] A similar use of silence, preceded by the *hate* leitmotif, occurs during the momentary confrontation between members of the two gangs at the fruit stand. Other confrontations are treated the same way, though to lesser dramatic degrees throughout the ensuing sequence leading up to the playground altercation.

Throughout these preliminary confrontations, no regular pulse or beat is aurally discernible in the music. Bernstein's score is written in a regular meter, but only for the musicians' sake. We do not hear the regularity of the pulse.

We return to the playground with the Jets engaging in a rowdy game of basketball. Riff accidentally passes the ball to Bernardo as silence again counterpoints the drama and heightens the underlying tensions.

[00:11:27] Muted trumpets and war drum sounds break the silence as the basketball is reluctantly returned. Only when the first deliberate and openly hostile physical events transpire does the regular duple beat assert itself, as the chase sequence begins. Even here, however, Bernstein disguises the phrasing, so that we do not feel that it is predictable and regular. The bass ostinato figure is juxtaposed across the regular phrasing structure we would expect, leaving us with a feeling of continuous ongoing running, enhancing the visual action.

[00:11:57] As the chase sequence begins, the music is not content to simply highlight the dramatic action. A fast, walking bass line begins the pacing as the snare drum hits a series of rapid sixteenth note figures, a musical onomatopoeia of running feet. Rather than using the running snare drum figure to synchronize exactly with the feet as a lesser composer might do, Bernstein synchronizes to the visual effect of the rapidly panning camera, mickeymousing the camera movement instead of the onscreen action, reflecting the underlying emotional state of the gang members (which way do they go, where do they run?) rather than just the action of running.

Chapter 3: Snowing the Coppers

[00:14:42] An authoritative police whistle interrupts the playground brawl as well as the rhythmic momentum of the music. The police whistle, itself a leitmotif in that it represents the voice of authority or adulthood, interrupts the children at play. We will see this archetypal intrusion of adults into the children's world played out with similar interruptions throughout the film.

After a brief and threatening discussion in the playground, Lieutenant Schrank and Officer Krupke force the Sharks out and leave the Jets in the playground. The ensuing rhythmic patter and pacing among the Jets' dialog is a technique I call *speech-rhythm*.   **[00:17:33]**

Speech-rhythm consists of a rhythmically accelerating series of verbal one-liners or single-word exclamations by individual gang members that inevitably result in a single, climactic, collective utterance, a sort of verbal orgasm by the entire gang. The sexual reference is not by accident. A psychosexual interpretation of these speech-rhythm moments and the nature of the gang members' interactions in general could lead one to the conclusion that there are sexual overtones to the various relationships.

Certainly the pattern of the speech-rhythm, accelerating rhythms to the speech, the inclusion of multiple partners (gang members), the mutually heightening of individuals' tension, followed by an climactic moment of release and subsequent relaxation of tension, follows a distinctly coital pattern, even if only by innuendo.   **[00:17:50]**

While this interpretation may seem a bit outlandish at first, we see support for this thesis throughout the film. When this pattern of speech-rhythm occurs, the climactic moment is either completed as described or interrupted by an authority figure before the climax is reached. A logical interpretation of this allegorical coitus interruptus is that the adult figures interrupt the children at play, usually before they hurt themselves or others. When the speech-rhythm is not interrupted, the participants reach a climactic moment in which they plan some action. In other instances, the speech-rhythm never really coalesces into a full-fledged climax. These moments reflect the disintegration or loss of cohesiveness to the gang as a whole. This curious speech-rhythm technique occurs throughout the film. We shall see these moments as our analysis progresses.

Chapter 4: "Jet Song"

The first example of speech-rhythm occurs as Lieutenant Schrank and Officer Krupke leave the gang in the playground. A second one begins as the Jets retreat to a dead-end alleyway surrounded by walls and chain-link fencing. We get a sense of rhythmic interplay and the use of one-liners to build tension.   **[00:18:30]**

The first fully formed speech-rhythm pattern begins as the character Action responds with the line, "I say, go, go." The exclamations begins but are interrupted by the stolid character Ice, who cautions the gang about the use of more dangerous weapons for the rumble. In this case, we have a gang member acting as the voice of caution or authority interrupting the flow of the speech-rhythm. It's a momentary pause, as Riff riles up the gang, again. The climax of the pattern is reached when Riff announces, "Okay cats, we rumble."   **[00:20:13]**

"Jet Song" is the first of a series of songs that functionally serve to amplify the feelings of the characters. Structurally, these songs have no significance for the movie other than adding to the character development. Richard Kislan calls these types of songs *charm songs*.[6] He explains that the choreographer Bob Fosse goes further, calling them *I am songs*. They do little to move the plot along other than fleshing out the character's state of mind or current per-   **[00:20:49]**

[handwritten margin notes] When not allowed to climax, those who participated in the speech rhythm are left with metaphorical "blue balls." They have to get rid of that unresolved feeling. → Think about this in terms of Billy, Sam + Pepper had it successful, part where Billy doesn't.

spective. Kislan describes them as happy, optimistic in nature. In *West Side Story*, the songs "Jet Song," "Tonight," "I Feel Pretty," "America," and "Gee, Officer Krupke" fit the bill. With the exception of "Tonight," all are ensemble songs. "Jet Song" is about brotherhood and friendship. "Tonight" is about the rapture of love. "I Feel Pretty" and "America" are both celebrations of life. Even "Gee, Officer Krupke" is about brotherhood, albeit among thieves.

From the perspective of musical theater (and musical film), these songs balance the singing load, enabling each of the principal singers and the various choruses (the Jets, Sharks, Lady Sharks, and others) to share a musical moment in the spotlight. The idea of balance and form in musical theater and film is beyond the scope of this book. There are several excellent books on the nature of musical theater that address the function of song in a more specific manner. We are concerned not with the form of the song itself, but rather its relationship to the visual material and plot development. Therefore, the discussion of these songs is limited here.

"Jet Song" establishes the familylike relationship among the gang members. It explains their raison d'etre:

> You're never alone,
> You're never disconnected!
> You're home with your own.
> When company's expected,
> You're well protected![7]

[00:21:07]   As the song begins, Bernstein deliberately obfuscates the beat by offsetting one of the repeating rhythmic figures by an eighth note, so that we are left with a disjointed feeling, almost like we are tripping over ourselves. The beat is further obfuscated by the quarter-note triplets sung by Riff and others over the repeating rhythmic figure. The net result is a rhythmic feeling that is deliberately tenuous and awkward, while simultaneously leaving us with a jazzy feeling. In terms of set design, the gang is surrounded by large, enclosing structures such as chain-link fences and multistory walls of buildings. This is a visual theme that will dominate the film. Gang members are repeatedly portrayed as being in jail, caged in, surrounded by their environment as if they were animals. This boxed-in illusion will become significant in a few later scenes as Tony sings about Maria.

Chapters 5, 6: "Something's Coming," Not Giving an Inch

The next significant musical cue for our discussion is the scene in which Tony (a former Jets member) and Riff discuss their friendship, plans for attending the upcoming dance, and Tony's search for something he is unable to define.

[00:26:03]   Tony's song, "Something's Coming," is by itself not unique or unusual. It is in duple, primarily consonant, and quite homophonic. Tony sings about his anticipation that something indescribable is about to happen, though he has no idea what it may be. One of his lines, "It's only just out of reach," will

---

prove to be fatally prescient. His final lyric, "maybe tonight," is a long note that is held as he gestures with his hand skyward. [00:28:28]

Orchestrationally, the woodwinds begin a rising musical line, musically paralleling his hand movement, as the camera follows the direction of his hand. We cross-fade quickly as the camera rapidly descends into a close-up of Maria. The woodwinds accompany the descending camera movement, with a descending chromatic line leading to a held note that harmonically resolves as the camera fixes on Maria's contented face. This completes the visual transition across the edit and the transition from song to dialog, and it serves as an example of the use of music as a sonic glue that simultaneously foreshadows future plot developments. Maria will be the *something* that is coming in Tony's future. This particular moment is one of the finest examples available of the cinematic marriage between lyric, dramatic gesture, musical composition, and camera movement and perspective.

Chapters 7, 8: Dance at the School, Love across the Lines

We first hear the *Maria* or *love* leitmotif as Maria begins to twirl in her new dress and announcing her excitement about being in America. Her exuberance provides the motion for the scene change as she twirls into a blurred mass of black and red, accompanied by a measured trill in the orchestra that sonically mimics the visual element. [00:31:23]

Throughout *West Side Story*, the dance sequences are among the most allegorically powerful in the movie. While the ambiguously scripted Master of Ceremonies (is he gay, is he straight?) organizes a get-together dance, neither Jets nor Sharks and their girls are eager to participate. They are cajoled into joining the contrived game of socialization, organizing themselves into a circle of boys and a circle of girls. The cue is titled "Promenade." The music commences as the two circles reluctantly and disdainfully revolve to what can only be described as merry-go-round music or perhaps circus music from hell. The form and orchestration are what we might expect from a band accompanying a circus, but the melody is shrill and decidedly dissonant, indicating that this is not a normal circus—not a circus you would want your children to attend. [00:35:54]

An examination of the harmony will reveal Bernstein's clever use of the musical intervals that define the *love/hate* leitmotif as a structural device. The bass line at each cadence or half cadence is defined by the interval of either a tritone or the perfect fifth, the defining intervals of the *love/hate* leitmotif. The entire phrase is nine bars long, not the usual eight, leaving us musically off balanced and unsettled.

Again, we hear the sound of the adults interrupting the teens at play. In this case the Master of Ceremonies blows a whistle to interrupt the moving circles, just as the police blew a whistle that interrupted the playground brawl. The whistle puts an end to this sorry state of socially engineered happiness, and a battle in the form of competing mambos begins to shape up between the Jets and Sharks. [00:36:16]

[00:36:19] After a brief confrontational pause, the drums break out into an uninhibited mambo beat announcing the "Dance at the Gym" cue. The use of the drums to announce the challenge-and-response is deliberately reminiscent of the film's opening aerial-view sequence and the tribal call-and-response that initially announces the *hate* leitmotif. The music and the gangs are unleashed. The Jets and Sharks take turns trying to outdance each other, cleverly choreographed to reflect the characteristics of their respective cultures. After an ensemble dance segment, the Puerto Ricans lead with sensual, understated hip movements, defined by a lower center of gravity. Shoulder shrugs and elegant lifts evoke a sense of placing the ladies on pedestals. The Americans respond with gyrating rock 'n' roll gestures, more sexually egalitarian combinations accompanied by frenetically flailing arm and leg movements.

In the "Dance at the Gym," Jerome Robbins presents us with a study of disparate cultures through his mastery of stylistic dance. Bernstein responds with carefully crafted rhythms and orchestrations that allow the jazz and Latin-laced melodies to gracefully and enthusiastically cross cultures. His music is wild and expansive, and it serves multiple functions here. It is source music, it *is* the music in the dance hall to which everyone is moving. It further underlines the psychological actions of competitiveness and rivalry between the groups as they fight for turf and recognition; in this case, the center of the dance floor.

[00:38:56] In the midst of all this choreographed combativeness, Tony and Maria spot each other. It is clear from their gazes that it is love at first sight. The music confirms this by melting into a mist of reverberation, a technically induced softening of the blaring trumpet and intensely brass and percussion scoring.

[00:39:30] The use of sound engineering tricks such as gradually increasing the reverberation of the music to simulate alienation or removal from the immediate setting is common in film music. As the orchestration softens, so does the lighting. The rival dancers fade into the visual reverberation of the background as Tony and Maria meet. The music becomes an unambiguous duple meter, with a wind staccato melody that is consonant and cute, light and delicate, as the future lovers explore their rapture. They dance the cha-cha, an intimate duet of a dance as they exchange their first declarations of passion.

[00:41:43] Tony and Maria's moments of intimacy and fantasy begin to fade as the reality of the world they live in comes back into focus, both visually and sonically. The surreal circus music cross-fades us back to reality, though the length of the cross-fade could indicate that both love and hate can coexist, if even for a few, fleeting moments.

[00:42:13] An adult figure again interrupts the teens at play. The Master of Ceremonies blows his whistle as Maria's older brother and commander of the Sharks, Bernardo, intercedes between Tony and Maria's intimations. The music reverts to a much more generic background figure more appropriate for the school dance source music that it is, led by an innocuous clarinet in its low and unobtrusive register.

Chapters 9, 10: Riff's Challenge, Maria

[00:44:14] Maria is whisked away from the dance, as Riff and Bernardo begin to arrange a rumble between the two gangs. Meanwhile, Tony is mesmerized by Maria and begins to chant her name over and over again. Repeated notes in a quasi-modal style, with text setting the rhythmic structure and phrasing, is characteristic of both medieval religious chant and Tony's rhapsodic musical musings. The beginning of the song "Maria" is deliberately Gregorian chant-like in its melody and phrasing, evoking a sense of reverence and spiritual awakening. Meeting Maria is a religious experience for Tony. The music underscores his psychological state, revealing his almost religious reverence and fascination for her and the innocence she represents.

At the same time, the seemingly innocuous set design comes into sharper focus. The setting for the dance has been the school gym, but as Tony begins his chantlike singing, lighting reveals the gym to be a churchlike structure, with great arching windows, cathedrallike corridors, and red wall covering. The lighting emanates from above. Angellike nondiegetic musical voices **[00:44:20]** from above echo Maria's name in response to Tony's callings. The religious overtones, conveyed by the synergy of musical style, lighting, and set design are undeniable. After this introductory material, Tony's song yields to a full **[00:44:41]** treatment of the *love* leitmotif, "Maria."

Tony is rhapsodic as he sings. The music reflects his uplifted state of mind, while serving as a sonic glue binding the various visual edits and fades as Tony drifts through his neighborhood and imagination. Even the lyric, "say it **[00:45:15]** soft and it's almost like praying," reflects his reverent inclinations. The song concludes with another Gregorian chantlike passage as he looks up toward **[00:46:23]** the light as the camera takes God's perspective, from above.

In these two sequences, the final moments of Tony's song "Something's Coming" and Tony's quasi-religious declaration of love for Maria in the song that bears her name, we see how the careful coordination and creative collaboration between the artists who control the various elements of film can produce a synergy of the arts, beyond that which each individual artist can produce. These collaborations yield powerful moments, dramatically, musically, and creatively.

Chapters 11, 12: "America"/"I Don't Wait"

In the original Broadway production of *West Side Story*, the female chorus sang the song "America." In the film version examined here, the Sharks join the girls, adding an additional level of sexual tension, sarcasm, and cynicism to the lyric. The result clarifies the differences between the Puerto Rican boys and girls. The girls sing about America being the land of opportunity while the boys describe it as a series of closed doors and quashed hopes.

After an impressionistic introductory passage that evokes the sense of a tropical island through the use of exotic tonal scales, reminiscent of the **[00:49:30]** work of Claude Debussy, this conflict is played out in Bernstein's rhythmic underpinnings for the song. The beat of the song alternates between the **[00:50:15]** following two rhythmic patterns, *123, 123* and *12, 12, 12*. It is a difficult number to sing; it is even more difficult to dance to because of this unusual alternation of beats.

Chapter 13: "Tonight"

The balcony sequence, set among the fire escapes of New York, provides an opportunity for Tony and Maria to proclaim their love for each other. As we shall see, the fire escapes serve the purpose of enclosing the couple in a prisonlike surrounding, much as the tenement buildings and fencing visually imprison the Jets and Sharks throughout the film. Vertical and horizontal bars in either the foreground or background surround Tony and Maria. The musical structure of the duet "Tonight" can be interpreted to represent the couple consummating their love. The combination of musical form and physical setting underscore that this is a forbidden love, one that cannot survive.

[00:56:18] After a gently orchestrated string introduction that underscores the tender-
[00:57:36] ness between the doomed couple, Maria starts the duet. Tony responds, and
[00:59:06] they sing together as they approach a musical (and allegorically, physical)
[00:59:20] climax. A brief musical pause follows as they begin again, together, acceler-
ating the tempo, and we follow the soaring melody as the camera blurs our vision, allowing us to only see the couple, clenched together and looking off into the distance or into each other's eyes. The lyrics, "shooting sparks into space," can be construed as having a sexual nature to them, but this may be subject to some debate.

[01:00:09] After the second climactic moment, the music again relaxes. As the couple embrace and are about to kiss, they are momentarily interrupted by Maria's father calling to her. This is a gentle reference to the subplot of authority figures interrupting the youths at play.

[01:00:54] As Tony begins to depart, we see Maria gazing at him through the bars of the fire escape, gripping the railings as an inmate would. The bars frame her innocent, love-struck face. A match shot shows Tony equally framed. The subtle musical underscoring continues as does the framing bars. Both Tony and Maria grip the bars, prisonerlike, as they make plans to meet later.
[01:02:11] A final parting verse is slower and gentler than the first two, perhaps reflecting a diminishing physical stamina, if one chooses to adopt the sexual interpretation of the scene.

Taken as a whole, the musical form for this tender balcony scene can represent an act of lovemaking, with the gentle caress of a beginning, the joining of two souls as they rise to meet each other, the mutually climactic moment, followed by tender moments of repose and then, an encore. Even the parental interruption can be conceived as an all-too-familiar part of teenage ardor. The final moments are the softest, most intimate of the encounter, spent as lovers would spend their departing moments, before each goes off to rejoin the realities that await them.

Chapter 14: "Gee, Officer Krupke"

In their operettas, Gilbert and Sullivan perfected the Italian comic opera form called the *patter song*. Stylistically, a patter song is a typical verse-chorus structure with a seemingly endless series of running eighth notes, each note linked to a single syllable of the text, coupled with satirically biting lyrics that mock the subject of the song. In "Gee, Officer Krupke," Bernstein adopts **[01:06:13]** the format in such a way that the Jets mock many of the adult figures and by extension, the society in which they live. Through the use of stereotype, the melodramatic staging and sarcastic lyrics take aim at the police, judges, psychiatrists, and social workers. Each is caricatured as the lyrics extemporize on the cause of juvenile delinquency and espouse one of the currently in-vogue solutions to the problem of alienated youth. The final shout chorus has an **[01:09:57]** almost chorus-line quality to it.

Chapters 15, 16: The War Council, Sweet Land of Liberty

The Jets adjourn to Doc's Candy Shop to await the arrival of the Sharks. Upon their entrance, both gangs assemble around Riff and Bernardo as they begin to negotiate the rules for the rumble. We see the emergence of speech- **[01:13:41]** rhythm as the negotiations begin to heat up. Each gang member's suggestion/ outburst ups the ante. Tony arrives just in time to interrupt this verbal fore- **[01:14:04]** play, once again highlighting the subtheme of adult intrusion into the lives of the youth at play. Tony convinces both sides to reduce the violence to a simple fair fight between two gang members.

Lieutenant Schrank strides into the candy shop, only to find the fore-warned Jets and Sharks buddying up with each other. This turn of events serves to highlight the gangs' shared hatred of authority figures. Schrank's own prejudices emerge as he orders the Sharks to clear out of the candy shop. They comply, offering their own sarcastic version of "My Country **[01:16:56]** 'Tis of Thee," as they leave. Their whistling, as clear an example of source music that exists, ends with a downward glissando, reflecting their lost love **[01:17:06]** of the American ideal.

Chapters 17, 18: "I Feel Pretty," What Anita Can't See

"I Feel Pretty" is another *I am* song in that it reflects Maria's feelings about **[01:20:54]** herself and does little to propel the plot forward. As she dances around the dress shop where she and the other Puerto Rican girls work, she coyly banters with her friends about her feelings, musically set to a hopelessly optimistic waltz tempo. It is the most unambiguously carefree song of the film, a song-and-dance number, much in the pre-*Oklahoma!* Broadway tradition.

Chapter 19: "One Hand, One Heart"

The dress shop scene is one of the most intimate and playful within the entire film. Tony meets Maria after hours in the dress shop where Maria works. They playfully engage in an imaginary wedding, using the shop's manne-quins as stand-ins for their family members. The music enters the scene as Tony and Maria's role-playing fantasy begins. Maria announces that "you do have magic." Tony responds, "Of course, I've got you."

Some note should be made of the colors that visually carry this scene. While the black formal suit and white wedding dress of the groom and bride are foregone conclusions, pastels and gauzy materials dominate the room.

The shop itself exudes a sense of warmth and coziness, with wooden planks for the catwalks. Even the god-light has been softened to a slight yellow.

The set reinforces the spirituality of the moment, with an overhead window's panes forming the shape of a cross as white light shines through. The camera shoots from the couple's perspective, looking upward into the light. But separating the cross and the couple is an iron railing; prison bars foreshadowing that this marriage is not to be. When coupled with the lighting, the cold, black, iron bars counterpoint the softness of the heavenly light. Tony and Maria gaze into the camera/altar as the iron railing separates them from the window with the crossed panes. A distinctly godlike light emanates from above and gradually grows with intensity. The shop itself is extremely narrow, made even more so by the four round supporting posts for the catwalk above them. We are left with the feeling that the ill-fated couple is still walled in by all that surrounds them, their hopes and aspirations limited by their environment.

[01:28:01]

[01:28:09] Bernstein begins to weave a wonderful pastiche as Tony and Maria's unrealistic hopes for their love finds expression in Bernstein's reprising of the introduction to the previously heard song, "Tonight." But he quickly dispenses with that theme as Tony and Maria's playful banter morphs into the cha-cha music from the dance, where their romance was initially kindled. They don the symbolic attire of a marriage, a bridal veil and top hat. As the prospective bride and groom kneel before an imaginary altar, they declare their vows in the duet, "One Hand, One Heart."

[01:29:56] The introduction to the duet references the song, "Somewhere," which appears in its entirety later in the film. It is an ominous foreshadowing of events, beginning with a monophonic string line that contrapuntally evolves

[01:30:21] into something more complex. A single pizzicato harp note gently hints at a church bell ringing.

[01:31:00] The music begins optimistically in a major key. But at the moment that Maria exclaims the unknowingly prophetic words, "until death do us part," the music takes a turn into the minor mode. It remains so, until Maria com-

[01:31:14] pletes the obligatory "with this ring, I thee wed," at which point it returns to a major key.

[01:31:19] After the introduction, the melody of "One Hand, One Heart" tenderly commences with a series of rhythmically equal repeating pitches. The opening figure is distinctly reminiscent of Gregorian chant and resembles the opening to the song "Maria." The chordal accompaniments ebb and flow, gently swaying, waves of love and passion carefully expressed by the strings and harp. The absence of percussion and brass is appropriate, but as we shall see, Bernstein will use this orchestrational decision to further the plot even more.

In a lesser film, this subtle harmonic movement would go unnoticed, a happy coincidence of dialog and musical composition, but Bernstein's careful coordination is apparent. The moments leading up to the change from major to minor and vice versa are rhythmically delayed (a rubato in musical terms), so that the dialog and musical statements can be perfectly synchronized. Bernstein concludes the duet by inserting several enunciations of the *love*

[01:32:36] theme into strings, recognizing Tony and Maria's momentary triumph of love

over hate. As if to support the intimacy of the moment, the other strings reinforce the *love* theme, resolving all their differences into the final cadence that accompanies the tender kiss of the faux newlyweds, blessed by the overpowering god-light from above. The strings complete the scene on a fragile high note; the cadence used leaves us with a sense of delicateness, incompleteness.

[01:32:49]

All of this, the delicate costuming, softened set design, lighting, and fragilely orchestrated music leaves Tony and Maria (and the viewer) in a state of blissful harmony. But this visual harmony, accompanied by its aural twin, is suddenly blighted out, replaced in an instant with all that can contrast it.

Chapter 20: "Tonight" (Ensemble)

A hard, direct cut replaces the pastels, gauzy lighting, and delicate costuming with the stark edginess of a black-and-red exterior scene: the rooftops of the neighborhood, replete with distraught and alienating angles and a red sky that sears us to our souls. Blaring brass and martial drums replace the warm and ephemeral strings of the *love* motif. Nowhere else in the film is the love versus hate urtext of the film so starkly revealed. Sight and sound unify the theme by a sharp division of all the elements in a fraction of a second.

[01:32:54]

The prerumble sequence is a tour de force of musical counterpoint in film. The power of the scene emanates from the five-part double imitative counterpoint Bernstein has written, reflecting all of the passionate love/hate expectations for *tonight* held by the Sharks, Jets, Tony, Maria, and Anita and the authorities.

The anticipations of all of the protagonists find expression in this climactic moment. Fueled by their hatred, the Sharks and Jets each hope to establish themselves as the supreme gang in the neighborhood. Maria sings hopefully about her rendezvous with Tony later that evening, supposedly after he has dispersed the rumblers. Anita also sings of her love, in this case for Bernardo, and their anticipated tryst after the rumble. Tony, ever hopeful, sings about his love for Maria and their meeting.

Bernstein's construction of the counterpoint is exquisite. The Jets begin the song announcing their expected trouncing of the Sharks with a running eighth-note motif, followed by the Sharks, who use the same motif to announce their intentions, the vanquishing of the Jets in the rumble. Thanks to Tony's earlier intervention, the rumble has in fact been reduced to a fistfight between Bernardo and Ice. While fully arming themselves with the weapons of the ghetto, both gangs announce their anticipatory anxiety about the fight escalating into a full, all-out rumble.

[01:33:00]
[01:33:15]

Bernstein allows each gang to establish their musical motif and weaponize separately, a wise compositional choice given the complexity that is to follow. This allows the listeners to firmly establish the musical motif in their ears and helps to clearly define the intentions of each of the groups.

A clichéd and somewhat sleazy saxophone riff announces Anita's moment. As she deploys her own arsenal in the form of sheer stockings, she reveals her intentions, to "get her kicks, tonight." Her musical line matches both gangs' motifs. The lyrics and their delivery, while reflecting her sensual

[01:33:53]

expectations, contain elements of aggression. It is not clear that she is talking about love or other instinctual behaviors, closer to that of the gangs. This may be why Bernstein chose to deliver her message with the same melodic phrasing as the Jets and Sharks.

[01:34:11]   Tony introduces the second contrapuntal motif with the melody from the song "Tonight." The use of the second theme here obviously reflects Tony's state of mind. His thoughts are not on the rumble, which he understands he must attend in the hopes of calling it off, but rather on his meeting with Ma-

[01:34:34]   ria later. Maria rounds out the phrasing by taking up the theme where Tony leaves off. She completes him, unlike the gangs who remain complete and independent in their vocalizations. Maria, however, does not sing her theme in its entirety, leaving the final part of the phrase to be replaced by a short

[01:34:57]   instrumental interlude, visually accompanied by a shot of Officer Krupke and Lieutenant Schrank in their patrol car. This severed phrase technique will become significant toward the end of the film. Schrank and Krupke are also anticipating tonight, but as authority figures, they interrupt the flow of the song as has been the case in previous adult/gang encounters. Metaphorically, this is what they are attempting to do, disrupt all of the anticipations of the evening's activities.

Schrank and Krupke's interlude is a wonder of orchestration. Trudging lower brass leave us with the feeling of centurions advancing to join the forces of evil in battle. The trumpet figures are as martial as they come, staccato sixteenth- and eighth-note figures blaring the fanfare of the forces of good.

Musically, this prelude to the rumble scene serves to complete the individual introductions of the main contrapuntal themes and to link the different themes and anticipatory associations with the characters involved. What follows is the joining of all of these anticipations into a musical mélange

[01:35:05]   that will culminate in the silence before the storm of the rumble. After the interlude, the Jets return with their theme, with Maria's lightly sounding "To-

[01:35:20]   night" theme soaring above them in counterpoint. A cutaway shot supports the music, revealing Maria on the fire escape. The Jets' theme is then taken

[01:35:34]   up midphrase by the Sharks, as we see them approaching the rendezvous
[01:35:39]   point under the highway. Anita joins the fray, singing a short phrase, similar to the gang themes, while she primps in front of the mirror. Tony leaves the

[01:35:45]   candy store where he has been working and joins Maria in their song. All of the themes have now been elucidated. Each of the protagonists have had their say, and as they all approach the moment and location of their destiny, the counterpoint goes full out, building to the now inevitable conflict. Both the Jets and the Sharks are walking toward the rumble point, reflected by the steel and concrete structures we would associate with an elevated highway's foundations. The pace of the film editing picks up and shots become shorter and shorter, just long enough to propel the action quicker and quicker.

At the conclusion of the song, we fade to red and a close-up of the geomet-

[01:36:14]   ric patterns of a chain-link fence, raging passion that is caged. The *hate* leitmotif returns, whistled monophonically, a call from the jungle, and a direct link to the opening musical theme of the film.

Chapter 21: The Rumble

The rumble begins, predictably enough, with this call from the jungle. Interestingly, the response to the call is from a ship's steam whistle from what must be the harbor nearby. The moral desolateness of the moment is achieved not just through the use of the monophonic whistle and the ship's response, but also from the contrast between the relative silence of this moment and the previous scene, with all five parts of the counterpoint reaching their climactic moment. Perhaps the ship's whistle announces the arrival of the first gang, the Sharks as they reach their port of destination under the highway. We find support for this idea when the Jets arrive. The same ship's whistle announces their arrival as well.

[01:36:20]

[01:37:00]

The rumble sequence brings together many of the sonic techniques that permeate the film. Yet, some are conspicuous by their absence. The speech-rhythm mentioned earlier is never heard. The Jets and Sharks are no longer just playing. The fight is for real. Mickeymousing is subtle but ubiquitous throughout the scene. Whether one considers the jabs of the knives and the body feints accompanied by musical gestures to be mickeymousing or choreographed *dance verite* combinations is irrelevant. Mickeymousing is usually used for comedic effect, but its more serious side, if carefully shown, will render physical movements even more effective from a visual perspective. This seems to be the case here.

Tony's interruption of the fight between Bernardo and Ice can be seen as the authoritarian interruption we've seen in several instances up to this point. It is less convincing than the other circumstances, however, since Tony is interrupting the drama rather than a musical event representing that drama. There is no musical interlude, no speech-rhythm, and no unfinished melody lines.

The rumble allows the set designer to make full use of the highway support structures and double-high chain-link fences to reflect the prison mentality that engulfs both gangs. The space is visually square, perhaps alluding to a boxing ring.

Riff throws the first punch, sending Bernardo sprawling to the concrete. His punch is accompanied by striking drum hits, used as a musical sound effect. In film-scoring terms, it is a *hard in*. The music is definitive, intrusive, and linked to a particular visual cue. There is no *sneaking it*, here. The initial musical figures are decisively disjunctive, with a jagged, rising melodic line and an awkward rhythm lending support to the moment.

[01:39:42]

A single rolled marimba/glockenspiel note that increases in volume draws us into the battle as both Bernardo and Riff draw their knives. Disjointed rhythmic structures begin as the knives flash in the light. The lack of a continuous, steady pulse serves to heighten the chaos and fear in the situation. Bernstein's command of musical language allows him leeway with the mickeymousing of the knife thrusts and parries. Rather than just punctuating important visual cues, Bernstein gives the brass held notes with crescendos built in, enunciating the *hate* motif and leading up to the moment of the thrust or parry. It's as if we enter the minds of the combatants, feeling the tension build within them as they attempt to anticipate their opponents' moves.

[01:39:48]

[01:39:55]

[01:40:06]

[01:40:15] Disjunctive melodic gestures rise in imitative counterpoint to each other. This simultaneously asserts the individuality of the opponents while acknowledging the necessity of their responding gestures.

[01:40:27] At the moment Riff, having lost his knife, appears to be cornered by Bernardo, the music simply disappears. This point of confrontation is underscored by silence. This may well reflect Riff's state of mind as he faces possible death, that infinitely long moment when one sees one's life flash in front of him. Many people speak of a deafening silence when confronted with the moment of their demise. Bernstein plays the psychology of the moment—Riff's psychology—and not the physical action.

[01:40:54] As Bernardo begins to taunt Riff with his knife, the music resumes its contrapuntal nature, the bassoon imitating the clarinet as the game of cat and mouse continues. As Riff counters Bernardo's thrust, a fully imitative coun-
[01:41:02] terpoint breaks out in the woodwinds and strings, reflecting all the thrusts, counterthrusts, parries, and feints of the fight. The counterpoint gives way to
[01:41:08] a more homophonic, though no less dissonant, brass figure as Riff recovers his knife and the battle equalizes.

[01:41:19] Tony intervenes, dragging Riff away from Bernardo, as the piano begins a rising arpeggiated masslike gesture that culminates in a single brass announcement of the theme's defining musical interval, the tritone. This
[01:41:25] matches the moment when Bernardo's knife fatally penetrates Riff's stom-
[01:41:27] ach. An intense moment of silence serves to reinforce our shock and astonishment (and Riff's) at the moment of his demise.

[01:41:40] A quietly introduced string figure, rhythmically jazzy and quickly imitated by other strings and later woodwinds, emerges as Tony, Bernardo, and both gangs realize the seriousness of what has just transpired. The intensity of the rising line, coupled with an increasingly dense counterpoint, emphasizes Tony's initial conflictedness and rising rage as he bends over the body of his lifelong friend. The various lines of counterpoint continue to rise and coalesce
[01:41:47] into a single melodic line, leading to the moment in which Tony stabs Bernardo in a rage-filled act of revenge.

The rumble becomes an all-out free-for-all, as does the music. Bernstein does not want the rumble music to become too predictable. He wants to keep us off center and uses atypical rhythmic structures without recognizably regular subdivisions of the beat to achieve his goal.

[01:42:09] During a brief lull in the fighting, the music allows the police sirens of authority to emerge. The mickeymousing (or dance verite?) that follows is the most blatant of the entire film as individual gang members deliver a final kick or punch accompanied by a musical punctuation mark (music as sound effect). A few musical hits are clearly coordinated with physical ones, but Bernstein, in conjunction with choreographer Jerome Robbins, quickly abandons the synchronicity. The point has been made; any more belaboring of it would have made the mickeymousing too obvious and rendered the scene almost comical. As the remaining gang members respond to the police siren and scatter, they leave behind the two mortally wounded gang leaders and an unconscious Tony. As the members of both gangs begin their escape, we are left with simply drums, communicating into the concrete jungle, as the sirens begin to dominate the soundscape.   **[01:42:16]**

The use of the siren is perhaps a more effective tool to communicate Tony's angst than anything Bernstein could have written for the moment. Tony slowly recovers and examines the bodies of Riff and Bernardo. The sirens are going off in his head. He is dazed but becoming aware of the ramifications of the death of his best friend and his killing of his lover's brother. But the siren also reflects his own feelings of inadequacy in averting the disaster as well as the hopelessness of his own situation. The wailing sirens reveal the angst that is at the heart of *West Side Story*.

The cat-and-mouse theme momentarily returns, initially delivered by the clarinet and then echoed by a pizzicato bass and woodwind combination, as Anybodys reenters the scene. Tony becomes the mouse, desperately trying to escape the spotlight of the squad cars as they arrive on the scene. Anybodys reemerges to coax Tony into abandoning the scene of the rumble. Tony climbs a chain-link fence to the accompaniment of a solo marimba tremolo. A nearby church bell begins to toll, simultaneously announcing the funereal scene, but also serving as a sonic glue or transition music, getting us across the edit point.   **[01:43:30]**   **[01:44:09]**

Chapter 22: Breaking the News

We see a midshot of Maria sitting on a rooftop dressed in white, dreamily gazing away the time while waiting for Tony to return. Ironically, the funeral church bells also serve as wedding bells for Maria, reflecting her fantasies about marriage. Again, the dual nature of love and hate is reflected in the sound of the film; Bernstein's carefully constructed love/hate theme and now the church bells find manifestation in the most intensely dramatic point of the film up to now.

Maria's romantic state of mind is revealed not only by her eyes, dreamily gazing skyward, but also by a variation of the "I Feel Pretty" theme. It is a quiet and contemplative moment for Maria, emphasized by Bernstein's use of the lower strings for the melody and an ascending musical pyramid, perhaps revealing her hopes of soaring above the fracas that is all around her.   **[01:44:35]**

Maria begins to lightly step to the cha-cha music from the "Dance at the Gym," where she first met Tony. This yields to a variation of the signature song "Maria." She is engrossed in her reverie. An ascending arpeggio based upon the *love* leitmotif concludes her moment of rapture.   **[01:44:58]**   **[01:45:35]**

This arpeggiated figure underscores Bernstein's clever intertwining of the *love* and *hate* leitmotifs. The arpeggio's initial two intervals define the *love* motif, but as the next note in the arpeggio is added, the *hate* motif is formed. Thus the arpeggio intertwines the *love* and *hate* themes by alternating the intervals that construct each of the motifs. Remember that both motifs are the same intervals, simply rearranged in order.

The arpeggio ends the cue as a disheveled and distraught Chino enters onto the roof. Chino somberly moves out of the shadows, his face bruised and sweaty in contrast to Maria's brightly lit innocence. Chino reveals to Maria

[01:46:57]

[01:47:26]

that the rumble did in fact occur. Her first is reaction is to ask about Tony's welfare. A horrified Chino reveals that "he killed your brother!" Music appears, instantly punctuating the devastating revelation. This is "Rumble" music, but it quickly becomes apparent that it is not just a reiteration of the rumble between the Jets and Sharks but now reflects the psychological upheaval within Maria as she realizes that her lover has killed her brother. The "Rumble" music underscores her psychological anguish. It is interspersed with momentary stationary chords, almost recitativelike, that allow the astonished interjections of offscreen characters to be heard, all in service of advancing the drama and heightening the impact of Bernardo's death.

Chapter 23: "Somewhere"

[01:47:56]

[01:48:02]

[01:48:17]

[01:51:03]

As Maria reels from the shocking news and her own inner turmoil, she rushes downstairs to her bedroom and begins to pray at the altar in her room. The spiritual connection between Tony and Maria finds manifestation in the seemingly innocuous use of stained glass doors as the entryway into Maria's inner sanctum, her bedroom. As Tony enters the room through the window, she turns and beats on his chest, first announcing, "Killer, killer," but then collapsing in his arms. The glow of the light through the stained glass doors illuminates her conflict. The doors are made of alternating panes of red and violet glass, colors often considered opposites. The tympani enter softly followed by low strings, and Maria sinks into Tony's arms. In the background the violet and red hues from the windows almost bisect the screen. When coupled with the figuration of the clenched couple, it is clear that although they may be together, it is the antagonism of their backgrounds, represented by the blue and red, that prevents their dreams from becoming reality. Throughout most of the scene, Tony and Maria are separately framed by the opposite colors of violet and red. The shadow of the brass headboard casts a prisonlike image on the violet and red surfaces, further enhancing the implied futility of their love.

The cat-and-mouse motif, first heard when the gang members began their escape from the scene of the rumble, reemerges here, as Tony comforts Maria and begins to plan their escape together. Tony's comment, "but it's not us. It's everything around us," reinforces the importance of the set design and the use of color and prison bars.

"Somewhere" is a quiet reflective work, a final moment together as Tony and Maria realize the futility of their situation and love for each other. The hopelessness of their situation is reflected by the camera's perspective, as it records their desperate duet, Tony and Maria's final one, through the bars of the headboard, the room awash in red and violet shadows. The bars and the contrasting colors never leave the framing, despite the exquisite intimacy and beauty of the duet. Orchestrationally, Bernstein relies almost exclusively on the gentleness of the strings to convey the moment. The music, along with the lighting and predominance of the red and violet light emanating from the doors to the bedroom, directly contrasts the ensuing scene, with its direct-cut editing, jungle drums, dark lighting, and harshly delineated exterior shots.

Chapter 24: "I'm Scared"

Bernstein accompanies the ensuing chase sequence with the jungle drums motif. Visually, we are treated to shot after shot of walls, buildings or old doors used as construction site barriers. The maze and corneredlike atmosphere is undeniable.

Chapter 25: "Cool"

The Jets regroup in an alleyway surrounded by walls and very foreboding fencing. As the Jets begin to sort out their feelings and plan their next moves, Action (the hotheaded character) begins to draw the others into the speech-rhythm patter that the gang so frequently used as a bonding technique. His first attempt only barely succeeds. There is little energy put into the first [01:54:19] climactic moment. The second attempt does not even take root. The syntactic structure of Action's gesture is similar to other speech-rhythm games we have seen: a rhythmic interplay of one-liners reaching a feverish pitch interrupted by a person of authority. But in this case the rhythm is weak and anemic. No one's heart is into the game, and they begin fighting among themselves. When a neighbor (seen from a position of authority by the camera), disturbed by the noise from the alley, sends a jar crashing to the ground in the hope of dispersing the gang, he is met with outbursts of hostility, not rhythmic foreplay. Ice, aptly named, herds the gang and their girls into an adjacent garage.

As Ice assumes the mantle of leadership of the Jets, faint signs of speech- [01:55:05] rhythm begin to reemerge as he interrupts Action's ranting by out-shouting him. He turns on the headlights from a truck inside the garage as a visual and sonic punctuation mark. Action begins his monologue, slowly, deliberately, and calmly. He is the reflection of coolness. He is the new Riff. His speech is abruptly punctuated by the rhythms of a car door opening and more headlights being turned on. The gang begins to respond. Action [01:55:22] wants to "bust," and Arab wants to "get even." Ice leads as the gang begins to regain its rhythm.

At first listen, the musical motif that forms the basis of the song "Cool" [01:55:51] seems to be the *hate* theme, but upon closer listening we find that it is really the *love* theme with an extra resolving note added on. This subtle musical construction reveals the true purpose of the song—out of their common hatred for the Sharks, the Jets regain their love for each other.

Stephen Sondheim's lyrics are about the Jets maintaining their cool under pressure. The music is written in the cool jazz style that emerged in the mid to late 1950s, led most conspicuously by jazz greats Lennie Tristano and Miles Davis, and defined by Davis's 1950 landmark album, *Birth of the Cool*. Johnny Green's orchestration for the film captures the essential ingredients of the style; slithery melodic lines punctuated by beboplike outbursts of brass and drum hits with dissonantly voiced harmonies played by a vibraphone, flutes in their lower registers, straight-muted trumpets, smooth saxes, and brushes on the drums.

Robbins's choreography reflects not just the musical characteristics of the cool style, but also its psychological underpinnings, the emotional state of the

Jets as well as the musical structure of the song. It is controlled turmoil. While on the surface, the music and dancing remains slippery and flowing, underneath is a powerhouse of emotional outbursts, volcanoes ready to blow at any moment. However disheveled, unorganized, and out of control the Jets may be at the beginning of the song, they recover their collective cohesiveness by the end.

Initially, dance combinations are individualized; each gang member is acting on his or her emotions independently and spontaneously. Their outbursts are irregular, only temporarily repressed and filled with emotional and physical rage. Their initial anarchy is reflected by the random musical outbursts of the drums, brass, and to a lesser extent by the woodwinds in a thinly textured counterpoint.

[01:56:51]   At first, the music is a veritable stew of musical exclamations, gestures, and riffs crashing into each other, spilling over each other. But structurally, a musical fugue emerges and provides some underlying organization to these seemingly random outbursts. The fugue is subtle, lying underneath a highly chromatic and rhythmic line. The fugue's subject is melodically and rhythmically simple, but its power lies in its dynamics, its change in loudness. Each subject's entrance starts pianissimo and crescendos to a sforzando. Each sforzando is matched onscreen by a character's emotional and physical outburst. The crescendo into these outbursts, then, reflects in the rising inner anger and tension within the character. The sforzando and associated onscreen movement is the release of these emotions.

[01:58:18]   But as the song progresses, the fugues disappear and the riffs and lines be-
[01:58:49]   gin to synchronize. By the end of the song, the individual gang members have coalesced into one unit, moving together as an ensemble again. By the final shout chorus, the dancers and the music have come together. Once they have collected themselves, the Jets settle back into their cool alter egos, ready to confront the world again. They emerge from the garage collected, organized, and in control of themselves.

Chapter 26: Gotta Find Tony

Anybodys rejoins the gang and informs them of Chino's plan for revenge. Ice takes control, issuing orders to each of the gang members, which are instantly obeyed with precision, enthusiasm, and a rhythmic patter indicating the recovered cohesiveness of the gang.

Anybodys seizes the moment and becomes the voice of authority now, disrupting the gang's planning. Having discovered Chino's plan, she dangles the knowledge of it in front of the gang until she is accorded her long-desired respect and acceptance. Music from the rumble scene returns as the gang takes to the street in search of Tony.

Chapter 27: "A Boy Like That/I Have a Love"

[02:02:33]   While brass and high woodwinds dominate the rumble, a lush string orchestration for Tony and Maria's bedroom scene provides a stark and comforting contrast. The scene's initial visual fade is an upward-looking exterior shot of Maria's bedroom, complete with jaillike fire escapes blocking the way. Another fade brings us to the bedroom interior, a delicately lit visual image that emphasizes the stained glass doors, along with Maria gently dozing in Tony's arms in her bed.

We hear hints of the song "Somewhere," indicating that, at least for now, Tony and Maria have found their place—in each other's arms, protected by the sanctity of Maria's churchlike room. **[02:02:40]**

The music carries us into the adjacent room as Anita enters, her head covered by a black-and-red scarf. As she calls to Maria and attempts to enter the locked bedroom, we hear gently rumbling tympani leading into a dissonantly constructed pyramid figure by the strings. This orchestrated crescendo presages the tension about to be released when Anita confronts Maria about her relationship with Tony. **[02:03:17]**

The relatively contrapuntal nature of the musical pyramid eventually yields to a unison statement of the *hate* theme as Maria unlocks the door and allows Anita to enter her inner sanctum. A disdainful and suspicious Anita pushes Maria aside and enters the room. Again, we see that any point of confrontation is highlighted not by a musically climactic moment, but rather by a silence that has been set up by a musical buildup. **[02:04:16]** **[02:04:24]**

"A Boy Like That" is a powerful demonstration of the conflict both women experience and their method of resolving it. Psychosocial theory would emphasize that the conflict is resolved through discussion and mutual acceptance and contrast this resolution with the wars concocted by the boys of the film. Musically, the rhythmic phrasing sets us off with its deliberately constructed awkwardness. The steady, underlying pulse is disguised through the use of multiple meters or divisions of time so that we never really have a sense of rhythmic bedrock. **[02:04:42]**

Anita's lyrics are venomous. She is filled with hate because of the loss of her love. She attempts to ward Maria off of Tony, proclaiming that "a boy like that wants one thing only." Maria counters that what is true for Anita is not true for her. Her vocal response is a gentler and loving proclamation, one reflected in the use of strings rather than brass and woodwinds as accompaniment. The climactic moment of the song is when Maria questions how Anita could have so much hate in her heart. She declares that if Anita truly loved Bernardo, she would understand Maria's dilemma. The pulsing rhythm of the song pauses for an instant, leaving a moment of breath to highlight the irrefutability of Maria's insight. The musical gesture is not unlike the dramatic pause in Franz Schubert's "Gretchen am Spinnrade," when the spinning wheel stops as the singer remembers being kissed. **[02:05:43]** **[02:06:07]**

Maria's wisdom triggers Anita's epiphany as she recognizes Maria's overpowering love. The musical nature of song changes at this point. The pulse returns, fluid but regular. Anita and Maria join in duet, closely harmonized, matching their rhythms. There is no counterpoint here. They have become of the same mind and heart. **[02:06:26]** **[02:08:11]**

Chapter 28: Anita's Message

Once the girls are resolved and set a course of action to save Tony, the music dips underneath their dialog only to be interrupted by a knock at the door. It is

of course the voice of authority interrupting this newest fantasy play. Lieutenant Schrank has come to investigate the murders of Riff and Bernardo. The
moment is perhaps the weakest musical editing of the film. The music simply

[02:09:11]

stops midphrase, with no sense of building or denouement. The interruption
of the music by the authority figure is less than convincing from a technical
and timing perspective. It is unlike any other moment in the film and causes
one to wonder if there was a momentary lapse in the editorial department.

Maria sends Anita to Doc's Candy Shop to arrange her meeting with Tony
so they can flee the hatred that is engulfing them.

Chapter 30: No Cure from Doc

Anita's entrance into Doc's Candy Shop is met by silence and the stares of the
remaining members of the Jets, who have gathered there upon learning that

[02:11:55]

Tony was hiding in the basement. The "Mambo" from the dance at the gym
returns, underpinning the simmering antagonism between the gangs. This is a
wise choice of music. Both gangs have shown respect and deference toward
the ladies. To underscore the confrontation between Anita and the remaining
Jets with rumble music would prematurely give away the loss of this respect
before it is actually revealed in the ensuing dialog and drama.

Initially, the Jets do begrudgingly show Anita respect. After all, the candy
store has always been neutral turf. But as Anita begins to inquire about Tony's whereabouts, the gang grows suspicious, and the speech-rhythm returns
as the Jets begin to verbally taunt Anita.

As the taunting escalates and Anita is physically accosted, the music

[02:13:47]

moves to a fast rendition of the *America* theme, no doubt a social commentary on the state of violence in America by the creators of the masterpiece.
Motivic elements of the rumble music surface as Anita is forced to the floor
and the Jets propel Baby John on top of her. Doc interrupts the scene, saving
Anita and confronting the gang.

[02:14:11]

As an interesting side note, the music ends on a full cadence just before
Doc interrupts the fracas. He does not in fact interrupt the music before it
ends, as has been the case with other authority figures. He may be the proprietor of neutral territory, but he is a resigned, timid little man. He has never
been the voice of authority, and both gangs treat him with little respect. To
have him disrupt the assault on Anita by interrupting the music would have
given him the same archetypal power that previous adult interruptions had
given to the character involved. Enraged at being assaulted, Anita falsely announces to the Jets that Chino shot Maria. Doc unwittingly passes the lie to
Tony, who bolts from the basement in which he has been hiding.

Chapter 31: Finale

The lack of music throughout Tony's hunt for Chino intensifies Tony's sense
of loss and despondency. He is under the impression that Chino has shot Maria.
His best friend is dead. He has killed his girlfriend's brother. His alienation is
complete. He is supremely alone. While a monophonic line of perhaps a flute or
violin may at first seem to be the logical musical choice to accompany him, the
starkness of the street and his state of mind is more appropriately reflected by

the absence of even a single melodic gesture. All we hear is the sharp clanging of chain-link fences as Tony pounds them in desperation.

The absence of any music and all but the most minimal of background sound makes Chino's killing of Tony all the more intense. The single gunshot punctuates the silence as no brass or percussion hit can. We are forced to confront our own sense of empathy toward Tony and to a lesser extent, Chino. And we are about to see how the entrance of the music at Tony's death underscores Maria's aloneness as she watches Tony slip from her arms into death.

As Tony begins to succumb to death in Maria's arms, she begins an unaccompanied, frightened, and forlorn rendition of the song "Somewhere." Tony is unable to join her, and the orchestra remains silent while we hear Maria's futile attempt at one last fantasy. She never completes the song. Just before the final cadence she falters, and the orchestra must finish her melody and the final cadence. Her fantasy, and Tony's, remains incomplete, unfulfilled. It remains for the music to bring home the final cadence and the final irony. **[02:20:45]** **[02:21:42]**

The orchestral conclusion to the song remains understated. Lush strings complete the melody, with no winds, brass, or percussion to be heard. Maria finally interrupts the orchestra (one final authoritarian intrusion) as she orders both gangs to "Stay back!" The music responds by stopping midphrase. Maria grabs the gun from Chino and announces that she, too, has now learned to hate. Maria's red dress stands out against the dirtied colors of both gangs. Her passion for love has now changed to hate, and the full flowering of the color red as a symbol of the duality of love/hate becomes strikingly obvious. **[02:21:47]**

At the end of her pronouncement, she drops the gun and collapses into tears onto the ground as "Somewhere" returns. She alternately looks to each gang, and we begin to see elements of remorse as each gang member begins to realize his own complicity, and the melody subtly builds. They comfort Maria while the music crescendos to a notable moment as members from both gangs join together to carry Tony's body from the playground as impromptu pallbearers.

The orchestration is flushed out with brass and ominous tympani that announce the funeral procession as it begins. The music, however, remains dissonant, reflecting the losses that have transpired rather than announcing that love has conquered and that the gangs will henceforth live in harmony. The gangs disperse, leaving Chino in police custody. There is no happy resolution here. An examination of the final few bars of music reveals that the intervals of the love/hate theme remain until the very end. While the upper chords resolve to a C major triad, the bass notes respond a tritone away, exemplifying the enduring dissonance and the residual hate. The final C major triad is not answered by the tritone dissonance of hate but by silence, leaving the final major chord resolved to a fragile consonance, one without a strong foundation and sense of resolution. We are left hanging, wondering about the fates of all whom have loved, hated, and suffered. **[02:24:38]** **[02:26:01]**

Chapter 32: End Credits

When it opened on Broadway, *West Side Story* was a daring and dangerous experiment. The show did not end happily, upbeat, and joyously, as did all other Broadway musicals up to that time.

But the end credit music does soften the blow to some extent. At first glance, the end credit music appears to be similar to the overture, a medley of songs from the film. It begins by reemphasizing Tony and Maria's hope with the song "Somewhere." But conspicuous by their absence are any songs associated with hate or alienation. We hear "Somewhere," "Tonight," "I Feel Pretty," and "Maria," all optimistic tunes expressing hope and love, but absent are the "Dance at the Gym," "America," "Gee, Officer Krupke," "The Rumble," "Cool," and other songs that reflect divisiveness and hate.

SUMMARY

Upon its opening on Broadway in 1957, *West Side Story* was immediately recognized not just as a great work of art but as a glaring social statement about the state of America. The music stands on its own merit. Bernstein's adaptation, *Suite from West Side Story*, continues to be one of the most performed band and orchestral works in the American music repertoire. The story, about American values and opportunities, hate, and forbidden love, remains as relevant today as it did when Jerome Robbins first began to fiddle with the idea of an updated *Romeo and Juliet* in the 1940s. But what makes *West Side Story* so powerful is the resulting synergy from all of its elements combined. Music, dance, screenplay, directing, acting, set design, cinematography, costuming, lighting, and all of the other elements that make filmmaking such a collaborative process are brought together to convey the artistic vision and message of those involved in the process. The result is an aesthetic and syntactic milestone.

NOTES

1. Geoffrey Block, *Enchanted Evenings: The Broadway Musical from* Show Boat *to Sondheim* (New York: Oxford University Press, 1997), 260.

2. Meryle Secrest, *Stephen Sondheim: A Life* (New York: Alfred A. Knopf, 1998), 123.

3. Greg Lawrence, *Dance with Demons: The Life of Jerome Robbins* (New York: Putnam, 2001), 288.

4. Arthur Laurents, *Original Story: A Memoir of Broadway and Hollywood* (New York: Knopf, 2000), 357.

5. Mark Eden Horowitz, *Sondheim on Music* (Lanham, MD: Scarecrow Press, 2003), 25.

6. Richard Kislan, *The Musical: A Look at the American Musical Theater* (Englewood Cliffs, NJ: Prentice Hall, 1980), 216-17.

7. *West Side Story*, vocal score (Milwaukee: G. Schirmer, 1959), 17–18.

Psycho

HISTORICAL CONTEXT

Much has been written about the music for Alfred Hitchcock's masterpiece, *Psycho*. Composed by Bernard Herrmann, the music is a terse and inspired score, using Herrmann's signature style, the development of small cells of musical ideas, then relentlessly varied over time. In Elmer Bernstein's *Film Music Notebook*, an article by Fred Steiner provides a solid framework for understanding why Herrmann chose to use only strings for the entire score, abandoning the well-wrought use of brass and percussion to build suspense.[1] In an interview from 1971, Herrmann indicated that "I felt that I was able to complement the black and white photography of the film with a black and white sound."[2]

Many scholars have noted Hitchcock's lifelong fascination with birds. The film *The Birds* may at first and obvious glance be about birds that mysteriously attack people, but Hitchcock has made it clear in writings and interviews that the film is really about the randomness of events in life. His penchant for feathered creatures finds it way into this film as well, as the allegorical story of the battle between birds of flight and birds of prey.

There has been some speculation that Hitchcock's almost fanciful fascination with birds could derive from the unique English slang of his time, referring to women as *birds*. This theory, if true, could certainly be supported by the story line of Norman preying upon women as well as the numerous strategically placed paintings on the set backgrounds. Closer attention to these background paintings reveals the ominous subject of women being either murdered or raped.

The term *bird* in Cockney slang is short for *jailbird* and has been around since the 1500s. The term as originally used referred to being caged and hunted. Newer use of the term referred to *doing prison time*, as in *doing bird*.[3] Hitchcock's mother was a Cockney, and no doubt he was familiar with the culture and its slang expressions. As we shall see, the archetypal plot for *Psycho* revolves around the prisons we either create for ourselves or are born into.

Bernard Herrmann's music for *Psycho* revolves around four essential leitmotifs, the *bird of flight* theme, the *bird of prey* theme, the *metamorphosis* or *transformation* theme, and the *madness* or *psycho* motif.[4] Virtually all of the musical cues reflect some melodic or harmonic treatment of these motifs. The musical themes reflect the screenplay on an allegorical level, telling the story of two protagonists locked in their own internal debates about their own capacity for good and evil. For Marion Crane, who steals $40,000 from her longtime employer to pay off her boyfriend's debts and marry him, the internal battle is moral and legalistic. For Norman Bates, who owns the infamous Bates Motel and has killed before and will soon kill again, it is his battle with psychosis and his multiple personality disorder, manifested by his assuming his mother's persona on occasion.

Marion Crane and Norman Bates both have their sweet as well as demonic selves. The four musical leitmotifs reveal the personas as they exist at that moment for Marion and Norman. We hear the *bird of prey* theme when either of them is planning or plotting an evil act, whether it is an escape, a deception, or a murder. We hear the *bird of flight* leitmotif when either character is fleeing from someone or a situation. We hear the *transformation* theme whenever Norman or Marion switches personas and motivations. And we hear the *psycho* theme whenever Hitchcock and Herrmann wish to indicate to us the notion of *crazy* behavior. The music gives us a map to what each of the characters are thinking and doing at that moment.

Curiously, the music from the famous shower sequence was almost an afterthought, not related to any of the defined leitmotifs. Hitchcock had in fact never intended music for the scene. He told Herrmann not to score it, but Herrmann persuaded Hitchcock to let him score it first and then decide. Hitchcock was pleased with the result, and the screeching strings became one of the most classic and famous moments in film-scoring history. Yet even here, we can aurally interpret the strings as the screams of the dying *bird of flight* and the aggressive screams of the *bird of prey* as Norman attacks, a musical sound effect reflecting the knife as it penetrates the skin, or just Marion's screams as she is assaulted.

Hitchcock was very detailed in his musical notes to Herrmann, indicating in meticulously typed memos to the composer the feeling of the music as well as very specific start and stop points. Having worked together on eight previous films, Hitchcock and Herrmann had already established a comfortable working relationship, trusting each other's judgments and decisions.

Herrmann was a master manipulator of short melodic and harmonic motifs. He wrote in a cell-like structure, using short, easily recognizable ideas that could be infinitely varied and repeated many times, occasionally adding other short motifs to expand the original idea. Graham Donald Bruce calls this a *developmental score*.[5] There is logic to Herrmann's musical ideas and their development, an almost clinical approach to developing these motifs. In most of his films, this creates a strong sense of cohesiveness and interrelatedness between each of the cues. Once the motifs have been defined and established, they can be traced throughout the film not just by theoretical analysis, but more importantly, by a sensitive and aware ear.

Psycho also carries a subtheme of voyeurism. In a sense, we are voyeurs, peering in on this little melodrama as it unfolds in a little town between Phoenix and Fairvale. Hitchcock brings us into the film from an aerial view, panning and swooping down, very birdlike, as we land on the windowsill of a very nondescript cheap hotel and peer in the window as Sam and Marion begin a dialog about their uncertain future. This *peering in* will manifest itself throughout the film. Let us not forget that voyeurism implies preying upon the innocent or unknowing subject of our gaze. We are as voyeuristic in watching this drama unfold as Norman is when he peeks through the peephole to watch Marion undress for her shower.

Chapter 1: Main Titles

[00:00:05]

The notion that one person can manifest multiple personalities is implied from the moment the film begins. The opening titles by Saul Bass display a series of black-and-white lines that split the screen in various ways. The titles enter the frame, then fracture and split, moving in opposite directions as they retreat off the screen. Though we are not yet familiar with it, the opening musical theme is the *bird of flight* theme in its fullest treatment of the film. It conveys a sense of urgency and franticness, as would be expected from a bird or person fleeing a dangerous situation. The opening chords define much of the musical material for the rest of the film. This minor triad chord with an added major seventh has been called the *Hitchcock chord*, since Herrmann was so fond of exploiting its tonal ambiguity in many of his collaborations with Hitchcock.[6] By itself, the chord is not novel, having been used in both classical and jazz compositions for decades. It is the starkness of the chord that is striking. It is not prepared by any other chords; nor does it resolve to any. It is what is called a *musical gesture*, complete and definable by itself. Its distinctive sound is derived from the combination of major and minor thirds, the basic building blocks of Western musical tonality. It is precisely this combination of major and minor thirds that gives the chord its unique ambiguity, not residing completely in any major or minor key.

Chapter 2: The Stolen Hours

With the *bird of flight* theme completed under the opening credits, Hitchcock gives us a bird's-eye view of the city of Phoenix. The setting of the film, Phoenix, Arizona, is no coincidence and is meant to reinforce the imagery of birds and especially the archetypal notion of transformation. During the opening panorama, one of the tallest and most distinguishable buildings in camera range features a rotating Thunderbird on its roof.

We are immediately introduced to another leitmotif that will have profound implications throughout the film, the *transformation* or *metamorphosis* theme. It is a gently lilting theme consisting of a series of ascending and descending block chords, meant to give us a feeling of alighting or landing. Indeed, this is exactly what the camera does as it moves from its panning of the city and begins to focus in, or descend on, a deliberately nondescript windowsill on a very ordinary building in downtown Phoenix. The camera lands as a bird would do, peering into the window on an unsuspecting couple just as a voyeur would. We see as it sees. We are the voyeurs. At first, the musical leitmotif seems to be accompanying the act of voyeurism, but as we will see and hear later, the theme will reemerge whenever a character is undergoing some form of transformation, evolving from one personality trait to another. For both of the main characters, Marion and Norman, this theme will return throughout the film as each transforms from an evil person to a good person and vice versa.

[00:01:55]

The introduction of the *transformation* theme at this point is admittedly a bit ambiguous. The fact that Sam and Marion are enjoying a midafternoon tryst in a seedy hotel does not at first glance seem to be cause for any form of transformation. We discover that they are normal, everyday people. She is an unmarried and trusted secretary for the same real estate firm for ten years. He is divorced and is a hardware store owner dutifully paying off his alimony, even at the expense of his own future. Yet, these seemingly upstanding individuals are in fact satisfying their more carnal desires, illicitly meeting during business hours for their dalliances. So, in fact, the *transformation* theme is relevant here. Both characters lead dual lives and move between them.

The dual nature of Marion's personality finds substance in costuming as well. In the room with Sam, she is wearing a white bra, while later in the film, as she packs her belongings in preparation for absconding with the money, she is dressed in a black one. This is a subtle costuming decision, one that might be misconstrued as a continuity issue, but given Hitchcock's known penchant for detail, the choice of costuming serves the allegorical good girl/bad girl theme that Hitchcock presents in other more obvious situations.

Sam and Marion's bedroom discussion centers on Marion's dissatisfaction with their current surreptitious arrangements. She threatens to break off the relationship unless they can be more public and therefore respectable in their meetings. Sam is resistant at first, but precisely at the moment he reconsiders

[00:04:36]

and agrees to her demands, Herrmann presents us with the *transformation* theme in varied form. Sam's mind has changed, and the music underscores his own transformation. He surrenders with his arms held wide open, palms upward and his chest bared as he slouches in the chair. Sam rises, donning his shirt and announces to Marion that "whenever it's possible, I want to see you, under any circumstances, even respectability." She responds, "You make respectability sound disrespectful."

It is a tender and revealing moment, supported by the lower strings in the midrange of their instruments, the lushest sounding orchestration available

[00:05:20]

to Herrmann. The final chord of the cue, the Hitchcock chord, is dissonant and harsh, however, and is heard just after Sam complains about the financial hopelessness of his situation. As Sam dresses in preparation for leaving, Marion reveals a sly sense of humor, indicating that all is well between them.

Chapter 3: Forty Thousand Dollars

Marion returns to the real estate office where she works. The barrenness of her life is reflected in the painting of a desert that looms above her desk. At first glance, the office appears to be no more than a well-dressed set. But Marion states that "you can't buy off unhappiness with pills." As we see her in a medium close-up, the desert landscape of the painting is clearly surrounding her. Later in the sequence, as Marion departs the office to deposit a cash transaction, the camera pauses on a companion painting of a lush mountainous landscape, reflecting Marion's upcoming decision to flee the barrenness of her current life for a more bountiful one with Sam.

[00:10:53]

As Marion and the camera gaze at the money on the bed in her room, we are introduced to the *bird of prey* theme for the first time. It is a tight, introverted, six-note melody, more of a gesture or even a Bach-like motivic fragment, the kind he would have used to develop his intricately woven counterpoints. The entire pitch range of the gesture is in only a minor third, a relatively narrow expanse for a musical idea. Rhythmically, the fragment is quite simple. A series of equal eighth notes convey the idea of a clock ticking and time passing. They are accompanied by a series of held chords that intensify in volume, drawing us into Marion's world. Herrmann then begins sequencing the gesture, transposing it to different notes while maintaining the overall contour of the line and preserving the rhythmic structure. In compositional terms, this is the classic cellular construction that is the hallmark of Herrmann's style.

One would expect a predatory leitmotif to be quick actioned and intense, but Herrmann, being uniquely attuned to Hitchcock's style of understatement, suspense, and implication, conveys the real imagery of a bird of prey—the stalking, plotting, and planning before the attack. The passage of time is musically conveyed by ticking eighth notes, which show the intricate preparations and planning that must accompany the successful plot. The intricacy of the planning is also reflected by the narrowness of the range of the melody, which is constantly being manipulated by Herrmann. The musical theme, then, is one of quiet preparation and planning.

Chapter 4: The Stolen Money

As Marion begins her escape from Phoenix, her boss, Mr. Lowery, happens to cross the street in front of her car while she waits for a traffic light. They acknowledge each other politely, though Mr. Lowery seems a bit taken aback at the sight of Marion, who supposedly had gone home ill from work after depositing the cash. The *bird of flight* theme enters a moment later as [00:13:00] the traffic light changes and Marion drives away. The *bird of flight* theme is an abrupt, pecking affair consisting of only two notes rather insistently repeated over and over again. It is as if we were watching a chicken pecking for grain from the ground. It is an agitated theme, the second note being deliberately clipped short, rhythmically, as if we were inhaling and suddenly became short of breath.

Whereas the *bird of prey* theme had accompanied Marion while she planned and prepared her embezzlement, the *bird of flight* theme now accompanies her as she leaves town. She has been seen leaving town and must flee with all due haste. Herrmann creates a series of tight, inwardly twisting melodies consisting of several notes without any large melodic leaps that are juxtaposed under a sweeping violin line, all the while accompanied by the pecking motif of the *bird of flight* theme.

The *bird of flight* theme accompanies a visual montage sequence as Marion continues driving and is designed to reflect a sense of time passing and distance traveled. The theme also represents the psychological distance Marion has placed between herself and her previous life. Daylight gives way to nightfall. Oncoming traffic begins to thin. Civilization (and civility) dwindles as Marion leaves Phoenix behind. The musical cue eventually dies out without [00:13:36] cadencing as the screen fades to black. The theme remains unfinished. It simply vanishes, unresolved. Clearly this escape is not over; it has simply paused as Marion gets some rest in her car by the side of the road.

Chapter 5: A Woman on the Run

The film's voyeuristic undertones are reinforced by a close-up shot of the highway patrolman peering into the window at the sleeping Marion. He wakes her up by pecking at the window. His gaze is expressionless, eyes hidden by dark sunglasses. Our perspective is Marion's. The patrolman dominates the screen, looking down from a position of power, a beaklike nose commanding the perspective.

After a rather confrontational discussion with the patrolman (one can hardly imagine participating in this sort of discourse today and not having to post bail afterward), Marion turns the ignition and drives away, having been cleared to leave by the officer. The *bird of flight* theme commences immediately as if attached to the ignition itself. Marion is on the run again. The incessant pecking of the theme becomes grating to us, though Marion maintains a steely gaze throughout the scene. The highway patrolman's car follows close behind her, visually supporting the *bird of flight* theme.

[00:16:16]

Chapter 6: The High-Pressure Customer

The *flight* music continues as a type of sonic glue or transition music, unifying a series of visual cuts designed to show Marion's continued escape from Phoenix. As Marion turns into a used car lot, the theme again simply dissipates, unfinished, unresolved, and indicating that there is more flight to come.

[00:17:33]

The *transformation* theme emerges as Marion eyes the used cars on the lot. Inevitably, we associate the *transformation* theme with Marion's molting of her feathers, the shedding of her old car for another one. Although the cue is short, it is reinforced by her curt and uneasy dialog with the used car salesman. Marion presses the salesman for a trade. The *bird of prey* theme emerges as Marion enters the ladies' restroom at the used car lot. She is plotting again, removing and counting large bills of money from her purse to pay for the new car. The theme disappears as she begins to execute her plan.

[00:17:47]

[00:21:01]

[00:21:55]

Having swapped her old car for another one, Marion drives away from the dealership as the *bird of flight* leitmotif immediately returns. For a brief moment during a fade we can see Marion biting her lip as the car salesman, mechanic, and patrolman watch her leave. The *flight* theme again serves as sonic glue, stitching together a montage, reflecting the passage of time and distance, but with the added voiced-over dialog between Cassidy, Lowery, and Marion's sister, Lila, as they initially worry about her before collectively realizing her intentions.

[00:23:11]

The *flight* theme intensifies in volume as the night grows longer and the weather turns considerably wetter and more hostile. For a few brief moments, the tempo of the music seems to be matched to the beating of the windshield wipers. Whether this momentary synchronization was intentional or not is speculative. While the wipers are shown five times, only the second shot is clearly synchronized. The others are not quite as decisive. Nonetheless, used in this fashion for a brief moment, the momentary audio and visual alignment does heighten the rhythmic value of the incessant pecking of the *bird of flight* theme and therefore our own sense of anxiety.

[00:25:38]

Chapter 7: The Bates Motel

The *flight* theme ends shortly before we see the Bates Motel through the windshield of Marion's car. This is important because Hitchcock does not

[00:26:14]

want us to make any initial association with the motel. For Marion, tired, a bit scared, and weary of the rain, the Bates Motel is simply the nearest port in a storm. The absence of music as she drives toward the motel office does not signal that there is any danger, just the mystery of a small motel on the side of the road. Marion honks her horn several times before the motel's proprietor, Norman Bates, descends from the house behind the motel.

As Norman has Marion register for the motel, their seemingly innocuous verbal exchange provides another moment for Hitchcock to emphasize the duality of Marion's nature. She stands in the hotel lobby next to a mirror that provides us with her reflection. The mirror simply allows us to see two Marions. The same mirror will serve to reflect dual images of other characters later in the film.

We enter a part of the movie in which the use of reflection, shadows, and mirrors provides glimpses into the twofold nature of both characters. As Norman shows Marion around her room, he pauses in front of the bathroom door, casting a shadow on the door frame. Two prints of innocent-looking yard birds hang on the wall. It is as if the pleasant side of Norman is oblivious to his shadowy other self, staring at the birds on the wall.

As Norman leaves and a very pleasant Marion wishes him good-bye, we catch a momentary image of her other self in the mirror on the vanity desk behind her. Hence, in a relatively short sequence we are treated to two characters, each with an additional reflection of themselves lurking in the background.

Marion begins to unpack her bag while Norman leaves to prepare dinner for them. The *bird of prey* theme returns as Marion unlocks her suitcase and begins to unpack. She searches her room for an appropriate place to hide the money, finally wrapping it in her newspaper and casually placing it on her night table. The motif fades as she accomplishes her task. She is drawn toward the window and becomes distracted by an argument between Norman and his "mother" in the house behind the motel. **[00:30:37]**

Norman then descends the steps from the house, accompanied by the *transformation* theme. The visual and aural linkage initially indicates that the theme is meant to reflect Norman's transformation from his privately argumentative self as he assumes his mother's persona to the complacent and congenial Norman he publicly portrays. The music supports the image of Norman's descending from the house and the safety of his private world. The *transformation* motif at this point is a series of descending chords, much like the film's opening sequence in which the bird (camera) descends to the windowsill outside the motel where Marion and Sam had their little matinee. **[00:32:48]**

As the *transformation* theme evolves, it becomes a sad, laconic, two-note motif, related to the *bird of flight* theme rhythmically. As was the case in the pecking rhythmic figure of the *flight* theme, the first note is long in comparison to the second note. But in the *flight* theme, the figure rises by a half step, conveying a feeling of nervousness, evoking the imagery of a bird feeding but abruptly raising its head every few moments to check around for predators. In this case, the *transformation* theme descends by a whole step, almost as if it were sighing. **[00:33:02]**

As Norman enters the frame and joins Marion on the porch outside of the motel lobby, we are treated to one of Hitchcock's extraordinary marriages of lighting, framing, and music. Marion remains onscreen with her back to our point of view. We are left to wonder to whom the *transformation* theme applies: Norman the inwardly rageous psychopath and outwardly meek motel keeper, or Marion, the outwardly pleasant, faithful secretary and inwardly angry, lonely larcenist?

Chapters 8, 9: Dinner with Norman, Mother's Problem

As Norman utters the ironically humorous line, "Mother is . . . she isn't quite herself today," we become aware of Norman's reflection in the window behind him. The *transformation* theme momentarily disappears but conspicuously returns as Marion backs up, gestures toward the open door, and invites Norman into her room. Whether the theme is referring to her return to the *innocent* Marion, or whether it is referring to the forwardness of her gesture, is unclear. Certainly, a Freudian interpretation of this moment would reference the female backing up, revealing an open space and inviting the man inside.

[00:33:28]
[00:33:56]

The sequence relies on the music to reflect the film's allegorical thesis about the conflict between good and evil within each of us. The *transformation* theme underscores two medium shots, one of Norman and then Marion. Each character is given their moment onscreen, accompanied by the same music, the *transformation* theme. The theme continues to underscore the dialog as Norman and Marion outdo each other with politeness, each inviting the other into their own world. Marion eventually relents, following Norman into the parlor behind the motel's office, a chamber that could be a taxidermist's trophy room.

Marion is momentarily taken aback at the sight of Norman's many stuffed and mounted birds. The camera lingers on the fierce-looking owls with wings spread as if they were about to pounce. Crows, mythological harbingers of death or at least bad luck, silently gaze from above. All sorts of birds of prey adorn Norman's walls. But looming even more ominously behind the birds are their shadows. Just as the bird leitmotifs lurk omnipresently in the soundscape of the film, so do the shadows in the visualscape; first Marion's, then Norman's, as they share the porch outside the parlor, and finally within Norman's nest, his parlor. The camera continually shoots the stuffed birds from slightly below, leaving us sensing the power that these birds and their shadows hold.

The marriage of visual elements, stuffed birds, shadows, and camera perspective is nowhere more evident than when a chivalrous Norman stands and invites Marion to sit down. Shot from below, looking upward toward a massive stuffed owl with wings spread and eyes forever focused on some unknown dinner prospect, the camera reveals the awesome power of the owl and its shadow. Norman leans over to place the dinner servings on a table. When he straightens up, his imagery replaces the owl in the frame. He is now that powerful, predatory bird. It is as if Norman has assumed the body of the predator with only the bird's wings and its shadow looming behind him, while he maintains his friendly and inviting demeanor. In this sense, Norman's predatory intentions are reflected by his shadow in the form of the owl, whose own predatory instincts are reflected by its own shadow. Marion sits and begins her meal while Norman takes a chair in the corner.

As Marion takes her first delicate bite of the meal or bait (Norman's surname is Bates, after all), Norman utters the line that can only be described as the icing on the cake. "You eat like a bird," sounds a bit ludicrous and even overstated now that we have so carefully dissected dinner, but the camera again focuses on Norman from below, giving him a larger-than-life persona. The dialog briefly focuses on birds and taxidermy as Norman and Marion politely dally around the real topics that are haunting them.

In the meantime, the music has gently faded out, allowing us to reflect on the allegorical significance of the ensuing dialog. Each character begins to reveal more about himself and herself. Marion is only politely interested in Norman's pastime of taxidermy. Norman's dialog is, however, quite revealing, and the fact that the camera continues to portray him as a powerful figure lends significance to that which he reveals about himself. Commenting on his taxidermist's choice of stuffing only birds and not other beasts, as he calls them, he reveals that "it's more than a hobby," as he gently strokes one of the smaller stuffed birds. The eroticism is unavoidable. After a very awkward pause, he further elucidates that "a hobby is supposed to pass the time, not fill it." His admissions reflect Norman at his most honest moments. Yet, the lighting continues to evoke Norman's shadow. Thus, innocuous small talk quickly becomes a thinly veiled allegorical discussion with such existential lines as, "Where are you going?" and "I'm looking for a private island." As each character begins to reveal more about himself and herself, they also begin to probe the psyche of the other, discovering that their innocence is only one aspect of their being.

[00:35:25]

The dialog serves as a platform from which Hitchcock invites us into his film and its subliminal debate. Norman philosophizes that "we're in all in our private traps, clamped in them, and none of us can ever get out." Norman may be revealing his inner thoughts to Marion, but the camera's perspective is that of Marion's. We have become her. Norman is talking to us, and in that sense, he is also talking about us. We, too, are caught in our traps, according to Norman.

Still the bird allegory is never far away. Norman continues, "We scratch and claw but only at the air." Norman's avian perspective finds later fruition as his physical movements begin to resemble that of a bird's.

When Marion gently probes Norman about his relationship with his mother, Norman responds compassionately enough, but as Marion's suggestions become more overt and direct, Norman becomes agitated, aggressive, and defiant of Marion. We see the other side of Norman, his shadow if you will; a hint of his aggression soon to come. The mise-en-scène reinforces the nature of the exchange, hinting at Norman's predatory ambitions by revealing two stuffed owls on the walls, wings spread, knees bent as if caught swooping down on their prey midflight—a moment fixed in time. Under each of these owls hangs a painting of an undraped woman being attacked by a dark, male figure.

Norman's anger and the shadow of his alter ego boils up and emerges as Marion suggests that he send his mother to a home. He leans forward, his eyes steely as the camera frames him presciently between two stuffed birds. At precisely the moment he utters the word, *madhouse*, the music reappears, with the distinct musical announcement of the *madness* or *psycho* motif, a series of three notes heard in the lower strings. This motif, defined as a sharp movement upward, then a deep drop downward, is striking, distinctive, and self-contained. It is a bastardization of the theme heard in the earlier motel scene with Sam and Marion. Whereas the earlier Marion motif followed the same contour as this *madness* motif (upward, then downward motion), it was harmonically consonant, almost loving, reflecting Sam's love for Marion. The current, distorted version is harmonically dissonant and grating, defined by musical intervals that seem extreme and unresolved. In a psychological sense, the concept of love as reflected in Marion's motif has become distorted, reflecting Norman's perverted sense of love.

[00:40:33]

[00:40:38]

With the entrances of the high strings, the music continues the transformation of the gentlemanly adult Norman to the homicidally angry child. The music becomes an extension of the dialog. Norman begins his transformation and verbal attack as Marion parries and retreats. He continues his diatribe, describing the horrors of living in an institution (old age for his mother, clearly a mental one for himself), as his eyes drift off, peering into another world. He is beyond Marion, beyond the stuffed birds; he is reliving another life. Eventually, he breaks his gaze and refocuses his attack on Marion, who again retreats, clearly concerned about the change of direction in their verbal pas de deux.

The camera again frames Norman between the two stuffed birds as he sarcastically pontificates, "People always mean well. They cluck their thick tongues and shake their heads and suggest, oh, so very delicately." Notice that the *madness* theme continues to underscore the entire scene with a wandering contrapuntal line in the upper strings. Norman flirts with insanity as he becomes more agitated, but he eventually recovers and retreats into his gentlemanly persona.

[00:42:16]

The *madness* music continues even as Norman successfully suppresses his inner anger. He asks Marion a simple question that causes her to reflect on her own dilemma. She responds to him, saying "Thank you," in a resolved tone of voice. The theme ends as Marion seems to recognize her own little madness. Her internal conflict between good and bad is resolved. She never overtly reveals whether she will continue with the larceny or return to her former way of life. Nonetheless, the allegorical dialog of the past few minutes causes us to understand that she will be returning to Phoenix to set things right. The subtlest, yet most unambiguous, clue as to Marion's decision is the disappearance of this remarkably dissonant and contrapuntal cue, a true musical resolution to this dance of musical and psychological lines.

The *madness* motif is related to the *transformation* theme in that both themes are constructed from similar, though not exactly the same, chords. While the *transformation* theme is derived from what is called a diminished chord, the *madness* motif is extracted from a minor triad with an added major seventh, the now familiar Hitchcock chord. Both chords are harmonically ambiguous. The sonic result is the same; we hear them as being similar. Support for this perception is found in the dialog of the scene where the *madness* motif makes an entrance. If we relate the *madness* motif to the *transformation* theme as I suggest, we can see that Norman's transformation from a calm, mild-mannered Norman yields to an angry, not-so-inwardly hostile one at precisely the moment that the *madness/transformation* theme enters and ends and when Marion has completed her transformation back to the honest secretary.

Though the music has receded and her mind is made up, Marion rises from her chair, as a rather prominently placed stuffed raven comes into the shot, precisely and presciently framed just above her left shoulder, opposite her head. Mythologically, the raven is an omen of doom and even death. The fact that it is lurking just over her shoulder should put to rest any concerns regarding the significance of the use of birds as an allegorical tool.

The *bird of prey* theme begins as Marion crosses between Norman and the camera. The camera lingers for a brief moment on the two paintings of a woman being attacked. A swooping, stuffed owl is framed between them. Norman rises between the two pictures, effectively replacing the owl as the central figure. **[00:43:11]**

Through some cunningly crafted dialog, Norman has previously discovered that Marion registered at the motel under a false name and address. The *bird of prey* leitmotif continues as Norman begins his plotting while reentering the parlor and standing between an owl (bird of prey) poised for attack and a guinea fowl–like bird (bird of flight). The framing is prescient. With the owl at his back and the guinea fowl in the foreground, Norman is physically (and psychologically) caught between the two.

He removes another painting from the wall to reveal a peephole into Marion's room. The painting is of a man accosting a woman. A close-up of Norman's eye reflects the voyeur subtext of the film. He watches Marion undress for her shower. The two paintings of birds on the wall behind her are given special prominence in the shot. Norman replaces the picture over the peephole and begins a series of posturings that can only be described as birdlike in their jerkiness. The owl continues to hover over his shoulder in the background, though the foreground guinea fowl remains out of frame. Norman's transformation is almost complete. The focus on the owl and the blurring view of the guinea fowl reveal to us which archetypal bird will win the battle for Norman's personality.

Norman climbs the steps back up to his house, forcing himself to detour to the kitchen and not up the stairs. This decision, underscored by the *bird of prey* motif, indicates that his planning is still incomplete. His indecision about whether to ascend the stairs and become his mother or to return to the kitchen and remain himself is brief. In support of this thesis, the music shifts to the *transformation* theme just before the next cut to Marion at her desk in her room. The music eases us across the edit to reveal that Marion is calculating how much of the stolen money she has already spent. The *transformation* theme, though begun in the last moment of Norman's scene, also serves as a transitional element to Marion's. The music simply fades out as Marion flushes her financial calculations down the toilet. Her transformation **[00:45:19]** **[00:45:33]** **[00:46:16]** is complete as she flushes away her sins. She intends to return to Phoenix and set things right. Marion turns on the shower and begins her ritual cleansing. But Norman, disguised as his mother, will never allow her to complete the symbolic ceremony.

Chapter 10: The Shower

Much has been written about the famous shower scene. From a musical perspective, the shrieking strings, representing the slash of the knife as it tears into Marion's flesh, is one of the most dramatic moments in the history of film scoring. Music as sound effect had already had a long history in film. The significance of Herrmann's shrieking string scoring is twofold. Rarely has such an avant-garde musical technique been used so brazenly in a film, and never had a musical effect been so strikingly linked to the allegorical aspects of a story. In addition, the musical gesture reflects not only Marion's screams but the shrieking of both the *bird of prey* and the *bird of flight* as well. It is a moment of brilliance, music as *both* music and effect, reflecting the physical calls of the allegorical combatants, the tearing of metal into flesh, as well as our own astonishment at what has transpired.

The silence preceding the slashing strings is designed to emphasize the violence of the slashing—the calm before the storm, if you will. The contrast between the silence and the ensuing dramatic physical and sonic gesture only heightens the intensity of the drama.

Hitchcock puts us inside the shower, looking out through the translucent shower curtain as the door to the bathroom opens. Norman is dressed as Mother, and with the knife raised, he pulls the shower curtain aside. [00:47:13] The music begins boldly and unadorned, with an intensity reflecting Marion's primal fear as well as the irrationality of Norman's psychotic drive. The music continues as Norman completes the murder and Marion collapses. We are left with the haunting images of blood-tainted water spiraling down the shower drain as Hitchcock dissolves to a close-up of Marion's lifeless eye. The attack is over, as is the shrieking of the violins. The relative silence, excepting the sound of the running shower, reflects on the consequence of the attack and Marion's death as well as Norman/Mother's disappearance. The camera pans around the motel room, momentarily pausing on the money-hiding folded newspaper, as an ironic, above-the-banner headline reads, "Okay." The scene closes with the sound of water disappearing down the drain.

Chapter 11: Cleaning Up after Mother

[00:49:37] After several exclamations by a now reintegrated Norman, we hear the shrieking strings return, in this case, reflecting his shock and panic about the murder. He descends from the house, stumbling as he goes. At first glance this is a sign of panic, but it can also be construed as the first misstep, the first fault in the charade he has managed to perpetuate for years. [00:49:46] The music abruptly fades out as Norman enters the bathroom and turns away in revulsion. It is a curious cut, almost as if the music had been taken from another cue and edited in. There is no attempt to musically resolve the structure of the cue.

After recovering from his initial shock, Norman begins to sanitize the scene of the murder. He closes the windows, turns off the lights, and retreats to the porch as a seemingly new series of themes are introduced. The first musical cue in this sequence, titled "The Office" in the written score, is only marginally related to the *bird of prey* theme. It, too, relies on the Hitchcock chord as its defining sonority. It has a similar underlying pulsing rhythm, although it is very much slower and much more static. While the undulating figure in the *bird of prey* theme is rhythmically clearer, the same type of rapidly alternating movement between two or three notes can be heard immediately after each series of chords in "The Office" cue.

The relationship between the two themes may not be immediately recognizable, however, perhaps reflecting Norman's shock at what his alter ego has done. More likely, the variation is a form of disguise. Norman has no immediate short-term or long-term plan to remedy the situation. He is forced to improvise, unsure of what he is going to do next. In all of the previous *bird of prey* cues, the character has had a plan and is quite assertive about accomplishing the task at hand. In this case, Norman shows hesitation and confusion at first. He is unsure about what to do and how to handle the mess.

The music reflects the pacing of the drama and the editing as it develops and becomes more complex rhythmically and harmonically. It starts with a **[00:50:24]** series of block chords and the rapidly alternating note figures, brooding in the midrange of the strings. The chords then develop in a downward musical **[00:50:33]** pyramid fashion, adding thickness at each beat. The figure then repeats over and over. The texture changes as Norman reenters the bathroom, pail and mop in hand. He begins to formulate a plan as a sinuous musical line weaves **[00:51:02]** its way downward, reminiscent of the *transformation* theme, intertwining with the recurring *bird of prey* motif. Norman has again transformed, from the astonished Norman discovering a corpse in a room to the brooding, planning murderer, covering his tracks.

Norman enters the bathroom with mop and bucket in hand, as the camera takes us through the same doorway. As he surveys the scene and prepares to clean up, his head replaces the showerhead, from the camera's perspective. The imagery of the voyeur surfaces once again. We have seen Marion's lifeless eye, peering up from the floor. We have seen Norman's peeping through the peephole, as well as the Arizona Highway Patrol officer peering through the car window as he investigates Marion sleeping in her car by the side of the road. We now have Norman, gazing down on the dead woman, just as the close-up of the showerhead revealed the same to us, moments earlier. He drags her from the bathroom and wraps her in the shower curtain.

Norman frantically begins his mopping-up operation, accompanied by a distinctly Wagnerian "Ride of the Valkyries" musical gesture. It is not clear if Norman has any organized plan to cover his felonious activities. The music **[00:52:51]** buzzes about with tremoloing strings as Norman hurriedly busies himself with cleaning the bathroom surfaces. The scurrying string and the tremoloing figures indicate both the increasing franticness of Norman's state of mind and

[00:54:10]

a musically onomatopoetic swirling of both the mop and water as he attempts to cleanse the room and his conscience. The musical drama deepens as the lower strings join the upper strings in playing a simple, rhythmic figure in octaves. Alternating octaves emerge, played with equal rhythmic value, reminiscent of the *bird of prey* theme, as it becomes apparent that Norman's plans to cover up his crime are now formed. The entry of the lower strings against a high string figure is a compositional technique that is almost always dramatic and foreboding. The present situation is no exception. Norman interrupts his cleaning to back Marion's car up to the doorway of the motel room. The

[00:54:54]

music resolves and ends after Norman opens the trunk and enters the room to retrieve Marion's body.

As we heard in earlier examples of the *bird of prey* motif, the motif ends when the planning and preparation is over and the execution of the plan begins. By now, Norman's instinctive cleansing has been replaced by an emerging organized plan, and he begins to dispose of the body and the collateral evidence. Norman lifts the body and deposits it in the car trunk, to silence. The aloneness of the silence is deafening and heightens our sense of shock and horror.

[00:55:44]

After the appearance of the *madness* motif, a distinctly contrapuntal texture emerges. It weaves a brooding line reflecting the convolutedness of Norman's thinking. Norman returns to clean up the bedroom, stuffing Marion's things into her suitcase, pausing to rehang a picture of a bird of flight he had knocked from the wall. The symbolism is almost comical. The term *bird* was a common slang expression for a girl in the England of Hitchcock's youth. Therefore, we may assume that Hitchcock, known for his dry sense of humor, had Norman *knock off the bird*, at least off the wall. Musically, the texture builds in complexity, adding a sense of increasing apprehension and franticness to Norman's actions. The defining *madness* theme is repeatedly interspersed throughout the rest of the cue. Norman places Marion's things, unknowingly adding the newspaper containing the money, into the trunk and then drives the car to the swamp, where he submerges the body and accompanying evidence.

Chapters 12, 13: The Swamp, Let's Talk about Marion

The film shifts to the hardware store owned by Marion's lover, Sam. Marion's sister, Lila, enters the store and discusses her concerns regarding her sister's absence with Sam, who was unaware that she was missing. Their dialog establishes a trust between them and a mutual concern for Marion's welfare. They are interrupted by a private investigator named Arbogast, who is anxious to follow Marion's trail in the hope of recovering the missing money.

Chapter 14: The Path to Marion Crane

[01:03:28]

As Arbogast leaves the hardware store and begins his gumshoeing, we hear the *bird of flight* theme. One would initially expect to hear the *bird of prey* theme as being more relevant, but Arbogast the detective is not chasing Marion for any malicious reasons. In his conversation with Marion's sister and Sam in the hardware store, he makes it clear that he is not the police, but rather a private investigator whose focus is recovering the money rather than prosecuting any individual. While his initial approach to Sam and Lila in the hardware store is a bit hard edged and adversarial, he warms a bit, announcing that "we're always quickest to doubt people who have a reputation for being honest." There is nothing predatory about his demeanor. The *bird of flight* theme is more appropriate as he searches for the bird that has fled. As Arbogast begins his search by canvassing every motel in the area, we are treated to a visual montage accompanied by the *bird of flight* theme.

Arbogast pulls into the Bates Motel as the *bird of flight* leitmotif segues nicely into chordal remnants of the *transformation* theme. The tempo begins to decelerate, as does Arbogast's car. Indeed, the final chord before the music ends is the same chord that forms the harmonic basis of the *transformation* theme. Arbogast is greeted by a remarkably relaxed and nonchalant Norman sitting on the porch, munching on a snack. **[01:03:44]**

Chapter 15: The Stammering Suspect

Arbogast begins to benignly interrogate Norman in the motel office. At first, Norman responds by appearing to be the picture of innocence. But their interaction becomes testy as Arbogast begins to unravel the inconsistencies in Norman's story. In an attempt to continue the charade of his innocence, Norman invites Arbogast to accompany him on his linen-changing rounds so Arbogast can inspect the rooms. The Hitchcock chord returns, accompanied **[01:09:46]** by an even more dissonant version of the *madness*'s three-note motif. As they leave the motel lobby, both characters immediately reveal their suspicions of each other by turning to go in opposite directions. As they reengage, the music turns even more dissonant. Norman's story begins to unravel under the scrutiny of the suspecting investigator. The *madness* theme in its original **[01:10:00]** form clearly emerges, underscoring the rising tension with Norman. The music slowly slips away under the dialog, having served its purpose of revealing the mutual distrust between the characters.

As Arbogast leaves the motel, the *madness* theme returns once more, to **[01:11:29]** complete the scene and confirm the intensity of the mutual suspicion. The cue ends with a slowly lilting violin gesture that ascends as we cross the cut, **[01:12:54]** lingering a moment longer than expected as Arbogast stops to call Lila from a pay phone.

Chapter 16: Back to the Bates Motel

After Arbogast's phone call, the scene shifts back to the motel, with a series of external shots showing Norman completing his linen rounds. A sinuously **[01:13:40]** ascending string line accompanies Norman, starting monophonically but then dividing into two and eventually more strands. The line becomes contrapuntal in nature, weaving several filaments of sound into a fragile sonic tapestry, reflecting Norman's now tentative grip on his situation and the psychological conflict raging within him.

[01:14:14]

[01:14:42]

[01:16:02]

As Norman drifts into the shadows of the motel, Arbogast returns, leaves his car, and enters the motel office. The three-note *madness* motif, its rising-falling contour preserved, emerges from the slithering counterpoint and returns to its monophonic roots as we are left with just Arbogast onscreen. As Arbogast enters the motel parlor, with its stuffed birds, the *madness* motif again splits into its contrapuntal texture. The *madness* surrounds Arbogast, both visually and musically. At this moment, we only see Arbogast along with the artifacts of Norman—his parlor and his proxies, the stuffed birds. Searching for Norman, Arbogast leaves the parlor and ascends the steps to the house, still accompanied by the *madness* theme. A series of tremolo figures with an occasional high violin gesture amplify the tension as Arbogast enters the house, looks around, and begins to ascend the stairs.

Chapter 17: Death and the Detective

[01:16:36]

[01:16:44]

[01:16:55]

As Arbogast ascends the stairway inside the house, the high string figures lose their rhythmic drive. The resulting tension matches Arbogast's apprehension as he begins his ascent. A single, low-pitched note crescendos as we see a door opening. The visual and aural elements combine, driving the shrieking-strings motif that abruptly returns as Arbogast is attacked. As we heard in the earlier shower sequence, the thrashing string sound is more of a sound effect rather than part of the musical landscape.

Compared to Marion's slaying in the shower, Arbogast's death sequence is short. The brutality of the stabbing act and the accompanying musical effect has already been established in the shower scene. We are simply reminded of the results, this time with Arbogast as victim. The beauty of Hitchcock's style is in its subtlety; he does not dwell on the obvious, leaving the viewer's imagination to fill in the gaps.

Meanwhile, back at the hardware store, Sam and Lila become increasingly concerned about Arbogast, since he had promised to be in touch after going back to the Bates Motel.

Chapter 18: Looking for Arbogast

[01:18:15]

As Sam goes to the Bates Motel in search of Arbogast, we experience the return of the *transformation* theme. This may seem a bit puzzling at first. After all, Sam really has no alter ego. To us, he is as he appears. The theme transitions across the dissolve, therefore the theme must refer to the image of Norman, quietly gazing into the bog. When the scene dissolves to Norman gazing at the swamp, implying that Arbogast's car has joined Marion's at the bottom of the swamp, we hear Sam calling Arbogast's name. The audible cue of the *transformation* theme leads us to expect to see Norman returning to his more innocent self. But as Norman looks toward the camera, it is by no means clear that he is transforming. His face remains taught and hidden in the shadows. He gazes untrustingly at the camera, his body stiff and erect. Norman is not changing. The evil within him has taken hold. The music, therefore, sets up an expectation within us, an expectation that is not resolved as expected.

The disquieting result intensifies our reaction to the image of Norman as he glares at the camera from the edge of the swamp that has swallowed yet another body in its automotive coffin.

Another interpretation may be that the *transformation* theme reflects the turn of events brought on by Norman's most recent murderous action. The theme may reveal that Norman's life, not personality, is changing. This is the beginning of the end for him. Sam is calling the name of the man Norman has just murdered and sent to the swamp. He has been found out, and he realizes it. Whereas Arbogast was on a "fishing expedition" when he ventured into the Bates Motel, Sam is headed straight for Norman. Norman knows that there is no longer any hiding.

Sam returns to Lila in the hardware store, having discovered nothing at the motel. Together, they agree to visit the sheriff, who provides them with little help, although the dialog does serve to deepen the mystery surrounding Norman's behavior. The *transformation* theme fades out under their dialog, [01:19:24] sonically gluing the entire sequence together, underscoring the turn of events . . . and Norman's personality. The hunter has become the hunted.

Chapter 20: The Late Mrs. Bates

After phoning Norman, Sheriff Chambers reveals to Sam and Lila that Norman's mother has been dead for ten years. Sam and Lila present the sheriff with conflicting information that causes the sheriff to question who was buried in Mrs. Bates's grave.

A series of chords reminiscent of the final moments of the *transforma-* [01:24:29] *tion* theme (the Hitchcock chord in various guises) carry us across the scene change to reveal a clearly perturbed Norman hanging up the phone, presumably at the end of the phone conversation with the sheriff. He ascends the steps to the house and goes directly upstairs to Mother's room, accompanied by a bare-bones melodic line that nonetheless retains the essential rising [01:24:57] motion of the second part of the *transformation* theme. The conversation between Norman and Mother becomes confrontational as Mother refuses to be moved to the fruit cellar. She continues to protest as Norman carries her down the stairs, *burying* her in the cellar. The bulk of the conversation is carried offscreen, while the camera circles the hallway from above, emphasizing the downward leading steps, highlighting both Mother's and Norman's imminent descent into their own individual hells. The accompanying chords [01:25:46] are the most harmonically dissonant and rhythmically static of the film so far. The orchestration is the most extreme of the film, with the strings holding on to the upper and lower extremes of their registers, perhaps reflecting the increased polarization that Norman is experiencing. The music and image both fade to an exterior shot of the local church on Sunday.

Chapters 21, 22: Mr. and Mrs. Loomis, Cabin One

A conversation between Sheriff Chambers, Sam, and Lila leaves Sam and Lila with no option except to file a missing-person report or go out to the

[01:28:03]
motel together to continue their own investigations, posing as husband and wife. As they approach the motel, yet another variation of the *transformation* motif emerges. They are now perpetrating their own subterfuge, so the theme is appropriate. We are treated to a cursory view of Norman peering out from the second-floor window of the house while the theme continues. Norman descends the stairs, meeting the couple at the foot and resuming his innocent, gentle self, though the music indicates that he has become just the opposite. As Sam and Lila check into the motel, their reflection in the motel office mirror reflects the illusory nature of their visit. Sam can barely contain his antagonism toward Norman, a fact not lost on Norman, judging by his thinly veiled politeness. The camera supports the tentativeness of the interaction, quickly cutting between reaction shots of Norman, Sam, and Lila.

[01:31:32]
After establishing their method of investigation in their motel room, Sam and Lila begin to explore the motel. The *transformation* theme reemerges in its most dissonant harmonic texture and continues until Sam notices that the shower curtain is missing in Room 1, the room in which Marion was murdered. Lila discovers a remnant of the calculation that Marion had made, and the two correctly conclude that Marion was at least in the room.

Lila leaves to find Mrs. Bates, while Sam attempts to deflect Norman's attention in the office by engaging him in a dialog. They meet, literally in the doorway to the office, both men uncomfortably close to each other, intruding on the other's space.

Chapter 23: Looking for Mrs. Bates

[01:34:33]
As Lila slinks around the back of the motel, views the house, and begins to climb the stairs to the house, a subtle variation of the *bird of prey* theme emerges. The cue consists of two simultaneous chromatic lines, each moving in the opposite direction, one going up, one going down. The lower, rising line is rhythmically related to the clock-ticking aspect of the original *bird of prey* theme. Its appearance at this juncture may seem puzzling at first. But consider that this is the first truly daylight image we get of the house. We see the imposing nature of the derelict-looking house, with overgrown grass and weeds on the lawn and sullen drapery hanging in the window. It is not at all clear that the house is habitable, though we know that at least Norman resides there.

This image alternates with shots of a nervous but determined Lila ascending what are left of the steps. The opposing nature of the two musical lines moving toward each other reflects these two perspectives, the looming, ominous image of the house that becomes less domineering as Lila ascends the hill and Lila's viewpoint as she rises to meet the house and her own fears

[01:35:21]
head-on. The competing, yet complementary, lines resolve into the Hitchcock chord as Lila turns the doorknob. The images of the house and Lila are joined together. Lila enters the house, looks around, and closes the door behind her.

The sequence continues with Norman and Sam continuing their tentative talks in the motel office, but we are soon taken back to the house, where Lila ascends the steps to Mrs. Bates's room, knocks, and upon hearing no

response, opens the door, enters, and begins to examine the room. A pulsing [01:36:15]
bass pizzicato figure begins, soon to be followed by an entirely new theme
not previously heard in the film. It should be noted that the steady plodding of
a tympani beat is one of the truly definable film music clichés, a sonic shorthand used by many composers to evoke anticipatory tension in the viewer.
Lila opens the closet door, notices Mrs. Bates's cluttered vanity, and along
with the camera, focuses in on a set of bronzed hands. While Hitchcock has
used the image of folded hands in previous films, its relevance here can be
tied to the issue of taxidermy. As we have seen, Norman is keen to stuff birds.
The folded, bronzed hands, delicately female, might well represent a more
permanent version of stuffed anatomical parts, the bronzing reserved for the
special hands of the bird he calls Mother.

As Lila returns her attention to the vanity, she is startled by her own image,
double reflected by two mirrors in alignment. At first she sees just another
person, behind her, causing her fearfulness. A moment later, she realizes that
it is her own image that has caused her alarm. Hitchcock's red herring is a
primarily a visual one. The musical figure crescendos slightly, anticipating [01:37:06]
Lila's sudden alarm, then decrescendos as she realizes she is seeing herself.
While the cue seems to fade out, the silence is momentary, allowing Lila and
us to catch our breath. The same pulsing figure reemerges as Lila continues
her investigations into Mrs. Bates's room. The scene ends with Lila noticing
the depression in Mrs. Bates's bed, obviously caused by the recent presence
of somebody, or at least, a body.

The sequence is intercut with a short scene showing Sam and Norman's
increasingly antagonistic conversation in the motel office. We return to
Lila's sleuthing as she enters what appears to be a child's room. The previ- [01:37:58]
ous motif returns, softened by bowed strings replacing the pizzicatos as the
source of the pulsations. Lila is surprised at the contents of the room. Aside
from a prominently displayed stuffed owl by the door, toys occupy a shelf.
A stuffed rabbit (the kind children prefer) sits on the disheveled single bed,
which is covered with a child's comforter. Lila's attention is drawn to an old
gramophone, and the camera pauses for a moment, revealing a recording of
Beethoven's *Eroica Symphony* on the spindle. She pulls a nameless hardback
book from the shelf.

The importance of the book is unclear, though the fact that Lila takes the
book and turns it upside down is of significance. The book's binding is sym-
metrical. We don't really know which way is *up*, and Hitchcock never shows
us the printing, so we remain ambiguous. It is as if the book, too, has assumed
a dual persona.

The pulsing figure first crescendos, then fades out as the scene switches [01:38:50]
to Norman and Sam's continued conversation. Sam becomes increasing
emboldened, while Norman becomes visibly agitated. Sam insinuates that
Norman has taken the money to open a new motel. He threatens to talk to
Norman's mother to discover the truth. Norman finally cracks when he realizes that Lila is nowhere to be seen and that he has been duped.

As Norman attacks Sam, hitting him over the head with a vase to the accompaniment of a lower-strings musical gesture, we know that the blow to [01:39:35]

[01:39:40] Sam's head is not fatal, because we do not hear the shrieking strings present in the two previous murder sequences. With Sam unconscious in the parlor, Norman rushes up the steps to the house to confront Lila. Herrmann employs scurrying strings in a contrapuntal fashion, mimicking Norman's frantic physical movement up the steps, as well as his panic-stricken thoughts as he attempts to cope with the rapidly unfolding events. The contrapuntal scurrying figures also accompany Lila as she flees toward the basement steps. The musical cue has become by now a very traditional chase music sequence.

Chapter 24: Mother

[01:40:28] The contrapuntal figures yield to a series of long chords as Lila descends into a basement room, seemingly safe for the moment. She discovers Mrs. Bates (at least what seems to be Mrs. Bates) seated in a chair, her back to the door. When Mrs. Bates does not respond to Lila's voice, she touches her on the shoulder, causing Mrs. Bates's chair to turn toward Lila, revealing the

[01:40:45] shriveled-up remains of a corpse. Lila screams, accompanied by the shrieking strings from the shower sequence. While the string effect enhances the portrayal of her emotional state at the moment and reflects yet another death image, it does not dissipate when she completes her scream. The shrieking strings continue as the camera focuses on the doorway in anticipation of Norman's entrance. The music tells us that Norman is about to enter with murderous intentions. He enters with a knife raised up, ready to strike, but a now-recovered Sam intercedes from behind. They struggle, and as Norman's

[01:41:01]
[01:41:12] wig falls to the floor (his unmasking if you will), we hear the resounding lower chords of the latter half of the shrieking-strings motif. The higher strings return with a diabolically frenetic ostinato that mimics the repetitive swaying motion of the light fixture that Lila has knocked in the course of the confrontation. The motion of the light evokes a vividly kinetic shadowing

[01:41:22] across Mrs. Bates's mummified face, and especially her eye sockets. The ostinatos end with a final, resolved chord, as we cross the edit to an exterior shot of the county courthouse. This final, resolved chord puts an end to the cycle of murders (remember that ostinatos are by definition cyclic figures). Therefore, we see the courthouse, the symbol of justice, and by extension, resolution in our society emerges in sync with the final, resolving chord.

Chapter 25: The Other Half

Chapter 25 is in many ways the weakest moment of the film. It revolves around the court-appointed psychiatrist's explanation of Norman's disease and tidies up the preceding events for those in the audience who may have missed what has transpired.

Chapter 26: I Wouldn't Hurt a Fly . . .

[01:47:59] A penultimate musical cue stealthily creeps in as we see Norman in the courthouse holding room, alone, draped in a blanket, accompanied by a voiceover that speaks his thoughts with his mother's voice. The music is elegiac, soft, and contrapuntal, no doubt reflecting the twistings and turnings in his mind. A momentary superimposition of Mother's skull on Norman's face is preceded by a gentle hint of the *madness* theme. The quiet inwardness of the cue is shattered by the strength of the unison celli, enunciating the *madness* theme unadorned, as we are left with the final, chilling image of a car being pulled from the swamp.

[01:48:03]

[01:48:07]

There is no end or credit music, Hitchcock preferring to allow the impact of the final sequence to speak for itself.

SUMMARY

Hitchcock's close collaboration with Herrmann over the span of eight films allowed both artists to develop an understanding of each other's thoughts and capabilities. Herrmann was able to extract the bird imagery from Hitchcock's filmic sense and translate it into musical terms. Herrmann's deep knowledge and appreciation for classical forms and structures allowed him to construct the leitmotif and musical cues in such a way as to bring Hitchcock's interior and subconscious themes closer to the surface while maintaining a structural integrity to both his music and the film as a whole. Though their collaborations would eventually end over artistic differences, with Hitchcock rejecting Herrmann's score for the film *Torn Curtain* under pressure from studio executives, Bernard Herrmann's compositional prowess will always be linked to Alfred Hitchcock's sense of psychological mystery and drama.

NOTES

1. Fred Steiner, "Herrmann's 'Black-and-White' Music for Hitchcock's *Psycho*: Part 1," *Film Music Notebooks*, ed. Elmer Bernstein (Sherman Oaks, CA: The Film Music Society, 2004).

2. Leslie Zador, "Movie Music's Man of the Moment," *Coast FM and Fine Arts*, June 1971, quoted in Steiner, Part 1, 33.

3. Kryss Katsiavriades and Talaat Qureshi, "Clichès and Expressions Origins," BusinessBalls.com, www.businessballs.com/clichesorigins.htm (accessed July 2, 2006).

4. The notion of a *bird of flight* theme is initiated by Steiner in his article previously cited in Bernstein's *Film Music Notebook*. I have taken his initial theory and expanded it to include the *bird of prey* and *transformation/metamorphosis* themes cited throughout this chapter.

5. Randall D. Larson, *Musique Fantastique* (Metuchen, NJ: Scarecrow Press, 1985), 119.

6. Royal Brown, *Overtones and Undertones: Reading Film Music* (Berkeley: University of California Press, 1994), 160–61.

SOUND DESIGN: THE UNIFICATION OF SOUND

The idea of unifying all aspects of a film's sound emerged as the concept of sound design in the late 1970s. While scholars point to Walter Murch's work in the 1979 film *Apocalypse Now* as the first clearly articulated example of the concept of sound design in film, its antecedents can be found in the responsibilities of the supervising sound editor for previous films. Prior to Murch's conceptual breakthrough, the three sonic elements of a film—dialog, music, and sound effects—tended to be conceived of and treated separately, only to be combined in the final stages of the film production under the auspices of the supervising sound editor.

In *Apocalypse Now*, Murch treated all of the sonic aspects of a film, diegetic and nondiegetic, as an organic whole, planning their relationships to each other as well as to the visual image. While balancing volume levels and to some degree tone color considerations between the disparate elements had always been a factor in mixing a film (as long as the soundtrack was *married* to the picture), everything was subservient to the dialog. Murch, recognizing the importance of the other sonic elements in telling the story, gave additional emphasis to the other elements. Thanks to new efforts in multitrack playback in theaters, sound effects could now indicate depth and direction, expanding a film's boundaries beyond the screen's edge. Music became all-encompassing, surrounding the audience with an aural atmosphere that made the *tone* of the film more personal for the audience. Between the sound effects and music, the audience became a part of the film, encompassed within it. Murch recognized this and unified a film's sound in total, as one large, all-inclusive element, much as a cinematographer would for all of the visual elements in a film. Today, it is understood that the sound design of a film can be as important as the cinematography.

Paul Théberge, noted film theorist, advocates examining a film's entire sound design, rather than each of its constituent components, indicating that it is better "to understand each of the sonic elements in their relation to one another as well as their cumulative contribution to the narration."[1]

In *Empire of the Sun*, Charles L. Campbell and Lou Edemann and their staff created a sound design that underscored the essential theme of the movie—the loss of innocence by a young boy held captive and coming of age and a nation (England) and lifestyle under siege. While John Williams's lush orchestral score, complemented by a boys' choir at strategic moments, successfully evokes the film's urtext through its traditional, classical Hollywood use of leitmotif, it is the overarching design of the music in relation to the diegetic, worldly sounds that supports the film's core experience.

The lush, romantic music and the sounds of machinery or crowds under siege battle for supremacy; they openly compete for our ears and our attentions. The sounds of war, mechanized in World War II as in no other previous war, assault the music, as the impinging conflict around the protagonist threatens to overpower the music that is his youth—his "Toy Planes, Home and Hearth," as Williams titles one of the crucial cues.

Therefore, if we understand the conflict within the sound design—music representing Jamie's innocence and childhood versus the mechanical sounds of war and disoriented crowds representing the adult world as well as his growing into manhood—we can better understand both the movie and what Jamie, aka Jim, experiences as his world is torn apart and reconstructed anew, albeit dramatically different from before.

BACKGROUND

Empire of the Sun represents a transitional work in the filmography of Steven Spielberg. Most of his early general release films are primarily fantasy-driven, escapist works based in childhood. They revolve around children, either their experiences or their relationship with the world around them. Spielberg encourages the audience to see the world through the eyes of a child, calling upon the viewer to remember childhood dreams, fears, and memories. *E.T.: The Extra-Terrestrial* and *Close Encounters of the Third Kind* are examples of these early themes. Though the story lines for the Indiana Jones series may seem adult enough, the plots are realized by Spielberg's fond memory of the Saturday afternoon serials at the local theater, the kind of fantasy, action-adventure film experienced by most American children of his age. Later works, such as *Schindler's List* and *Munich*, are reality-based pieces with decidedly adult and moral themes.

But *Empire of the Sun* reflects a confluence of, or transition between, childhood and adulthood story lines and themes. We see elements of both worlds colliding in terms of treatment and perspective.

By his own admission, Spielberg indicates that

> from the moment I read the novel,[2] I secretly wanted to do it myself. I had never read anything with an adult setting—even *Oliver Twist*—where a child saw things through a man's eyes as opposed to a man discovering things through the child in him. This was just the reverse of what I felt, leading up to *Empire*, was my credo. And then I discovered very quickly that this movie and turning forty happening at almost the same time was no coincidence, that I had decided to do a movie with grown-up themes and values, although spoken through a voice that hadn't changed through puberty yet.[3]

Most certainly, *Empire of the Sun* is an archetypal story about a boy's coming of age. It can also be seen as political allegory, as England loses its *children*, its colonies overseas during and immediately after World War II. And more directly, the film is about a child's growing into adolescence, confronting the loss of innocence of childhood and the inevitable onslaught of adulthood. Jamie, the son of a British capitalist living in Shanghai, endures all this while coping with the loss of family and his detention in a Japanese internment camp in China during the war.

Spielberg constructs this battle between childhood and the adult world in the sound design for the film. As we shall see, the music of childhood, both diegetic and nondiegetic, will be continually interrupted and drowned out by the sounds of adulthood, the harshly real sounds of daily life, and eventually the war that engulfs Jamie's childhood and family.

So the archetypal story, the inevitable intrusion of the adult world into the secure, fantasy world of a child, is played out in the sound design, sometimes called the soundscape. The music associated with childhood is overpowered by the worldly sounds of adulthood, an allegory we all experience as we leave our own childhoods to enter into our adult lives.

Chapters 1, 2: Forward, The Choirboy ("Suo Gan")

After an introductory scroll and voiceover explaining the nature of the Japanese/Chinese conflagration that earmarked the beginning of World War II, *Empire of the Sun* opens with the sounds of gently rolling waves lapping against an object, a boat or perhaps a shoreline. "Suo Gan," a Welsh lullaby, emerges, sung by a prepubescent boys' choir. As we fade in, we see dark and gently rolling waters, with flowered wreaths floating in from the right side of the frame. They finish their journey across the screen, disappearing to the left as a partially shattered casket floats into view from the lower right corner.

[00:01:11]

[00:01:22]

English translations of "Suo Gan" vary to some degree; no doubt each translator adding their own poetic sense to the lullaby. For our purposes, the translation below will suffice.

> Sleep my baby, at my breast
> 'Tis a mother's arms round you.
> Make yourself a snug, warm nest.
> Feel my love forever new.[4]

The song conveys a sense of security and comfort as would be expected from a lullaby. "Mother will protect you" is the urtext. This will become one of the major themes that Jamie, the protagonist, will confront—the loss of the security and safety that his mother provides, the loss of his home and way of life, his Britishness, and most importantly his childhood. "Suo Gan," therefore, becomes the first leitmotif defined. Its association is with the safety and security that represents Jamie's childhood.

The introduction of "Suo Gan" is less associated with the floating funeral than with the serenity of the moment—the expression of life through the image of death, counterpointed by a gentle song, gently sung by a choir of prepubescent boys.

"Suo Gan" continues as the casket follows the wreaths' path. The camera fades and pulls back to a medium shot from above, revealing five additional caskets floating in the water. They are simple boxes, the others in better shape than the first. While a simple burial at sea is a normal state of affairs, five caskets hint that something unusual is afoot. The calmness of the scene is abruptly interrupted by an overwhelming, battleship-gray Japanese navy boat, whose bow plows into the array of caskets, arrogantly brushing them aside in the water. The sound of the engine intrudes on the gentle voices that sing "Suo Gan," just as the boat intrudes on the visual serenity of the caskets afloat. In this moment, we see and hear the story of *Empire of the Sun* as it will play out over the next 154 minutes. The reality of the adult world,

[00:01:54]

represented by the harsh sounds of war and the cacophony of the world as it exists, intrudes upon and often overpowers the lullabies and music of the innocence of childhood.

"Suo Gan" continues over a series of establishing shots—the Japanese flag aboard the boat as it passes the Shanghai skyline, a bucolic scene showing a Packard automobile, and a man carrying a bag as if on Sunday morning errands. The camera pans down from the steeple of a decidedly English church, seemingly transplanted stone for stone from the motherland. In front of the church, we see more cars, impeccably clean, with Chinese drivers dressed and acting like proper English chauffeurs, lulling about and waiting for their charges to reappear after the choir practice indoors. Interior shots of the cavernlike and richly decorated church reveal a maroon-jacketed boys' choir in rehearsal. It is unmistakably English, it is unmistakably England; England transplanted from thousands of miles away to Shanghai, China, within a secure (at least for the moment) diplomatic and capital womb called the European Settlement.

[00:03:00]   Their faces freshly scrubbed, hair cleanly cut and combed, the choirboys follow the conductor. Jamie becomes the focus of our attention as he sings the solo, to the other boys' accompaniment. He sings well, though it is obviously dubbed. Spielberg wisely allows the sound of the dubbing to be slightly out of tune (the high note noticeably so), thus showing us that Jamie is not a superstar. He is a normal boy with above-normal talents, occasionally called upon for solo passages. But as we are about to see, he is still a boy, bored by the lack of excitement, with a mind that wanders. Given to daydreaming, he is repeatedly called back to the reality of the rehearsal by the conductor, who emphatically snaps his fingers and raps the podium to remind Jamie of his upcoming entrance, and by his Chinese nanny who must tap the pew to remind Jamie of his cue. Even here we see the story line unfold in the sound. Jamie's daydreaming and the accompanying boys' choir are interrupted by the actions and sounds of the adults tapping and snapping their fingers to draw him away from his childish reverie.

This scene reveals much about whom Jamie is and the qualities that will allow him to survive the upcoming upheavals. He is a daydreamer, yet quickly
[00:03:33]   able to respond to the immediate situation as needed. Witness his abrupt, yet perfectly executed, solo entrance after being startled out of his reverie.

A series of establishing shots reinforce the image of normalcy that surrounds the European Settlement; a close-up of the flying bird hood ornament on the family car, a 1937 Packard Super Eight Touring Limousine; tile-roof houses; and carefully walled and gated plots of land in the background. The continuation of "Suo Gan" serves as the sonic glue throughout these establishing shots. It not only links the visuals together but also reinforces the perspective that nothing is amiss; everything is as it should be in the European Settlement Zone in Shanghai.

We next find Jamie alone in the backseat of the family car. His driver and nanny occupy the front seat. He is reading a comic book titled "Wings," intimating one of the subplots of the film, the young boy's fascination with airplanes and flight. While author J. G. Ballard notes that as a young boy, he was always interested in airplanes, Spielberg and screenwriter Tom Stoppard transform the idea of airplanes and flying into a metaphor for the innocence and freedom of youth.

As the car turns into Jamie's driveway, the lullaby is sharply interrupted by a beggar tapping his tin cup on the ground, pleading for food or money. **[00:04:06]** The nature of the sound mix becomes of interest with this interjection. The tapping of the tin is mixed louder than one would expect, even given the beggar's proximity to the camera. The moment reinforces the initial premise that the harsh reality of the adult world intrudes upon the reverie that is Jamie's childhood.

The camera's perspective further reinforces the significance of the scene. Jamie views the beggar through the car's window, a classic cinematic technique used to portray a character's emotional and psychological distance from the object of his/her gaze. Jamie and his music are within the womb of his family's car. The reality of the world in which he really lives bangs a tin cup on the ground from the other side of the window. Jamie is protected, just as the lyrics to "Suo Gan" say.

Chapter 3: Luckier (Chopin *Mazurka*)

"Suo Gan" ends, only to be replaced by the middle section of Frederic Chopin's *Mazurka*, op. 17, no. 4, played by Jamie's mother at the family piano. **[00:04:24]** The camera dollies back to reveal framed pictures on the piano, with Mother vacantly staring off into space as she plays. She, too, is in her own reverie. Dressed in a flowing white gown, with nothing particular on her mind, her family close at hand, playing parlor music for no one in particular, she is content. This music, then, is a continuation of "Suo Gan" in the sense that it represents safety. The subtle difference between the use of "Suo Gan" and the Chopin *Mazurka* is relatively minor. "Suo Gan" becomes the leitmotif for the concept of innocence of childhood in general, while the *Mazurka* comes to represent the safety and comfort of Jamie's home and Mother in the specific. Indeed, the soundtrack for the film lists these two pieces of music as one, titling the cut, "Toy Planes, Home and Hearth."[5]

Mother continues playing the piano while Father practices his golf outside. Jamie mischievously pedals his bicycle around the grounds, holding a flaming model airplane and teasing his nanny. As we move outdoors for the **[00:04:49]** exchange between Father and Jamie, his mother's playing remains sonically indoors, source music for the quaint English moment between father and son.

Jamie engages his father in a chat about the war. The beggar's banging **[00:05:44]** reemerges from beyond the estate's wall, suddenly intruding on this father/son dialog and mother's piano playing. The volume and lack of reverberation of the banging is again disproportionate to the setting, given the distance between the beggar outside the family compound and the father and son inside. The beggar's audible intrusion is larger than life, reflecting its importance.

Jamie professes his admiration for the Japanese air force and his intention to sign up. This declaration disturbs his father's "chip across the water." Two Japanese airplanes are heard offscreen. As they fly into the frame, their engines **[00:06:06]**

drown out Mother's music. At least for the moment, the sounds of war overtake
and render inaudible the safety and security of Chopin.

Across the scene change, Jamie is preparing for bed by pouring himself a
glass of milk while ordering his Chinese nanny to give him some biscuits.
She explains that his mother does not want him to eat before bed. In a curious

[00:06:51]   yet subtle gesture, Jamie rubs his cheek the way a mother would encourage a
baby to suckle, while informing his nanny that "you have to do what I say."
It is a small but important gesture if we are to understand Jamie's maturation
process throughout the film. His symbolic gesture is one of omnipotence,
signifying a child demanding food from the adult.

At an early stage in their development, babies feel a sense of power. They
simply cry and others attend to all of their needs. That Spielberg devotes
screen time to this scene and the fact that Jamie rubs his cheek with the hand
that is also holding the glass of milk would seem to confirm the importance
of the gesture. Jamie wins the muffins, which he carries to his room, passing
his father in his study, who is examining documents and then casting them
into the fireplace. Unlike earlier, we hear no music from the radio. Instead,
we hear the very adultlike news of the war that is already raging and about
the British evacuations from Shanghai.

Chapter 4: Upward Dreams

[00:07:43]   As Jamie's mother puts him to bed, a curiously dissonant cluster of notes
played by a celesta merges with the sound and visual flare from a cigarette
being lit by Mother. The sonic gesture is a bit startling. Model airplanes suspended from the ceiling of Jamie's bedroom loom over his mother's shoul-
ders. When Jamie looks up from his bed at his mother, he sees her as well as
the airplanes. He sees the freedom and fascination of his childhood and the
protection his mother provides.

She calls him "Ace," his nickname, indicating that he is the champion
of flying, the master of freedom and his childhood. The issue of childhood
freedom is reinforced by the curiously metaphysical dialog between Jamie
and his mother as she kisses him goodnight. He talks of God and dreams, and
whether God is our dream or vice versa. His mother responds predictably that
she knows nothing of God. Indeed, throughout the entire film, we see nothing
to indicate her level of intelligence. She is merely the icon of love, the trophy
wife and piano-playing mother. She is the manifestation of love and family
in image and action.

[00:07:49]   Careful listening will reveal the violins holding a high G that seems to remain curiously suspended above the dialog and the musical gesture played by
the celesta. A sustained, high-pitched violin note as is heard here is often used
by a skilled film composer to evoke a feeling of uneasiness or anticipatory
anxiety, a remote, distant sense of foreboding. Something is going to happen,
though perhaps not immediately.

The use of the celesta in the orchestration is appropriate for a child's
bedtime scene. It is delicate and light sounding, evocative of a toy piano.
But the musical gesture used by Williams is designed to enhance the pre-

scient nature of the high violin notes. The melody is assuredly dissonant and avoids any sense of cadencing or ending. It sounds incomplete, leaving us hungry for resolution.

As Father enters Jamie's bedroom, Mother tells Jamie to "dream of flying." The *toy planes, home, and hearth* motif momentarily emerges from the dissonance at the precise moment that Spielberg's mise-en-scène pays conscious homage to Norman Rockwell's quintessential all-American painting/illustration titled *Freedom from Fear*.[6] The imagery is unmistakable— the pose, the camera angle, the lighting. The only difference, a trivial one in terms of the message of the painting/shot, is that Jamie has no sister being tucked in beside him. The background wall is awash in model airplanes, kites, and all things flight-worthy. Jamie's childhood is filled with the wonder of freedom as represented by images of, and a preoccupation with, flying. As his mother turns off the light, yet another long, high string note comes to the forefront. A flurry of dissonant notes announces the arrival of the darkness. Jamie looks up at his airplanes, and in the waning light, continues to wonder. **[00:08:40]**

[00:09:01]

Chapter 5: Partygoer Procession

The blackened screen segues to a close shot of a phonograph playing the Chopin *Mazurka*. As both source music and the musical embodiment of Mother, Spielberg spends a few moments of screen time to visually underscore the theme's prominence within the film. The image is reinforced as the music becomes nondiegetic, and we are treated to an exterior scene of Jamie's house, genteel and serene, with Chinese gardeners diligently at work. Yang, the family chauffeur, is resting his eyes at the steering wheel of the family Packard as the family emerges from the home. Jamie leads, costumed as Sinbad the Sailor, carrying his oversized glider. Mother and Father emerge dressed as thinly disguised stereotypes of the English in China at the time. Father is a pirate, a representative of economic redistribution that formed the basis of many capitalist ventures in China. Mother, vacuous as ever, is dressed as a sort of hapless-looking clown, the quintessential Pierrot. **[00:09:20]**

[00:09:26]

The music, however, indicates that nothing is amiss, as it is lyrical and happy. It turns briefly to the minor key as the Chinese servants dutifully applaud the costumed family, but it quickly returns to the original major key of the Chopin *Mazurka*. As the car departs, we see the house servants waving farewell through a half-opened (or closed) car window. The communication between the Chinese and European worlds is only partial in its nature. The view is not complete. An extended violin note subtly emerges as the family leaves home and the servants behind. The Chopin *Mazurka* blends with the violin's pitch and Williams's musical extension of its melody, and "Suo Gan," resulting in a three-faceted cue that briefly turns minor as the family leaves their compound, foreshadowing their respective fates. **[00:09:59]**

[00:10:22]

As the car emerges from behind the estate walls, the beggar's banging resumes offscreen. Fascinated as all boys at that age are with the outside world, Jamie climbs to the window and looks out. The image is carefully reinforced by the camera's perspective from outside of the car looking in **[00:10:27]**

[00:10:35]   at Jamie through a closed window. The music again turns dissonant at the
precise moment when the car exits from the walled estate and Jamie spies the
beggar banging on the ground. Close listening reveals that the still-present
high violin note continues until the direct cut to the following crowd scene,
when all the music disappears and we witness the clutter and crowdedness
of the Shanghai streets from an aerial shot. The crowd is noisy and excited.
Car horns blare and bleat; the carefully encapsulated home life of the English
family has been surrounded.

    The montage that follows is a remarkably well-crafted moment in sound
editing and reflects the best collaborative efforts between the visual and

[00:10:57]   audio forces in film. It begins with a shot of the car's hood ornament as it
leads the car through the crowd. The car remains in focus; the surrounding

[00:10:59]   crowd does not. The music turns even more dissonant than before, eerily
atonal, lending a ghostly air to the car as it glides through the morass of
humanity. It increases in intensity, as we now see Jamie in costume, excitedly staring out the car window.

    The confrontation between the sounds of adulthood and war and the music
of Jamie's childhood is highlighted by the alternating camera shots from
inside and outside the car. Images of the massive size and crowdedness of
Chinese society give way to the seemingly effortless gliding of the European
car cutting a swath through the crowd. Jamie's family views the crowded
chaos that is China from the spacious safety of their car. Only the sounds
intrude into the car's interior—the voices from within the crowd and the
ugly *thump-splat* of a piece of meat as it hits the window, smearing blood
on the meticulously buffed car. A Chinese street urchin approaches the car,
presciently shouting, "No mama, no papa, no whiskey soda."

[00:11:43]   But rising above this morass of humanity are the angelic voices of Jamie's
church boys' choir. If the sound from the street scene is short, choppy, and
full of competing sounds (a sound-effects counterpoint), the church choir is
singing uncomplicated, sustained notes. They provide the harmonic counterpoint to the crowd's internal dissonances.

    And so music battles the sound effects, vying for our attention, reflecting
Jamie's awe of, and amazement at, the world surrounding him as he travels
within the comfort of the car's womb. The visual confusion evoked by the
collage of images seen by Jamie is reinforced by the sound design. The sound
effects and music alternately vie for our attention. Just as we are visually
unable to linger on any single image, our ears are constantly pulled between
the soaring strings, the noise of the crowd, and the overwhelming presence
of the innocent, prepubescent boys' voices. Furthermore, Spielberg is careful
not to let one aural or visual image dominate, nor does he synchronize the
visual and aural shifts. This helps reinforce the vagueness and instability of
the moment while highlighting Jamie's experience, the overwhelming assault
on his senses and his ability to comprehend the external world around him.

    At the same time, the strangeness of the English predicament in China is
emphasized by this disconnectedness of the music and the visuals as the car
moves through the Shanghai crowd. Williams uses the boys' choir to counterpoint the drama, simultaneously revealing the English family's alienation

from the events surrounding them while heightening the surreal quality of the visuals—pirates, clowns, and adventurers in bright costumes and colors gliding through the gray grittiness of the world around them.

During this montage sequence, the choir voices cross-fade into a childlike **[00:12:34]** piano sound and evoke a balanced, Mozart-like melody and accompaniment. Just as we see a Chinese peasant woman carrying her child, a very foreboding barbed-wire fence separates her from the camera and us. We then see the British car with the costumed revelers inside behind the same barbed wire. The children inside are dressed as clowns, bees, and flowers. The camera lingers on one woman noticeably dressed as Marie Antoinette as she peers warily out of the car window. The nod to history is inescapable. Tympani and **[00:12:51]** strings join the boys' choir, propelling the scene inexorably forward, just as the British contingent in China is moving toward its fate.

Chapter 6: Hospitality ("Swing Is in the Air")

The ensuing lavish masquerade party contrasts the gray and dark tones of the previous street scene. The house interior is all gaiety in pastels. While politics may be the topic of conversation, the music is stylistically appropri- **[00:13:43]** ate for the era: swinging source music that reinforces the Western civility of the conversation, despite its fatalistic overtones. With the ongoing Battle of Britain and the Japanese movements on the mainland of China very much the insinuated topic of conversation, destruction of the British status quo lurks in the background throughout the entire dialog as well as at the party itself.

In the next scene, shot outdoors, the jazz band source music continues as we are treated to a lone Japanese airplane circling overhead, the drone of its **[00:14:28]** engine intruding upon the gaiety of the song's trombone solo. Despite the festivities of the British community, the war drones overhead, ever present.

Chapter 7: Engaging the Enemy

Jamie leaves the party to "see something," taking his glider in tow. He launches it toward the open fields and shortly thereafter, the boys' choir be- **[00:15:30]** gins to soar as well. The choir sings a cappella as Jamie looks in wonderment upon a derelict Japanese fighter that has been shot down and abandoned in the field. The orchestral strings join Jamie in his wonder as Spielberg treats us to **[00:15:44]** the full shot of the downed Japanese *Zero*. Jamie climbs into the plane and enters the cockpit as his dreams and fantasies find full fruition. He imagines himself in a dogfight, guiding the plane and firing upon the enemy, his glider.

Visually, this can only be described as the perfect Spielberg moment. Jamie **[00:16:03]** the adventurer, resplendent in his passionately red costume, shares the screen with the gray, busted-out windshield of the warplane. The passion of youth, with its flowing silks and red, feathered turban is surrounded by the dull, gray steel and broken glass of adulthood. The frame within the frame, the medium shot of Jamie in the cockpit as seen though the broken windshield, is a study in contrasts, a dramatic counterpoint exquisitely executed.

[00:16:14]   What is about to be heard is equally vivid. We hear the playful theme of Jamie's home, *toy planes, home, and hearth,* lyrically performed by strings and
woodwinds. Plucked strings join with the choir to strengthen the fantasy. The
[00:16:30]   winds and strings rise to their higher range as Jamie's eyes follow his glider
across the open sky as he engages in his own private dogfight. He succeeds in
play-shooting the glider down, as it descends just over a ridge a short distance
away. The music is happy and victorious as it fades away, with less than a
[00:17:34]   fully resolved cadence, indicating that there is still more to come to the scene.
     Jamie leaves the plane to retrieve his glider as we hear the gathering thun-
der in the distance. Jamie walks toward the ridge, a spot of bright red against
an ever-darkening landscape, as gray cumulus clouds render the grass a deep
grayish green, muting the future Jamie is headed toward.
     Jamie climbs the ridge only to be surprised by the sight of an encampment
[00:17:55]   of Japanese infantry. Tympani and log drums, the sounds of war, accompany
Jamie's startled response. There is no definable steady beat; Jamie's war has not
yet begun. The Japanese are waiting. A colorfully festooned Jamie and an olive-
drab uniformed soldier share the screen from opposite edges of the frame, visually underscoring the childhood versus adulthood dilemma Jamie is confronting
[00:18:29]   for the first time. The drums pause for the briefest of moments, intensifying the
focus on the image of a brightly festooned Anglo-Saxon child staring at an olive-
drab uniformed Asian soldier. As Jamie's father rushes to his aid, the intensity
[00:18:35]   and contrapuntalism of the music increases as if headed for its own confrontation. But the music simply fades away as Jamie retreats down the berm.
[00:18:59]   A solo shakuhachi flute soon accompanies the drums as other Japanese
soldiers climb the ridge, moving toward what appears to be a confrontation.
But the Japanese will wait, as will the tempo. The Japanese soldiers disappear
back over the ridge. There is no full confrontation, just as there is no finality
to the music—it simply fades away, unresolved.
     The overcast weather of the countryside yields to the darkness of the city as
[00:19:50]   the scene changes. A closed, repeating arpeggio, with a childlike theme in the
piano, couples with the droning, high-pitched strings, leaving us with a surreal
juxtaposition. The lightness of childhood counterpoints the drabness of a city
under siege and about to be overrun. An interior shot of the Packard finds Father worrying about the family's future in China and suggesting that the family
[00:19:56]   move into town for a bit. The choir voices return as Chinese voices from the
real world intrude into the family car. The string drone continues throughout the
passage, unsettling us just enough to feel the tension that Father feels.
     As Jamie and his family somberly return from the party, they pass through
a barbed-wire security gate that slams shut behind the car as it winds its way
[00:20:33]   through the streets. The gate also abruptly shuts the ethereal music off. The
final flourish, an exotically arpeggiated scale upward by the harp, only reinforces the bizarre quality of the scene: clowns and pirates gliding through a
dismal world, only faintly aware of what is to befall them.

Chapters 8, 9: Shanghai: December 8, 1941, Lost in the Crowd

After the gate has been shut, closing the door on the music as well, we
are treated to an aerial view of Shanghai harbor from Jamie's hotel room.

As he plays, we hear only the harbor sounds: motors from junks, horns from   [00:20:36]
freighters, no music or sounds from his childhood. All is dark; we hear only
the sounds of the world that is about to engulf Jamie.

From his hotel window, Jamie witnesses Japanese warships entering the
Shanghai harbor. The first salvo fired from a ship sends him reeling from
the window. Father frantically enters the room, announcing that the family is
leaving the hotel in three minutes. The following scenes of panic, first by the
European hotel occupants as they try to flee the hotel and subsequently by the
general chaos in the streets, is powerful enough to succeed without musical
accompaniment. From an upstairs window, Jamie witnesses the converging
forces of the Japanese army and the Chinese resistance.

After the appearance of Japanese soldiers rhythmically marching in step,
scurrying strings seemingly devoid of a beat or rhythmic structure loosely   [00:23:17]
reflect the uncoordinated movements of the resistance fighters and the
panic-stricken civilians. Tonality is abandoned. A series of crescendos in   [00:23:33]
the strings, punctuated by drums and brass, heighten the effect of panicked
breathing by the frightened Chinese civilians.

Attempting to reach their chauffeur and car, Jamie and his family struggle
through the streets, finally reaching the car that is now surrounded by the fleeing crowd. The low brass enter as the Japanese soldiers march onto the street.   [00:25:08]
Brass and percussion figures gradually overtake the strings. As the dissonant   [00:25:16]
music increases in volume, Jamie and his family abandon their car and driver
and become consumed by the crowd as they head to the waterfront. The frantic
chaos of the crowd scene is underscored by a bed of string chords, with the
brass, high woodwinds, and percussion emitting sharp-edged gestures with
increasing frequency and volume. The figures are short, declarative, and biting.

Now separated from Father, Jamie and Mother struggle against the crowd.
The string sounds merge with the engine noises of airplanes overhead. Jamie   [00:26:18]
looks up at the airplanes, as does the camera. He is momentarily entranced, so
much so that he loses his grip first on his toy airplane, and then on Mother's
hand. Jamie's fantasy and real worlds merge. At the precise moment that   [00:26:31]
Jamie loses Mother's hand, we hear a long and loud trumpet note, the first
really decisive brass figure in the extended cue. It is Jamie's scream as it
is his mother's scream, while it simultaneously serves to underscore the
psychological terror of the breaking of the mother/child bond. The use of
this musical sound effect for dual representative purposes is reminiscent of
Bernard Herrmann's shrieking strings in the shower sequence in *Psycho*. It is
the most identifiable music effect yet, and it is echoed shortly afterward by
a harmonized brass figure, reflecting the emotional panic felt by Jamie as he   [00:26:48]
realizes Mother is lost.

The tumultuous crowd sequence eventually yields to the coordinated
marching of a column of Japanese infantry as they move onscreen. The
chaos-evoking musical figures yield to the clear beat and precisely defined
chords that match the columns' step. The Japanese soldiers scatter as resistance fighters attack them. The rhythmic and harmonic organization of the   [00:27:18]
music breaks apart as well. The ensuing dissonance never fully resolves;
it simply fades out across a cut to the Shanghai skyline shrouded by the   [00:28:12]
smoke of battle.

Chapter 10: Plunderers

Jamie's solitary walk home to his now abandoned house is devoid of any musical accompaniment, as is a midshot of his house. No voice or music responds as he calls for Mother. Even a pullback shot from the piano (a visual reference to Mother) reveals the family photos on the piano, yet no one is seated at it.

[00:30:08]   As Jamie ascends the staircase toward the bedrooms, dissonant high strings begin a wandering, elegiac, melodyless gesture. Instead, a gently serpentine-like texture unfolds as Jamie looks around his parents' ransacked bedroom. His confusion, loneliness, and anxiety are embodied in this string texture. It will gradually vanish, much like the powder on the bedroom floor, soon to be carried away by a gust of wind from the shattered window.

At first, Jamie smiles as he sees what seems to be Mother's footprint in
[00:31:00] the spilled powder on the floor. The boys' choir returns, reflecting his fleet-
[00:31:05] ing recollection of the security his mother represents. But dissonant strings emerge as the camera offers up signs of a struggle in the powder. The skirmishing strings and comforting choral voices compete for our attention before the wind carries away both the traces of the struggle and the musical
[00:31:30] conflict. The elegy returns as Jamie witnesses his former servants carrying the family belongings away.

Chapter 11: Home Alone

[00:33:04]   This wandering elegy is replaced by the coldly mechanical ticking of the mantel clock; the reality of the external world now defining Jamie's existence. The clock soon ceases to function and the elegy returns, taking a more noticeable form as the piano takes on a simple arpeggiated character heard earlier. The undulating figure of the arpeggio simulates the passage of time, replacing the now dormant mantel clock. For Jamie, his life and his childhood stopped when the mantel clock did. For the viewer/listener, the continuing music reflects the passage of time, as do the onscreen fades and alternating scenes of night and day.

Accompanied by the elegiac string line, a forlorn and lonely Jamie takes
[00:35:28] his bike and leaves home. The music underscores his loneliness as he observes Japanese soldiers loading European heirlooms into their trucks from a neighboring house. A truck full of English refugees drives past him. He furiously pedals to catch up but cannot reach their outstretched arms. The truck leaves him forsaken in the dust.

Chapter 12: English Boy Surrenders

Jamie pedals into town and unsuccessfully attempts to surrender to a Japanese patrol. He continues to wander the streets, stopping to reflect upon a massive billboard that consumes much of the screen, advertising the film, *Gone with the Wind*. *Gone with the Wind* is, of course, about the destruction of a city, a love, and a way of life, and Jamie's wandering in front of the looming billboard is an obvious reference to his unfolding experience. The wind is especially poignant; a not-so-subtle allusion to the previous sequence in which the last traces of his mother (her cosmetic powder) blows away, swept out of the window.

A series of dissonant chords and the boys' choir momentarily returns as Jamie gazes upward at the billboard, reflecting all that he has lost; the angelic voices of his childhood just a haunting memory, now. The worldly sounds around him disappear under the choir, the aural equivalent of *panning in* on his emotional state. [00:37:47]

The choir music is interrupted as the real-world sounds return. The Chinese street urchin from the previous market montage sequence calls to Jamie, another rude, sonic interruption of his musical reverie. During the confrontation between the scrappy urchin and the still well-kept Jamie, a more war-like chase sound using temple blocks and gongs, as well as other percussive instruments, emerges, underscoring the tense conflict. [00:38:10]

[00:38:46]

The urchin chases a terrified Jamie through the streets of Shanghai, accompanied by an increasingly dissonant barrage of orchestral sounds. As Jamie's attempt to surrender to still more Japanese troops is rejected, the drums momentarily organize the beat as a contingent of soldiers marches by. The complete orchestra led by the brass emerges with a more regularly rhythmical approach, dissonant, sharp edged, and caustic to the ear, as the chase reaches its full drama, consuming the aural landscape. [00:39:07]

[00:39:39]

Chapters 13, 14: Making Frank's Acquaintance, Shanghai Jim ("South of the Border," "These Foolish Things")

Having been rescued by an American named Frank, Jamie is taken to a hideaway, a safe location, now home to Frank and an aptly named American, Basie. A radio incongruously plays "South of the Border," a light and fancy-free song whose melodic line and lyrics directly counterpoint the dark oppressiveness of the visual image. Jamie adopts Basie as a surrogate father. He is seemingly sagacious, practical, and at least at first glance, caring and compassionate. He renames Jamie as Jim, a decidedly un-British and very American-sounding moniker. He offers Jim food and teaches him how to eat in this new life. "Jim, chew your food. Chew every mouthful six times, to get the benefit." [00:43:46]

Chapters 15, 16: Journey to Opulence, New Occupants

As Jim, Frank, and Basie cruise the streets of Jamie's old neighborhood looking for the opportunity to pilfer from houses, Jamie steers them toward his old house in an effort to be accepted by his new family. As the truck turns into the driveway of Jamie's old estate, the camera perspective is strikingly similar to the earlier driveway shot in which Jamie notices the beggar, though no beggar is now to be found. Spielberg's repetition of an earlier shot is designed to lure us into believing that Jamie is returning to familiar turf. Even the Chopin *Mazurka* returns, appearing to come from within the house. Is Jamie's mother at the piano? An excited and hopeful [00:52:31]

Jamie catches a glimpse of someone in a diaphanous gown inside. His excitement is palpable as he expects a family reunion.

But what we hear is not Mother playing the piano. In fact, Jamie does not hear the music at all. Spielberg and Williams toy with our expectations, using the music to tell us who (his mother) and what (the innocence of his childhood) Jamie expects to find. We *hear* Jamie's hopes and emotions.

[00:53:24]

[00:54:00]

The robed figure turns out to be a Japanese soldier, a very displeased one. The *Mazurka* disappears as the soldier and his associates pull Basie from the truck and begin beating him. From a sound design perspective, Jamie's childhood reverie has again been interrupted by the very adult war that engulfs him, and now his new parents. A brief return of the Chopin theme accompanies a visual fadeout as a clearly distraught Jamie whispers Basie's name. He fears losing yet another parent.

Chapters 17, 18: Chow Time, the Truck to Soochow

[00:54:36]

Awakening in an internment camp, Jim is attended by a woman as well as a gentleman adorned in a curious Santa Claus coat, incongruously singing "Good King Wenceslas." His gentle awakening, however, is accompanied by hundreds of beggars banging their tin cups. The banging intensifies, eventually overpowering "Good King Wenceslas." Even Christmas has been interrupted by the sounds of adulthood and war.

The psychological transition from Jamie to Jim and the burgeoning confusion associated with his emerging adolescence is illustrated in the scene in which English prisoners are selected for the lorry ride to another detention camp. Jamie finagles his way onto the truck by convincing the Japanese soldiers that he knows the way to the camp. Jim triumphantly clambers onto the top of the truck's cab, where he bangs his tin cup like the others in the crowd and points the way to his own future. The symbolic significance of his cup banging cannot be lost. He has become that which he formerly viewed only through the isolating window of his chauffeured automobile, an adult. As such, he adopts the sounds of the adult world.

Chapter 19: One with the Planes

[01:06:52]

As Jamie makes his way through the internment camp in which the antlike business of building an airstrip is taking place, a laconic version of the *toy planes, home, and hearth* music returns. Again, it is the sound mix that tells the story. The sounds of the camp—the construction sounds, the welding, the rock breaking—are matched with a gentle and introverted orchestration of the *toy planes, home, and hearth* theme, reflecting Jamie's continuing childlike wonder at the world in which he now lives. But the music also signals that this is Jim's new home, at least for the duration of the war.

Musically, the *toy planes, home, and hearth* theme is treated with block chords reminiscent of a church chorale. The sounds of the camp become muted, almost filtered as the music rises to reveal Jamie's innocent fascination with all that surrounds him now. Sparks from a welder's torch become

a fireworks display in Jamie's fervent mind (and the camera's framing). **[01:07:09]**
The melancholic orchestration yields to lush string voicings of the same
theme, while the camera gives us a midshot of Jamie from slightly below,
empowering him and signaling his emerging confidence in this new world.

The significance of the reverent, churchlike block chords becomes apparent as Jamie approaches a parked Japanese airplane, an enduring object of
fascination for him. The imagery of an airplane represents the duality of Jim's
experience, the freedom and fantasy of his childhood as well as the machinations and complexity of the adult world.

It is significant that the spiritually orchestrated *toy planes, home, and
hearth* music continues despite Jim being confronted by a Japanese guard
as he sensually strokes the airplane. There is no break in the music; the reverence continues unencumbered. As three Japanese aviators approach the
airplane and Jim, horns enter with the melody, ennobling the theme. The **[01:07:48]**
strings play through a sweeping gesture that brings them into their upper
register. Jim draws himself to attention and salutes the pilots, who return the
respectful gesture as the orchestration expands with soaring strings, now ac- **[01:08:08]**
companied by the disembodied angelic voices. It is a climactic instant musically and dramatically, reinforced by the visual of the sentry pausing, as if
he, too, feels the moment. The certainty of war is momentarily suspended
as the fantasy-pilot Jim earns and returns the respect of the real pilots; opposing parties brought together by the allegory of flying, the symbol of
childhood freedom and adult ability.

Chapter 20: Kindred Spirits

The *toy planes, home, and hearth* theme continues across the fade to the
image of a red rising or setting sun and a Japanese boy launching his toy
glider across a open field, much as Jamie did at the prewar masquerade
party. The sequence is an intentional comparison between the experiences
of both youths.

In the masquerade party sequence, we saw Jamie running away from the
camera into the distance, his arms outstretched as he prepares to launch his
glider. In this scene, the Japanese boy is running toward the camera, while his **[01:08:20]**
arm and glider assumes the same position as Jamie's in the first scene. Jamie
was colorfully dressed, while the Japanese boy is adorned in muted tones.

The music cements the commonality between the two boys and their
growing-up experiences. The carefree, playful atmosphere incited by the
melody and orchestration from Jamie's glider flying scene continues under **[01:08:24]**
the Japanese boy as he flies his own toy plane. In both scenes, underscored
by the same music, a child encounters a real airplane while pretending with
his own. In Jamie's case, it was an abandoned Japanese *Zero*. In the current
scene, it is a working one. The music turns momentarily mournful as barbed **[01:08:38]**
wired cuts across the camera's perspective, only to reemerge cheerfully as we
see Jim staring at the Japanese *Zero* through the wire as it takes off.

The parallel between the two scenes continues as the Japanese boy accidentally launches his airplane across the barbed wire into Jim's side of the

[01:09:04] camp. Jim ascends the berm separating the two sides. He retrieves the toy plane and returns it across the wire to the Japanese boy. But here, underlying music veers away from the earlier scene. Unlike the first scene in which the drums and nonrhythmic sounds of war emerge at the moment of confrontation between a Brit and a Japanese, the music in this scene continues unabated. The Japanese boy recovers his toy airplane as the two boys, torn apart by the war and the wire, exchange understanding glances and thanks in Japanese. Though a single strand of barbed wire cuts the close-up shot of a now smiling Jim, the music continues its optimistic course. It fades out under the din of two airborne Japanese *Zeros*. A fleeting childhood moment has returned.

Chapter 21: Tricks of the Trade

While one of the primary uses of music in a film is to establish the time and place of the narrative, another is to help establish a sense of time passing; to evoke the passage of a longer period of narrative time in a short amount of film time. Chapter 21, titled "Tricks of the Trade," uses music in such a capacity.

We are treated visually to a series of short vignettes about the everyday life in the internment camp. These vignettes are connected together in two ways. The first is by Jim's continuous running through the camp, from vignette to vignette, while engaged in a rather sophisticated business of bartering goods and services. He trades cigarettes for cabbages for clean laundry for chewing gum for shined shoes and so on. Jim has adapted by taking charge of his life. In short, he is learning to be an American, a flourishing entrepreneur, reflected by his American flight jacket that provides bulk to his still developing masculine frame.

But his activities alone do not indicate the passage of extended time, nor do they reflect *how* the years have passed and normalized his captive experiences. It is the contrast between the previous scene and this one that amplifies the change in Jim's life.

[01:09:50] The music that accompanies Jim's business rounds is happy, sprightly tempoed, clearly in a major key and could easily underscore the cosmopolitanism and commerce of a bustling New York in the 1940s or 1950s. It is the music of business, the music of optimism. The camp is alive, as are the people in
[01:11:26] it. Jim passes the camp thespians and offers his elders advice on golfing. The music continues, albeit muted in its orchestration. He crosses to the Japanese side of the camp to deliver the newly polished shoes to the Japanese comman-
[01:11:38] dant. The music returns to full enthusiasm as he returns to the internees' side.

Jim momentarily pauses in his rounds to shoot marbles with some children. He is invincible, an expert marksman, winning and collecting all of the marbles on his first shot.

[01:12:11] But the excitement of the music diminishes as Jim approaches the camp hospital. The atmosphere in the hospital is grave; death and despair counterpoints the unbridled enthusiasm reflected in Jim's gait. The buoyant and bubbling music yields to a high string figure, lingering like the dying patients in the hospital. The doctor presses Jim into applying CPR to a dying woman.

Jim is aware of the seriousness of the situation, but despite his efforts, the patient is declared dead. He continues his pumping actions, however, and the woman's eyes momentarily shift toward Jim as if she is looking at him. Excited by his apparent power, Jim declares that "I've done it. I can bring her back to life. I can do it again." The patient *is* dead, however, and the eye movement simply a mechanical response to blood being pumped to the brain by Jim's movements. Nonetheless, this imaginary sense of power will be paralleled in a later scene.

Chapters 22, 23, 24: The Antidote, New Word: Pragmatist, the University of Life

The next several chapters are devoid of music as the film establishes the relationship between the doctor and Jim. The doctor works with Jim on his studies, but the discussions inevitably return to the issue of the war. The nature of the dialog serves to reflect Jim's confusion; he admires the bravery of the Japanese fighters but recognizes that they are the enemy. His confusion is understandable, especially for a teenager who has been stripped of his identity as he has known it and struggles to discover who he is. He is British, but he has never been to England.

Jim leaves the hospital and continues with his entrepreneurial chores, which eventually take him to the American barracks and Basie. Ever the schemer, Basie convinces Jim to cross the wire to trap a pheasant for the upcoming Thanksgiving meal in the American barracks. Ever the adventurer and tired of the British dorm, which he describes as "lethargic," he hopes to move to where the action is, the American barracks.

The parallels between the two new adult males in Jim's life are clear. Both attempt to educate him—the doctor more formally with Latin and poetry, Basie with pragmatic lessons in survival, the "university of life," as Jim calls it. Both refer to reading materials; the doctor with a grammar book, Basie with *Life* and *Reader's Digest*.

Chapter 27: Setting the Traps

The next day, Jim approaches the barbed-wire perimeter of the camp carrying two pheasant traps and sporting his newly acquired English golf shoes. Driven by his desire to be accepted by Basie and the American POWs, Jim sneaks through the barbed-wire perimeter, crawling through the mud to avoid **[01:31:58]** detection as the war drum theme returns. A Japanese sentry sloshes through the reeds to investigate.

The music's orchestration and texture is similar to the confrontational music heard earlier in the film, when Jamie, dressed as Sinbad, climbed a berm only to discover a contingent of Japanese soldiers in their encampment.

Militant snare drum figures, cymbal scrapes, reverberant clave hits, and other sparse drum gestures dominate the sonic landscape, emphasizing Jim's slithering stealthiness. He scurries through the reeds, stopping to lie facedown in the muck as a Japanese sentry investigates. A breathy shakuhachi flute **[01:33:50]** gesture responds to high-pitched dissonant string figures as the guard discovers Jim's golf shoes and begins the hunt. The music rises in overall pitch, while its density and rhythmic activity increases as the sentry moves closer and closer to Jim. The music becomes increasingly contrapuntal, even adding piano and strings as the hunt intensifies.

[01:35:56]   It reaches its most intense moment as the guard looms above a well-hidden Jim, but it quickly dissipates as he moves away, oblivious to Jim's presence. Jim's Japanese friend calls to the guard, diverting him. The music continues to vanish, as does the danger, as the sentry moves past Jim. The guard departs as Jim and his friend exchange knowing glances and salute each other.

Chapters 28, 29: In America Now, Nagata's Revenge on Basie

[01:36:54]   As the scene changes, a very muddy but triumphant Jim marches with his suitcase from the family dormitory to the American barracks. A celebratory "Grenadier's March," a fife and drum affair, accompanies him throughout the scene. To the salutes of its occupants, Jim enters the American barracks, his

[01:38:07] bravery rewarded as he is shown to his new cubicle. The march cross-fades to a series of comfortingly resolved major chords, reminiscent of family as

[01:38:25] Jim enters his new home. He opens his suitcase and replaces the girlie picture on the wall of his cubicle with his magazine cutout of Norman Rockwell's

[01:39:05] *Freedom from Fear*. The string chords resume, becoming increasingly dissonant as a haunting variation of the march's melody reemerges. The scene fades out as the camera pulls back from Jim, who stares at the ceiling, with only the Rockwell picture accompanying the shot. His real home is just a memory now, as is the piano's sound; the safety of the consonant chords are as evaporative as his memory of his family.

Chapter 32: Kamikaze Dawn ("Umiyakaba," "Suo Gan")

The scene opens with an air of tranquility as the sun rises over the camp and airfield. Jim is asleep on the ground, caught in a no-man's-land between the American aviator and British family compounds. He belongs to neither of the two worlds, American nor British, adult nor child, as the new day dawns. Jim rises to witness a Japanese officer congratulating three pilots before the rising sun as they partake in the ritual reserved for kamikaze airmen. Barbed wire separates him from the men.

[01:49:52]   As part of the ceremony, the airmen begin to sing "Umiyakaba," a patriotic Japanese song popular during the war. While witnessing this and noticing that his Japanese friend is also watching, Jim draws himself to attention and

[01:50:11] begins singing "Suo Gan" as he salutes the Japanese flyers, British-style. It is interesting to note that Jim begins "Suo Gan" just as the camera catches the reaction shot from his friend, as if the song is meant to comfort his Japanese counterpart. The two songs briefly overlap, but "Suo Gan" soon consumes the sonic environment.

    "Suo Gan" continues over a sequence of shots revealing the contemplations of the key players—the Japanese camp commander as he gazes out the window overlooking the camp, Mr. Lockwood as he collects firewood, Basie as he recovers from his beating inside his barracks.

The song, now harmonized by the boys' choir, continues as the camera **[01:51:11]** returns to the tearing-up camp commander, then Mr. Victor lost in thought as he clutches his pipe, a dispirited and pale Mrs. Victor, and finally the pilots as they run to mount their planes. The song, now fully orchestrated with organ **[01:51:42]** and voices, has momentarily replaced the sounds of war.

The haunting sweetness of the music has brought a moment of reflective memory of childhood and a happier time to all of the people whose images we have just seen, thus underscoring even more poignantly the futility of the events that have transpired during the course of the past several years.

Nonetheless, the sounds of the planes begin to overwhelm the music. The song approaches a cadence point as Jim watches the planes rise to meet the sun. But the completion of the cadence is violently severed by the sound and **[01:52:18]** sight of one of the planes exploding in midair. Along with the characters involved, we, too, have been lulled into a temporary reverie, visciously interrupted by the suddenness of the explosion. The effect is startling to both the viewer as well as the characters onscreen.

Chapter 33: Bombs and Rapture

The plane explosion signals the beginning of an American air attack on the airfield adjoining the internment camp. Though everyone else runs for cover or prostrates themselves on the ground, Jim, in his excitement, grabs his luggage and runs to the top of the barracks to witness the attack. After his anticipation and anxiety has been established, music sneaks in under the sound **[01:53:26]** effects of exploding bombs and machine guns firing.

But we do not hear Jim's anxiousness reflected in the music. We hear his awe and wonderment, the same theme as when he flies his glider across the field at the masquerade party. It is the excitement of his childhood returning.

Only now do we understand the significance of his gestures, his holding himself cross-armed, self-cuddling, reassuring himself. He has grabbed his luggage because the attack triggers his hope for returning home to his parents and his childhood. Whatever anxiety he feels about the battle (remember he is standing in a rather exposed position for an air attack) dissipates as his smile emerges. The American P-51, the "Cadillac of the Sky" as he calls it, becomes his symbol of freedom. To reinforce Jim's sense of wonder, Spielberg flies one plane in slow motion toward Jim. We hear only the ethereal boys' **[01:53:41]** choir, no bombs or engine noise, as the plane approaches and the pilot waves from the open-canopied cockpit to a mesmerized Jim.

Jim's cathartic exclamation is less about being liberated than about the joy of experiencing the airplane and childhood it represents. His outburst brings us back to the reality of the moment, while the sound effects of the battle return.

Still, Jim's confusion eventually overwhelms his sense of euphoria. He begins to unravel, "I touched them. I felt their heat. I can taste them in my mouth." These are very physical, childlike expressions. He rants about British bones in the runway. He begins to claim ownership of the runway, but he is

[01:55:16] brought back to the moment by the camp doctor who has joined him on the roof in the hope of drawing him down to safer quarters. The joyousness of the strings and boys' choir gives way to dissonant string chords, reflecting the strangeness of Jim's thinking and the conflict raging within him.

[01:55:49] The doctor shakes him back to reality by admonishing him to "try not to think so much." The dissonant strings underscore Jim's confession that he cannot remember what his parents look like. The boys' choir softly returns, a gentle reminder, and he reverts to mindlessly conjugating Latin as a parachute from heaven descends in the background. Jim's regression is complete as the doctor carries him down the steps to safety, much as a parent would carry a sleeping, or in this case, injured, child. Jim continues to recite his Latin, harkening back to his days in the church. The choir gradually diminishes under a series of shots that focus our attentions on a burning airplane (a childhood up in flames) and the loss felt by the camp commander as he sits dejectedly on the ground. We are left with the image of untouched remnants of the kamikaze ceremony, two white-clothed tables and the ceremonial china settings. But no one is in attendance.

Chapter 34: Return to the British Dorm

Jim's regression continues as he returns with his things to the British family dormitory. Mrs. Victor, despite her own physical and psychological condition, rises from her bed to help him settle back into their corner of the dormitory. She leans toward him as if to kiss him and welcome him back, but she instead takes his suitcase while her husband rearranges their beds. She unpacks his bag while the camera focuses in on the Norman Rockwell picture [01:57:44] Jim has carried with him throughout his ordeals. Musically, we hear a variation of the music from chapter 4, in which Jim's mother puts him to bed. The melody is a dissonant variant of the leitmotif from the earlier, happier times in Jim's life. The first part of the melody is played by the flute, followed by the oboe, with horns and strings adding a gentle sighing figure, emphasizing the faint longing for the previous family lives of Mrs. Victor and Jim.

Mrs. Victor hangs the Norman Rockwell picture and even places Jim's toy Japanese airplane, the one he dropped at the moment he lost touch with his [01:58:35] mother, by his bedside. It is an achingly poignant moment, as the original orchestration from the previous chapter reemerges with the melody momentarily in a major key. A close-up of Mrs. Victor, her hair still emphasizing her femininity, shows her innocently tending to the needs of a child. The moment is not lost on Jim as he looks at Mrs. Victor, remembers his mother, and [01:58:55] begins to cry. The harmoniousness of the major key yields to an unresolved dissonance as the screen fades to black.

Chapters 35, 36: Broken Promise, Failed Mission

With the end of the war in sight, the Japanese begin to move the detainees to Nantao. Jim discovers that Basie has already escaped, abandoning him and breaking his promise to Jim.

The music at the beginning of chapter 36 is different from anything we have heard previously. It can be considered episodic music, reflecting the difficulty of the trek undertaken by the internees.

As the prisoners begin their march, a crane shot reveals the crowd of ragtag, disheveled, and disheartened Europeans and Americans as they walk through the camp entrance's archway. The music, fully orchestral in nature, **[02:01:05]** begins with the low strings. The slow, plodding nature of the tempo matches the weariness of the prisoners as they walk past a sole pilot (Jim's Japanese friend) partaking in the kamikaze ritual. A long, languorous English horn **[02:01:11]** solo rises above the morose strings, reflecting the futility we see onscreen: both the Japanese aviator undergoing the kamikaze ritual and the European and American prisoners death-marching, all of them resigned to the fates that circumstances have thrust upon them.

Jim is alarmed as he sees his Japanese friend mount an airplane. His friend's own trek—passage from innocent child to kamikaze pilot—is thwarted by a balky airplane engine. The Japanese youth is left in the cockpit **[02:02:52]** in tears, as the horns arch their countermelody upward. The visual image cross-fades to the marchers in their misery, as the higher strings assume the **[02:03:03]** melody, accompanied by the boys' choir.

Chapters 37, 38: March to Nantao, the Olympic Stadium

The march to Nantao is a visual montage of death and tragedies underscored by tragic and plodding episodic music. Ponderously slow, with soaring angelic voices hovering overhead, it hints at the impending death of many of the refugees. One lost soul maintains a stoic rendition of "It's a Long Way to **[02:03:07]** Tipperary," but no one else rallies to the tune. Jim babbles nonsensically in Latin as he gazes at the metallic trinkets hung on the backpack of the person walking in front of him.

A repetitive figure in the lower brass simply plods forward. It has no **[02:03:14]** momentum; it is just an endless ostinato, lugubrious and unrelenting. As the camera pulls back, we see the scale of the misery, hundreds of walking human skeletons trudging onward, their will all but destroyed, accompanied by the brass ostinato. The ostinato increases in loudness and intensity as the camera draws back, emphasizing the scope of the tragedy.

This ostinato yields to an ethereal, atonal section, evocative of the night- **[02:04:10]** marish images we see as well as the passage of time. The camera catches the silhouette of Jim on the bank of a body of water. Jim stares for a moment, and then tosses his suitcase filled with the sum total of his life into the water. Gone are his toy airplane and Norman Rockwell picture and all that is precious to him. By discarding all that he is, his belongings and therefore his identity, he abandons all hope of the future and seeing his parents again. Crescendoing choir voices accompany his act of banishment, and then float **[02:04:36]** away as wistfully as Jim's suitcase. All that is left is the dissonance of his current existence.

Williams's orchestration is unusual in that he calls for glass tubes to be gently bowed, along with more traditionally played instruments such as the piano, glockenspiel, and harp. The voices, superimposed above this texture, are not called for in the original score and may have been added at some postproduction phase.

[02:04:56]   A mournful, lushly orchestrated melody in the violins' darker midrange continues, as does the endless march of the refugees, through a series of establishing shots designed to reflect the passage of time and continued misery and dying. We then cross-fade to the image of Jim, incongruously walking in his golf shoes across a barren landscape. He begins to encounter a strange assortment of objects from a previous civilian life—umbrellas, violins, birdcages—all scattered along his path. The music assumes a lushness not heard before, a more lyrical and legato string melody that simultaneously maintains the episodic quality while hinting at an air of optimism.

Jim's journey leads him and the other survivors to an arch of bronze angels and birds at the entrance to the Olympic stadium, abandoned and now filled [02:05:30]   with Japanese spoils of war, Western relics from the past. The angelic voices briefly return, and Jim looks up to the arch with a sense of wonderment. The [02:05:34]   music momentarily reveals the child that still lingers within him. The boys' choir returns, unaccompanied as the camera pans around the archway, revealing the intricate details. Angels look and grasp upward, but more importantly, birds, the symbol of freedom, complement the imagery.

As Jim and the other refugees stumble into the stadium, they find it filled with the spoils of war: all of their belongings, the contents of their houses, their cars, pianos, the bric-a-brac of their past lives. The refugees wander among the detritus. The boys' chorus dominates the aural landscape, reinforcing the ghostliness of the entire scene. The chirping of the birds briefly returns, evocative of a more peaceful time. It is one of the rare occasions in the film in which the natural world sounds complement rather than counter-[02:06:20]   point the music. One woman sits at a white grand piano playing music last heard when the British cars headed toward the masquerade party in prewar Shanghai. The piece itself triggers Jim's reflections and memory, and he visually homes in on the swan hood ornament of a car, his family's Packard. [02:06:33]   An extended high string dissonance overlays the piano music, a clash of tonalities that underscores Jim's surrealistic experience. Additional string tone clusters subtly underscore the transition to nighttime.

Chapter 39: "Pretend You're Dead"

Hints of the sounds of war return as the Japanese officer orders the refugees [02:07:00]   to continue their trek. We hear a reverberated shakuhachi flute accompanied [02:07:19]   by harp arpeggios and various rumbling percussion effects as Jim administers to the now-dying Mrs. Victor. The intensity of the earthy but dissonant duet increases as Jim convinces Mrs. Victor to fall to the ground and play dead, so she will no longer have to march.

Chapter 40: Heavenly Light

As morning dawns, we are treated to a series of still-life images of objects in the stadium. The final image in that still life is a statue of a Greek goddess

in repose. The image cross-fades to one of a now-dead Mrs. Victor, roughly **[02:09:02]**
assuming the same position. The only sounds we hear are that of a mourning
dove, followed by other morning birdsongs.

As Jim gazes on her body, the sounds of wind chimes indicate an approach-   **[02:09:55]**
ing breeze, an aural cue that a new *wind* is about to blow. Jim witnesses a
flash of white light like the sun and sees a shock wave traveling from the
source. Jim has mistaken the light and shock wave from an atomic bomb explosion for Mrs. Victor's soul leaving her earthly body. The image of her as-   **[02:10:05]**
cending spirit is poignantly highlighted by the return of the angelic-sounding
boys' choir. Jim looks skyward in awe as the choir fades out and the screen
fades to almost white.

Emerging from the white light of the atomic bomb is a downtrodden Jim
walking. The accompanying choral figure morphs into a plodding tympani   **[02:10:19]**
mimicking a now-starving Jim's listless gait. He stumbles upon a chaotic
scene of Japanese soldiers and Western civilians scavenging a destroyed out-
post for food. A blaring radio provides a voiceover explanation that the Japanese have surrendered under the weight of two atomic bombs. Jim stumbles
about looking for food while the voices rise in volume, accompanied by a   **[02:11:34]**
lush upper string orchestration as Jim begins to understand the scientific basis
of what he saw. Even the childhood image of a soul ascending to heaven is
decimated by the adult world's intrusion, a radio announcing the scientific
root of the shock wave. Neither the voices nor the strings cadence as they
rise in volume and pitch, however, leaving the resolution for the next scene.

Chapters 41, 42: Reunion, "I Can Bring Everyone Back"

The choir and strings resolve their line as we cross-fade to Jim aimlessly   **[02:12:00]**
wandering in a rice paddy. We hear a return of the *toy planes, home, and
hearth* theme, luxuriously orchestrated in the midrange of the string section
of the orchestra. The incongruous quality of this sound, the lushness, has
not been heard since Jim was still Jamie and he was home with his parents
in the womb of the International Settlement. Jim's salvation is heard before
it is seen. The music effectively announces that manna from heaven is arriv-
ing via parachute in a series of metal canisters. The Americans have begun
dropping canisters of food and emergency provisions. One may consider
that the lushly orchestrated leitmotif representing salvation began the moment the food bombs were released from the airplanes overhead, thus the
reason for the music appearing before the actual visual image to which it is
to be associated. The theme continues to build as more canisters drop and
Jim races to an open one.

Overcome with joy, he frantically cuts open a can of milk, the universal
symbol of Mother, as the *toy planes, home, and hearth* theme is capped in its   **[02:13:02]**
full glory by the clarion-sounding trumpets at the precise moment he takes
a sip. It is noteworthy that these were the same trumpets that announced the
loss of his mother when he let go of her hand in the panic of the Japanese
attack in Shanghai.

The music turns more introverted as the winds play with snippets of the   **[02:13:19]**
melody in a less declarative fashion. Jim returns to the Soochow Camp he

was liberated from, dragging a parachute full of goodies. He encounters his youthful Japanese counterpart, thrashing about in the paddy, delirious with failure as a kamikaze pilot. Jim and his counterpart meet, and the camaraderie of their youth is reflected in their eyes and smiles. It is a powerful reunion

[02:13:35] of childhood friends amid all that they have both endured. The boys' choir returns as the salvation theme continues. Gently orchestrated with strings and voices, the theme is left unresolved and unfinished as it fades away, the Japanese boy overcome with confusion.

A bandit-filled truck barrels through a wooden fence as two American renegades emerge from the truck, firing weapons in the air as a show of force and intimidation. The intimacy of the moment between Jim and his Japanese

[02:14:43] friend, the lingering vestige of childhood, is again shattered by the sounds of war and adulthood. When the camera returns to Jim and his friend, he offers Jim a mango as a token of friendship. The camera shoots Jim from above, giving him power, with his friend clearly in a subservient position.

Basie has returned as one of the marauders. He recognizes Jim and calls to him from afar. Jim and his Japanese friend share a playful moment while Jim attempts to eat the mango without first cutting it open. His Japanese friend laughs and offers to slice it open with his ceremonial sword. Basie perceives the raised sword as a threat to Jim and runs toward the boys as another bandit fires his pistol, killing Jim's friend. Jim is overcome with rage and attacks the culpable bandit. The fracas that follows draws Basie into the water where the fight is taking place.

Basie attempts to engage Jim in a discussion regarding possible places to pilfer supplies, but Jim is oblivious while he gently lays his friend out. Jim gazes at his hands while soliloquizing about the new word he learned today. The mo-

[02:16:36] ment is quite surreal, especially given the nature of the music introduced: gentle string and choir gestures associated with the happier times of his childhood.

Jim delivers a monologue about the flash of the atomic bomb he witnessed, likening it to "God taking a photograph." Jim believes he has mystical hands, that he has the power to perform the miracle of giving life.

The camera shoots upward, positioning Jim in power as he applies CPR to his dead friend. He reaches down, almost toward the camera and us, the sun at his back. He begins to methodically pump his friend's chest, while chanting, mantralike, "I can bring everyone back." The dialog is a reference to an earlier scene in which he attempts to resurrect a dead woman in the camp's hospital. The pace of his pumping and the editing rallies into a series of visual flashes. Images of the dead boy and Jim's frantic pumping alternate with the boys' choir, providing continuity for the sequence.

[02:18:30] The music unfolds, chorale-style. The screen flashes only for a moment on the image of Jim, pumping the heart of himself, dressed in his red schoolboy uniform. He is literally pumping the life back into his own childhood. He has become an adult by choosing to become a child again, perhaps the ultimate freedom. The music soars to a climax as his self-empowering gesture takes hold.

[02:18:40] The music turns dissonant and minor as Basie pulls Jim off his dead friend. "Jim, didn't I teach you anything?" "Yes, you taught me that people will do anything for a potato." The other bandits laugh and mock Basie, exclaiming, "Three years with him?"

At first Basie doesn't get it. He entices Jim back into the adult world by offering him the fantasy of childhood, offering to take him back to his family and fill up the family pool and retire. The promise is accompanied by eerie, dissonant music. One wonders from what Jim should retire until it is clear that Basie refers to the horrors that have surrounded them. But Jim doesn't fall for the false fantasy of childhood offered to him by his false father, Basie. The music, dissonant as it is, simply fades away, leaving us with a very *loud*   [02:19:05] silence at this crucial moment in Jim's life. He glares at the uncomprehending Basie. The camera assumes Jim's point of view, standing above and behind Jim, looking down on Basie, mired in the murky water of the paddy. At one point, we see only Jim's torso. His neck and head are unseen above the frame, while his knees and lower legs extend below the frame. He is a giant, a true man, according to the camera.

Jim confronts and ultimately rejects Basie, who has been his protector, guiding light, and teacher during their internment. The significance of the awkward pause at that moment of confrontation, followed by Basie's smile and acknowledgment of Jim as more than a pawn in his own designs, becomes apparent.

Chapter 43: "I Surrender" ("Exsultate Juste")

A series of establishing shots places Jim alone in the deserted camp. We experience Jim as he begins to recover elements of his childhood by riding a bicycle through the American dorm in the camp, his home away from his real home. This sequence parallels an earlier one, in which a mischievous Jim first rode his bike through the deserted dining room in his own house, just after the Japanese invasion.

The music builds in its joyfulness from the moment we see Jim somberly   [02:20:20] pedaling around to his upward gaze of wonderment at the falling supplies being dropped from airplanes. The music is in a major key, and when the boys' choir finally arrives singing "Exsultate Juste," they are not just vocalizing but   [02:20:28] singing the lyrics, filled with an enthusiasm we've not really heard since the first few minutes of the film. When the next manna from heaven in the form of a food-packed cylinder crashes through the roof, the chorus can be heard   [02:20:47] singing the lyric, "Hallelujah."

Jim's continued pedaling and laughter takes him outside of the dorm as he winds his way throughout the camp. When confronted by newly arrived American soldiers in their neatly pressed uniforms, the chorus momentarily   [02:21:29] disappears (though a playful oboe and harp interlude continues), only to return as Jim assumes the submissive posture he has learned under the Japanese. He offers his can of milk to the American officer, and exclaims, "I surrender." At first glance, this seems humorous and ill scripted, but taken in the context of the past few scenes, it is clear that Jim is surrendering his adult persona in favor of recapturing his youth. He rejects all that the adult world has forced upon him. At the moment in which Jim surrenders to the

American, the camera presents us with an upward-looking close-up of Jim, indicating his power as he makes his decisions.

Chapter 44: Tired Eyes ("Suo Gan")

Choral sounds carry us across the cut to a crane shot of a somewhat run-down conservatory that houses European displaced children. We hear the cacophony of children playing games as the camera takes us inside. The children gather together, as a group of parents looking for their children enter the conservatory. The anticipation is palpable as parents begin to recognize their lost children and vice versa. We see Jim's mother and father looking into the crowd, while a sullen and morose Jim, still in his American flight jacket, just stares off. Jim's father does not recognize his son and walks right by him. [02:23:49] But the theme "Suo Gan" returns, sung solo by the voice of a prewar Jamie, a moment before his mother turns and begins to recognize him.

In this case, the music presages the reunion that is about to happen, but only by a second or so. "Suo Gan" becomes louder and more powerful as his [02:24:06] mother calls him "Jamie," his childhood, prewar name. The full chorus begins to accompany the solo voice as the sounds of the children, parents, and conservatory disappear, leaving us with only the lullaby and the image of mother and son reunited in their embrace.

The lullaby continues above a crowded street scene in Shanghai, as the population fills the street and celebrates with fireworks. Jamie's solo voice carries us into the images of a once-again peaceful harbor scene, sampans being steered, barges being pushed by tugboats, and Jim's suitcase, the sum total of his experience, floating in the water.

Chapter 45: End Credits ("Exsultate Juste")

[02:26:08] The joyous choral work, "Exsultate Juste," returns fully orchestrated over the closing credits. While we are left with the proverbial Hollywood ending, the story is based on the truth as experienced by one boy confronted with the realities of the world around him and his own place in that world.

SUMMARY

In *Empire of the Sun*, we see another way in which both music and sound is used to further the plot as well as an underlying archetypal story. In the movie, a young boy's inner conflict between the innocence of his youth and his ensuing maturation into a man is manifested in the larger sonic framework called sound design. Youth and innocence, accompanied by dreams and fantasies, is represented by the film's music, as initially established by "Suo Gan," a mother's lullaby, with all of its reassurings about safety and protection.

Adolescence, the crossover from childhood to the adult world and its accompanying realities, finds form in the sound effects, often in the form of machine noises or real-world sounds that impinge upon the songs of youth.

"Suo Gan" and the Chopin *Mazurka* serve as the primary reinforcements for childhood fantasy, while buzzing airplanes, banging cans, and warlike drum figures (are they sound effect or music?) underscore the reality of war and its intrusion into and destruction of Jamie's childhood.

Visual leitmotifs such as Norman Rockwell's illustration *Freedom from Fear* and images of airplanes flying, on fire or exploding, represent the destruction of the freedom of childhood and the harsh reality of adulthood. The visual elements become all the more significant and powerful when coupled with their aural counterparts, rendering the film a masterwork of sound/music collaboration in the overarching concept of sound design.

NOTES

1. Jay Beck and Tony Grajeda, "The Future of Film Sound Studies," in *Lowering the Boom: Critical Studies in Film Sound*, ed. Jay Beck and Tony Grajeda (Champaign, IL: University of Illinois Press, 2008), 5.

2. James Ballard's autobiographical novel, *Empire of the Sun*, on which the film is based.

3. Joseph McBride, *Steven Spielberg: A Biography* (New York: Simon & Schuster, 1997), 392.

4. Composer unknown.

5. *Empire of the Sun*—Warner Bros., 11753, ISBN 0-7907-6165-3.

6. *Freedom from Fear*—One of Norman Rockwell's most famous oil paintings, it was part of a series called Four Freedoms, based on a State of the Union speech by President Franklin D. Roosevelt, and it was used as a war poster during World War II.

American Beauty

OVERVIEW

In *American Beauty*, Thomas Newman writes some extraordinarily evocative nontraditional film music, while using it in a very traditional manner. Newman begins with musical color. "My approach normally is to start from a point of color, meaning do I hear woodwind sounds or do I hear plucking sounds or bell sounds, and I try to build up. I normally start from a point of color as opposed to a point of melody."[1]

Leitmotifs are more oriented toward texture and color than melody, similar to John Corigliano's approach in *Altered States*. Nonetheless, Newman's leitmotifs are quite definable once one develops an ear for his style of composition. At the same time, Newman is able to create an overall musical ambience, a signature sound that becomes identifiable with the movie as a whole. In this sense, he creates a monothematic atmosphere, a singular, omnipresent air that permeates the entire film. Balancing these two seemingly opposite approaches to film music composition, a leitmotif-based approach and an atmospheric-based gestalt, is difficult, but Newman is able to accomplish it through his choice of instruments for the score and his compositional approach.

Thomas Newman comes from a film music family. His father, Alfred Newman, is credited with developing a film and music timing system that revolutionized the film and music synchronization process. Other family members in the business include his uncle, brother, and two cousins. He is credited with scores for *The Shawshank Redemption*, *The Player*, *Finding Nemo*, *WALL-E*, *Road to Perdition*, and *The Help*, among others. His score for *American Beauty* was nominated for an Academy Award, one of many nominations.

In an interview, Newman explained that he "typically records with a small group of players. . . . Then I will go in with an orchestra and overdub to these kind of 'stages and vibes' that I have set up and then I start to mix."[2] By stages and vibes, Newman seems to be talking about the sonic placement of individual sounds within the overall soundscape and the general tone of the film that he is trying to capture. We will see this approach applied to *American Beauty*.

American Beauty is British director Sam Mendes's first film, having previously established himself as a fine director of theatrical productions at the Royal Shakespeare Company and Royal National Theatre in England. For his freshman efforts in film, he was rewarded with an Academy Award for Best Director. He has gone on to direct *Road to Perdition* and *Revolutionary Road*, among others, while maintaining an active stage directing and film producer career.

Newman's score is an eclectic mixture of rhythmic ostinatos and intentionally incomplete-sounding melodic gestures played by traditionally scored string sections, nontraditionally tuned instruments, non-Western percussion, and organized by structured improvisations as well as more conventional scoring techniques. Not all of the cues are notated in orchestral form. Some cues do not even exist in written form. In general, Newman seems to rely on a core group of instruments and skilled improvisers to provide an overarching sonic coherence to the entire score. "A lot of times I will go in with an idea that is skeletal. I'll go in with an idea of how I want to dress it up and I will really be able to deal with issues like transition in ways that you never would if you put a pencil to paper or worked with notes. Then when something works I ask myself why."[3] Most cues have very similar tempos, varying only slightly. This, too, adds to the consistency of the film. Tension within the film itself is built through the pacing of the editing, plot, as well as the remarkable skills of the actors.

If we are to characterize the basic musical elements of the score, we clearly hear repetitive figures in the marimba and piano. More often than not, synthesizers are used to create musical pads or beds. They will occasionally provide a fleeting, nonstructurally important gesture. Melodies are fragmentary, less forthcoming, and often hard to clearly delineate. They add to the texture created by the other instruments rather than commanding it.

This is what makes the score so unusual and difficult for our ears. But once we examine the subtle use of instrumentation and define the gestures or sly half melodies thrown at us by Newman, we begin to hear and see how Newman defines his motifs and uses them in a very traditional way to advance the story.

Newman's leitmotifs do not apply to the characters directly. Rather, they apply to abstract personality traits or moral statements intended by the filmmakers, as first represented by the characters. Therefore, the motif Newman associates with *Mental Boy*, as identified by his own title for the cue on the soundtrack CD, is first identified with Ricky, the seemingly strange, aloof boy who spent time in a mental or detoxification facility. But the *mental boy* motif is later applied to Angela, the all-American, cheerleading, slut-talking, wannabe model whose worst fear is to be considered boring. At the climactic moment in the film, we come to recognize that the *mental boy* leitmotif is really director Sam Mendes's and writer Alan Ball's biting social commentary on our society's idea of normal and abnormal behavior.

The *American beauty* leitmotif also provides the vehicle for Mendes's and Ball's commentary on our contemporary society and its concepts of beauty. The *dead already* leitmotif reflects the emotional state of whomever it is underscoring, while the *lunch with the real estate king* motif represents the concept of empowerment. It will emerge whenever a character is feeling optimistic and in control of his or her life. The *power of denial* leitmotif reflects the subconscious denial of a reality by the character with whom it is temporarily associated. This theme will later evolve as each character's subconscious denial is confronted on a conscious level toward the end of the film.

The *arose* leitmotif is attached to a sense of optimism and self-fulfillment, not to a specific character. In this sense, it evokes those same emotions within us as the viewer, creating a sense of empathy with the character experiencing the same emotion. The leitmotif then, supports the general premise of the film, an introspective glance at our own existence. When we see the onscreen characters taking control of their choices and therefore their lives, we experience the same excitement and sense of empowerment. We become them at that moment, which, of course, means that we also become them when they regress to their old habitual activities or states of powerlessness. While we can relate to the many personal facets of Jane's, Lester's, Carolyn's, and Ricky's experiences, the subtle exposure to the *arose* leitmotif at strategic moments profoundly reinforces the experience on a subconscious level.

Newman's orchestrations reflect a minimalist sensitivity. The piano plays a prominent role in almost all cues. The bass makes liberal use of glissandos between notes. But the most striking orchestrational choice is Newman's use of deliberately detuned mandolins to evoke a sense of wildness, playing outside the normal boundaries. It is a harsh, almost primal sound, a signature sound that becomes associated with this *beyond normal* idea that permeates the film. The use of an Indian tabla and other hand drums, rather than a more traditional drum kit, provides the rhythmic drive.

Much of the credit for the success of the film goes to the mixing engineers and music editors, whose choice of source music, subtle control of volume, as well as musical form of the source music cues also sheds light on the dialog, set, and movement in the film. Indeed, the use of musical form to reveal the psychological implications of a scene is masterfully controlled in a way rarely seen in other films. It is naturally evocative of the characters involved and their predicaments at the moment.

Chapter 1: The High Point of My Day

The *dead already* leitmotif fades in a moment before an aerial shot of Lester's [00:01:10] middle class, all-American, suburban neighborhood. The houses are not quite dissimilar, not quite the same. The opening figure of the motif played by a marimba and set against this view is a bit disconcerting. It does not establish time or place. It seems to hesitate before it gets going, like an automobile whose ignition needs to be turned several times before the engine kicks in. But the cut to the scene of Lester Burnham waking to and performing his all-too-usual morning routine interrupts the music just as it begins to get started. A brief glissando, a glassy slide downward from the reclusive reverie of sleep [00:01:37] into the mundane of the awake world, gets us back into the theme and gets Lester out of his blissful dreams and into the conscious world. Lester awakes to being *dead already*.

In a sense, this brief bass glissando reveals Newman's ingenuity in tweak-ing our sense of cliché. In music for film, a downward glissando figure has long represented the idea of descending from a higher point of existence to a lower one (witness the same use of a downward sliding motif in *Altered States*). Newman relies on the film viewers' previous associations with the downward musical gesture to indicate that Lester's lower state of being is actually his waking, conscious existence. In short, when Lester wakes up, he slides from the harmony of his dreamworld down into the rut of his waking life as an advertising executive. The not-so-subtle bass drum hit at the end of [00:01:39] the glissando only heightens the effect.

The repetitive nature of the music underscores the boredom and mun-daneness of Lester Burnham's life. His opening monologue speaks to the *normalcy* of his existence. He lives in a typical suburban house, decorated in closely coordinated colors that do nothing to excite the senses. He spends his days in a typically gray cubicle, staring at a computer screen while talking to customers on his headset telephone in what can only be described as an an-noyingly happy telemarketer voice.

As the monologue progresses, Lester looks out of the window of his house, as if he is already dead. His voiceover is delivered in a slightly monotone and depressed fashion. Visually, the alienation Lester is experiencing is reinforced by our view of him through his living room window, removed from the world, as his wife, Carolyn, cuts a variety of rose called American Beauty from her garden while chatting with their neighbor, Jim. An exterior shot focuses on the banal conversation between Carolyn and Jim in the front yard.

The *dead already* theme continues as Lester describes his daughter Jane's typical teenager-related angst. He describes her as lost, confused, and without direction. A shot of her face reveals her depressed, flattened demeanor. She is dressed in dark, baggy clothes, a monodimensional look that matches her pancake-makeup-basted face.

Lester's voiceover monologue continues as he sleeps in the backseat of his wife's car on the way to work. He sits, or rather slumps, alone in the backseat, certainly a peculiar arrangement. The fact that his wife and daughter occupy the traditional front seats of empowerment further demonstrates just how emasculated Lester has become. He is alone in a dreamworld, oblivious to the world passing him by. A brief shot of the blue sky, outside the car that insulates Lester, reinforces the notion that he is oblivious to the world around him. The voiceover catches the short moment of blue sky with the line, "It's never too late." The music and the scene end together, delineating the prologue from the dramatic body of the work.

[00:04:17]

Chapter 2: Job Description

As we view Lester at work in his cubicle, the tightly controlled clutter of his life is manifested by the set design. The cubicles in the office are neatly arranged, with only occasional elements of personal decoration visible. The color of the decor is that gentle, nondescript gray that seems to permeate all workspaces that are *pleasant* to work in. As we zoom into Lester's space we see the detritus of his job strewn across his desk. One item draws our gaze: a motivational sign placed in a position of prominence by Lester, which says, *look closer*. While this sign may reveal something about Lester's inner yearnings for more meaning or at least more excitement in his deadened existence, its placement encourages us, the viewer, to look beyond the initial superficiality that we will experience throughout the film. It is an invitation to cleverness, an enticement to actively engage in the spectacle that is the undoing of all of the characters involved in the film.

Lester's supervisor, Brad, enters the screen looking slick and formidable, an image reinforced by the camera's low angle, emphasizing his position of power over Lester. He is immaculately coiffed, and dressed in a suit that blends a little too well with the office decor. Brad asks Lester to join him in his office for a chat.

The set design and camera placement for the conversation between Lester and Brad is anything but subtle. It opens with a low-angle shot of Brad, his nameplate prominently placed and lit on his desk, which spans the entire frame. The room's decor, even the painting on the wall behind Brad, is so color coordinated that it leaves us with a bland but pleasant feeling. Nothing in the mise-en-scène is designed to excite or shake us up. It is the background of Lester's life, pleasant, planned, and devoid of any excitement. We view

Lester from a distance, alone in an armless chair in the middle of Brad's office, his jacket unbuttoned. He slouches in the chair, legs conspicuously spread, open for attack—even the design of Brad's office belittles him with its carefully hued expansiveness. The lighting leaves him in the shadow, unenlightened. Lester is disempowered by all that surrounds him.

Lester and Brad's verbal bantering reveals a side of Lester we have not yet seen. He quickly sees through the corporate rhetoric being spewed at him and coaxes Brad into revealing that a downsizing is afoot and Lester must justify his position at the company. His retort, about another executive's misappropriation of funds for a personal sex-capade, makes it clear that Lester does have the capacity to *look closer*, to see through the falseness and banality that causes him to feel *dead already*. He does, however, appear to lack any motivation to do anything about it.

A short, establishing sequence brings Lester home from work after having been picked up by his wife in her car. He grumbles about the events at work, only to be belittled by his dominating wife. The nature of their relationship is now set for the dinner sequence that follows.

The introduction to "Bali Ha'i," a song from the 1954 musical *South Pacific*, coordinates with a dolly shot that brings us across the cut to the interior of the Burnham family dining room. We are treated to a meticulously decorated and coordinated dining room, with close-up shots of family portraits, accompanied by a vase overflowing with neatly and perfectly arranged American Beauty roses. Lester and Carolyn's daughter, Jane, complains about the choice of dinner music, but Carolyn's sarcastic response only reinforces our image of her as the dominating force in the family. This is her Bali Ha'i, her Shangri-La, not her daughter's. Jane's reflexive nastiness toward her parents can be construed as typical teenage angst. The dialog also reinforces her sense of alienation. **[00:06:48]**

Carolyn's choice of dinner music underscores her unrealistically idyllic perception of the world. She exists within her own Bali Ha'i, with a husband, a daughter, a color-coordinated dining room, and pleasant music with dinner. Her husband is depressed, unmotivated, and completely beaten down. Her daughter is sulky, uncommunicative, and lost. Carolyn is in denial about how dysfunctional her family really is. Yet the lyric of her choice of song describes an idyllic tropical paradise, where there are no cares, no troubles. This is Carolyn's world, a denial of the unhappiness that surrounds her. Unfortunately for Lester and Jane, Carolyn's paradise leaves them deadened to their own worlds.

Jane departs the dinner table in a huff, leaving Carolyn and Lester to share what could be a fleeting moment of parental solidarity. The camera is careful to include the American Beauty rose centerpiece in the reaction shot of both spouses. But the moment is short lived as Carolyn's gestures only provoke Lester's disgruntlement even more.

"Bali Ha'i" ends as Lester leaves the room and Carolyn is left alone in her paradise. The conclusion of the song coincides with the end of the scene, leaving us with a sense of completeness. Lester and Jane's estrangement from each other is apparent as they converse while cleaning the dishes after dinner. **[00:08:39]**

The dialog between father and daughter about the loss of communication and closeness is established within the kitchen, but the discussion is then shot from the exterior looking in through the kitchen's window, removing us from the sounds of the kitchen. Each character is framed in his or her own windowpane, separated and alone. A vase of American Beauty roses is visually bisected by the window frame, revealing the fractured nature of this *beautiful* American family. Although the dialog is lost in the silence, the tension is not.

[00:09:12]   The *mental boy* leitmotif (so named by Newman on the soundtrack recording) interrupts the silence as we watch the argument through the window.

The *mental boy* motif is the essential musical core of the film. It is one of the primary vehicles used by Mendes and Newman to comment on their notion of *true beauty*. Their message is that what is considered *mental* or *out of the norm* may be truly beautiful, especially in the face of all the superficiality and psychological denial that surrounds it.

The motif itself is a slow, laconic affair, set in a minor key. It hints at the melancholy of a Chopin prelude, with the piano performing both the melody and a harmonically and rhythmically simple accompaniment, occasionally supplemented by gentle string pads. The motif is haunting and creates a deep sense of intimacy. It reappears throughout the film in unaltered fashion, clearly recognizable at each occurrence. In this sense, it is very much like the classical composer Hector Berlioz's idea of a musical idée fixe, a singular, recognizable melody representing an ideal, which reoccurs unaltered and intact at crucial moments in a musical story to convey an ideal.

The *mental boy* theme takes us across an edit to a close-up of the Burnham's new teenage neighbor, Ricky Fitts, surreptitiously shooting video of Lester and Jane's kitchen conversation. It is clear now that the image we saw through the kitchen window was Ricky's perspective, through the camera lens, as he hides in the shadows outside the kitchen window, totally absorbed in his voyeurism. At first, we associate the *mental boy* theme with Ricky and his voyeurism, but as we shall see, the theme is more promiscuous than that.

Ricky sees the world through the viewfinder of his camcorder. It is his tool of choice for dispassionate observation of the dramas that surround him. Necessarily, it also reflects his sense of alienation since the use of a glass barrier between the observed and the observer is one of the essential signifiers in film semiotics. But as we will see, only Ricky (and later Lester who has been influenced by Ricky) clearly sees (with the aid of his camcorder) the machinations of the external world. This allows him to survive and exist within his own world of beauty. Though the *mental boy* motif seems to first be associated with him, it is the banality and disingenuousness that surrounds him that feeds the leitmotif.

Ricky's intense gaze is essential to the film; his unwavering eye causes a nervous and unsettled self-reflection or denial in those who become the object of his gaze. He rarely blinks. It is as if he has the ability to see through the charades and facades fronted by people, to see the *real* beauty underneath.

Jane leaves the kitchen while Lester finishes the dishes alone. The camera slowly zooms in on a series of family photographs on the countertop, pictures of the family from a happier time. Lester literally (and symbolically) throws in the dish towel in frustration. It lands next to the Burnham family portrait.

Chapter 3: "I Will Sell This House Today"

The previous scene yields to an upbeat Carolyn staking her real estate sign outside a new home. She unloads her car, preparing to clean and prepare the house in anticipation of the day's open house. She is excited, motivated, chanting her mantra, "I will sell this house today," as she squeegees the window. The accompanying music is slightly faster and more optimistic than we have heard in some time. It provides no discernible leitmotif, although with an emphasis on marimba, its orchestration is reminiscent of the *arose* leitmotif, which itself is a theme of optimism. The continual rhythmic pulse provides continuity through a series of vignettes as Carolyn shows the house to a series of bored or skeptical couples. The happy, enthusiastic nature of the cue also provides a humorous counterpoint to the obvious disinterestedness of the clients. [00:10:45]

The music fades out underneath the last vignette as Carolyn desperately tries to maintain a lesbian couple's interest in the house. The music vanishes as she recognizes the futility of her efforts. The scene ends in silence, interrupted by Carolyn's frustrated sobs and self-admonishments about maintaining control of herself. The silence and her aloneness are emphasized by the final image of a floor-length curtain gently swinging, shot from inside the darkened and barren living room, a house vacant and unloved, feelings denied by Carolyn. [00:12:20]

Chapter 4: The Gym

The ensuing high school gym sequence begins with a series of establishing shots before we see Carolyn and Lester conversing in the family car. Lester's moroseness and boredom dominates the conversation. Ever the optimist, Carolyn explains that Jane has been working very hard and secretly wants them to see her perform as part of her cheerleader squad.

If Carolyn's fantasy is the paradise of her own dining room, Lester finds his on the high school basketball court, though it is not the game but the halftime cheerleader show that arouses his interest. A series of musically opposite cues and disorienting visual elements draw us deep into Lester's fantasy world.

As the halftime show begins, we hear "On Broadway" over the school's PA system, an apt musical choice as the cheerleaders perform on their version of a stage. The camera slowly draws us in as we focus on Angela, the sexy, blonde cheerleading centerpiece of the routine. She stares directly at the camera that is assuming a slack-jawed Lester's perspective. A reaction shot captures Lester, gazing back at the object of his desire. The lighting casts the other girls into the shadow, focusing us on Angela and reflecting Lester's rapidly developing tunnel vision. [00:15:10]

The catchy rhythmic and tonal features of "On Broadway" is obliquely interrupted by the ethereal sounds of the *fantasy* leitmotif, announced by a provocatively placed upward glissando, reflecting Lester's succumbing to his libidinous side. It is a musically onomatopoetic moment; the upward movement can be heard as an analog to Lester's rising emotional (and perhaps physical) interest, and perhaps even the revelatory exhalation experienced by some who are in the presence of consummate beauty (or lust in this case). We can still discern a beat, though it has little relation to the pop song of the cheerleading routine. It is as if we have entered another world, Lester's fantasy world. A single spot shines on Angela as her dance becomes overtly provocative, a for-Lester's-eyes-only, hip-swinging gyration. The gym floor is absent of all others—no cheerleaders, no basketball players, no audience, no Jane.

The *fantasy* motif's interruption of "On Broadway" is not just rhythmically and texturally complete. While "On Broadway" is solidly in the key of F major, the *fantasy* motif hovers around Bb major; though it is much more ambiguous in terms of its tonality. The result of these sudden shifts in texture, rhythm, and key is an emphatic support of the visual image showing Lester's real-world existence being overwhelmed by his emotions and libido.

The fantasy continues as Angela provocatively unzips her sweater. Rather than the lascivious sight of teenage breasts, rose petals emerge, flying toward the camera (and Lester's perspective), launched in slow motion as Angela tilts her head back in ecstasy. The image, accompanied by a series of unsettling and expanded upward glissandos, is a powerful and magical moment. We don't see the reality of her breasts emerging from her outfit; we see Lester's conception of perfection, American Beauty roses.

Just as we are lured further into Lester's reverie, "On Broadway" returns along with the final pose of the cheerleaders on the gym floor, with Angela again as the centerpiece of the formation.

After the game is over, Lester recovers his composure to some degree, though he remains flustered and a bit too solicitous when Jane introduces Angela to Lester and Carolyn. Angela returns his flirtations, much to the shock and disgust of Jane and the self-absorbed obliviousness of Carolyn.

Chapter 5: Spectacular

In the subsequent sequence, yet another leitmotif emerges, the *arose* theme. Lester is lying on his back, staring up at the ceiling as his wife sleeps beside him. A single rose petal begins to fall toward a smiling, contented Lester, who is lost in his dreams, presumably one involving Angela. The melodic line thickens as we see Angela nude, in a sea of rose petals. It is a happy theme; decidedly major in key with the melody harmonized in thirds. Lester's voiceover declares that he is "just now waking up," indicating that he is rediscovering his long dormant passions. The overhead shot of a happy, contented Lester is replaced by the supine Lester's perspective of his ceiling filled with rose petals and a nude Angela languorously lounging in the pile. Unlike the first image in this sequence, however, the petals are flowing toward the floor. Our perspective, via the camera, has merged with Lester's. A quick reaction shot of a smiling Lester shows the petals flowing down on him; Angela's energy, her youth, all the *beauty* she represents being absorbed by a blissful Lester reveling in his newly rediscovered appetite for living.

The music does not fully cadence, however, as it lingers across the cut to the following scene with Angela and Jane conversing in the car. The use of the musical cue gently connecting these two scenes is designed to show the simultaneity of the events—middle-aged Lester in bed with his dreams and the two teenaged girls in the car with theirs. [00:20:04]

Angela and Jane share a joint in the car as they listen to the radio and discuss the day's events. The choice of song on the radio, "Use Me" by Bill Withers, amplifies the nature of the girls' relationship. The outstanding lyric, "You just keep on using me," reveals the psychology underlying Angela and Jane's relationship. Angela dominates the unconfident Jane, masking her own insecurities about being *just ordinary*. Jane, on the other hand, looks to Angela as a mentor. She is *trying on* her personality, as teenagers often do. Remember that in the film's opening monologue, Lester explained that Jane is lost and trying to find herself. Thus the source music emanating from the radio accompanies both Jane and Angela, making a larger psychological statement rather than a specific, character-related one.

The abrupt cutoff of the source music and ensuing silence matches the cut-away to Jane leaving the car and returning home. The graininess of the visual image makes it clear that we are seeing her through the lens of a camera, the mechanical eye of a voyeur. She is at first oblivious to the camera that stalks her. She then realizes that she is being observed. Annoyed, she verbally responds to the affront, as her neighbor Ricky stands up and moves into the light while holding the camera. Notice the careful lighting of the American Beauty rose in the lower right corner of the image. [00:21:14]

Silence fills the remainder of the scene, indicating the surreptitious nature of the characters involved. As Jane moves into her house unnerved, she runs to the window to see if Ricky is still spying on her. All she sees is his empty chair, still lit by the porch light. She pauses for a moment, and then smiles, perhaps relieved that he is gone but more likely intrigued by the notion that someone has noticed her. She is not *ordinary*, a fate that Angela has just previously declared the worst possible one.

The bossa nova that opens the following scene may or may not be source music from the dining room (remember Carolyn's penchant for pleasant dinner music in the house). Nonetheless, the sensuousness of the beat reflects Lester's newly awakened lecherous qualities as he phones Angela using the number found in Jane's address book. While the song's introduction vamps as Lester dials Angela's number, the opening lyric, "Open the door . . ." occurs precisely at the moment Angela answers the call. The song has the undeniable beat, with a melody and vocalization characteristics of Antonio Carlos Jobim's seminal song about a man's lust for "The Girl from Ipanema." The remainder of the audible lyrics confirm Lester's salaciousness and yearning. Before the direct cut, we hear the songstress Betty Carter sing, "Open the door, dear. I must get in your heart! You're making it hard to be true." [00:22:26]

[00:22:46]

The music continues underneath as Jane is disgusted by the realization that her father has called Angela. An external shot interrupts the sequence as it becomes clear that Ricky is again filming her, framing her within the window panes, the distant, disembodied image of his fascination.

[00:23:23]   This external perspective masks the sound of Jane and Angela's phone conversation, replacing it with a distant relative of the *arose* theme. The *arose* motif, one of the few optimistic ones in the film, seems out of place here, but we can interpret Ricky's gaze as one of hopefulness. Support for this interpretation can be found by the fact that he removes the camera from his eye, baring himself, opening himself up. A series of additional shots bond Jane to Ricky.

Chapter 6: Welcome to the Neighborhood

Ricky is called away from the window for breakfast. A look into Ricky's domestic environment is bizarre, to say the least. His mother forgets that he doesn't eat bacon. His father orates from the table that "this world is going to hell." When the doorbell rings, everyone is astonished, as if aliens were canvassing the neighborhood. Colonel Fitts, retired USMC as he is fond of saying, answers the door and is slow to realize that his version of aliens, a gay, professional couple, has brought a housewarming gift of pasta, fruits, and flowers to welcome the Fitts family to the neighborhood.

[00:25:27]   As the colonel drives Ricky to school, he hums a nondescript, unrecognizable melody. In an effort to engage his son, the colonel reveals his revulsion for his gay neighbors by declaring, "How come these faggots always have to rub it in your face? How can they be so shameless?" Ricky offers a matter-of-fact explanation, indicating that gays don't feel there is anything to be ashamed about. A bit more incensed colonel emphatically declares that "it is." Sensing that he needs to submit to his father, a survival skill he has developed over past years, Ricky reinforces the colonel's perspective, aping his anger and emphasis. The colonel, eventually satisfied that he has again steered his son on the straight and narrow, begins to hum the "Battle Hymn of the Republic," specifically the section indicating triumph: "Glory, Glory, Hallelujah." He has triumphed, at least for now.

Chapter 7: "I'm Just Curious"

The ensuing scene establishes the nature of several relationships, as well. In this case, it becomes clear that Jane is modeling herself after Angela. The two girls posture in the shadows of the school, sulking and complaining. After a brief dialog with two very average school friends, designed to reinforce Angela's fear of being just average and her faux hypersexuality, Ricky walks over to introduce himself to Jane and then Angela. Angela is as disdainful as ever, treating him as *mental boy*. Jane acts out a similar response, but she is clearly intrigued by the intensity of his gaze and his ability to remain unfazed by Angela's verbal assault.

A short but disturbingly peculiar scene follows as Ricky returns home after school, joining his parents on the couch to watch what looks to be a military training/comedy routine on the television. Prior to Ricky's arrival, it is the only time we see the colonel at ease, laughing in response to the television. His wife is distant, off in some unknown universe, only minimally responsive to anything or anyone in the room. The colonel returns to his stoic posturing upon Ricky's arrival. The solemnity of the scene is disrupted by a deliberately contrasting, festive rumba beat that heralds the ensuing cocktail party scene.

[00:29:53]

Chapter 8: "My Personal Hero"

The source music wafting out from the reception for the Realtor's convention takes us across the scene change. It is cocktail music in its most prosaic form: a rumba, no doubt watered down as much as the drinks. What makes the source music of interest is its subtle marriage of musical form to spoken dialog. The editing of the musical form is a carefully crafted example of understatement and perhaps even subliminal manipulation. The form of the songs performed by the live jazz band underscores the ebbs and flows of the dialog. The use of silence at crucial moments in the dialog or drama demonstrates an attention to detail not found in lesser films. This is a type of *photograph and negative* approach to sound. The contrasting black of sound against the white of dialog is designed to emphasize the dramatic awkwardness of the scripted silences.

[00:30:00]

When Carolyn ascends the stage to pay her respects to her competition, Buddy Kane the Real Estate King, the established melody of the song, called the *head* by musicians who play these events, continues underneath their conversation. Carolyn introduces Lester to Buddy, who feigns recognition of Lester. Lester recognizes that he is unrecognized by Buddy and waits for Buddy to stew a bit before bailing him out with a politely social and banal comment. At precisely the moment when Buddy tries to remember Lester and the dialog awkwardly grinds to a halt, the head of the song cadences. This completes the form of the music, rendering a musical silence that is both musically appropriate while intensifying the social awkwardness of Buddy's nonrecognition.

[00:30:36]

[00:30:54]

The form of a typical cocktail jazz tune calls for the head, or melody, to be followed by an open and extended improvisation section. A return to the original melody after the improvised section signals the conclusion of the song. We've already examined the use of the head and its cadence to reinforce the social awkwardness of the moment, but what happens next is even more decisive.

In response to Carolyn's earlier admonishments to Lester to behave and be socially appropriate, Lester has until this moment behaved like a well-trained husband. But as soon as he sarcastically retorts, "I'll be whatever you want me to be," he wanders off Carolyn's social script. He begins to improvise, and he confronts her with an overly demonstrative and pretentious kiss directly in front of Buddy and his trophy wife. Carolyn is as astonished as Buddy's wife

[00:31:13]

[00:31:17]

is disdainful. Lester's improvisations, his wandering off the established *melody* of proscribed social niceties, happen precisely as the music enters its improvisatory phase with a full-bodied saxophone solo. The sarcasm of Lester's gesture is further highlighted by the increase in loudness of the music, rather than its disappearance (as we might expect) during the kiss. This draws our attention to the awkwardness of the *context* of the very public kiss, as Buddy averts his gaze. In short, the use of underscored source music is coordinated in such a way as to emphasize the awkward moments of silence in the dialog and action, as well as the emotional awkwardness of the characters involved.

[00:31:40]

[00:32:00]

Lester finishes his exaggerated affections and excuses himself in search of a drink. The sequence cuts to Lester hanging off the bar, having his glass replenished. It is clear from his posture and wilting look that some time has passed and it is not his first drink. In the background, the pianist has assumed the improvisational chores, indicating that Lester is still *off script*, as far as social behavior is concerned. The saxophonist musically rejoins the pianist for the head of the song, forming a duet just as Ricky, working as a waiter for the party, enters the frame. He approaches Lester, and after introducing himself as the new neighbor next door, asks him if he likes to party, a euphemism for getting high.

[00:32:37]

In the meantime, Carolyn and Buddy, who has apparently ditched his wife (or perhaps, she, him), are sharing an intimate moment at a table. A tipsy Carolyn is opening her professional heart to Buddy, flattering him and revealing her enviousness of his stature. Only the piano is heard, rhythmically free, with a slower tempo, piano-bar-like, a musical signal for intimacy if not loneliness. Carolyn propositions Buddy by asking if she could meet him for lunch for professional purposes. When he says yes, she practically chokes on her olive. Both Buddy and Carolyn gaze into each other's eyes, and then look away, as the music cadences with a final arpeggiated flourish, a musical *winking eye*.

[00:33:40]

The comedic awkwardness of the moment carries over to an exterior scene in which Ricky and Lester share their own intimate moment by smoking a joint outside the party. When confronted by his boss, Ricky assertively declares that he quits the job, thereby instantly becoming Lester's hero. Ricky reveals that he deals drugs for his real money. Carolyn finds Lester outside and calls him back into her world.

Chapter 9: "I Love Root Beer"

[00:36:28]

The kitchen sequence that follows is one of the most tensely hilarious scenes in the film. Lester is innocently enough raiding the refrigerator at home when Angela, who has joined Jane for a sleepover, runs into the kitchen, ostensibly to get a root beer but in reality to tease middle-aged Lester. Lester's fantasies take hold as Angela reaches for the root beer. The camera focuses in on her hand as it stretches toward the refrigerator, but the angle is such that we assume Lester's vantage point and perceive her hand reaching for him. The music takes us down into Lester's fantasy world with a series of glissandos and cymbal scrapes and an eerie, pulsing rhythm (Newman's fascination with ethno/exotic instruments comes to the forefront here) that again leaves us with the sense of descending into a more libidinous state. Lester's transformation (and ours) into this fantasy state is reinforced by Mendes's editing, which repeats Angela's arm movement toward Lester three times, each with a different speed. It is as if time has not stopped, but progressively slowed down.

The brightly lit kitchen has yielded to a shadowy, silhouette-evoking any-place, devoid of set or setting as Angela's arm makes contact with Lester's shoulder. He embraces her and leans in to kiss. The kiss is passionate and re-ciprocated by Angela as the camera slowly spins around the lovers, showing us their raw emotion from every angle. Angela drifts away from the shot, and a rapturous Lester draws a rose petal from his mouth. He has tasted beauty, at least in this fantasy. All of this occurs in a bit of slow motion, a blissfully relaxed pace designed to pull us out of our, and Lester's, normal existence.

The music ends on a clearly delineated glissando in the bass, as we are abruptly brought back into the reality of Lester's kitchen with Angela mis-chievously declaring, "I love root beer, don't you?" Lester is caught staring at the bottle of root beer in his hand, stymied and bewildered by what he has just fantasized. **[00:37:25]**

The slumber party sequence that follows finds Angela and Jane chattering away in Jane's bedroom. We see Lester eavesdropping at the door, with the song, "We Haven't Turned Around" emanating from the girls' bedroom. The music fades out as Jane and Angela move to the window, where they discover that Ricky has etched Jane's name in a small fire burning on the ground un-derneath her window. **[00:37:48]**

Excited by the prospect of being filmed by him, or more precisely by her chance to tease him, Angela begins to pose provocatively in front of the win-dow. The graininess of Angela's image as seen from outside of the window looking in indicates that Ricky is filming the girls' room, just as Jane had predicted. We might expect that Angela's provocative posing would be any teenage boy's fantasy, as she is wearing only the briefest of panties and a tube top. And in fact, the camera's perspective begins by framing Angela's body as she flirts and taunts. But as the camera begins to pan in, encouraging our own sexual voyeurism, Angela's head moves out of frame. Her *decapitation* leaves us with just the mindless image of pure sexuality. As the pan contin-ues, the camera captures the image of Jane reflected by a mirror in her room. The pan moves past Angela, fixing on Jane's visage innocently gazing down-ward, smiling in contentment with some unknown inner thoughts, a portrait of inner beauty. It is a tender moment, the camera using our own voyeuristic avarice to draw us beyond the superficial lusting and toward a deeper beauty.

The underlying musical leitmotif throughout this sequence is the *weirdest home video* motif, a gentle, sensitive melody, sweet and innocent, played by the strings as an ensemble in their lusher midrange. The choice of this theme reinforces the unusual nature of Ricky's filming and his direction of focus. We would expect a more *normal* home movie shot by a teenage boy to be one of Angela at her titillating best, but Ricky's focus looks beyond the sexpot to a deeper subject, Jane, the true object of his fascination. Hence the use of the *weirdest home video* leitmotif applies to Ricky's non-normal perspective, given our expectation of what would be of interest to the *normal* teenaged **[00:39:18]** boy. Simply put, his decision to choose inner beauty over superficial sexiness is *weird* by the norms of the society as reflected in the film.

Chapter 10: America's Weirdest Home Videos

[00:39:53]

The music also crosses us into the interior of Lester's garage as he thrashes around in the exiled detritus of his middle-aged life. The texture and modality of the music suddenly changes at the moment he discovers the new object of his desire, a set of old dumbbells. The shift is subtle. The *weirdest home video* theme is clearly structured in the key of G minor, a sad and laconic key. Newman accomplishes Lester's emotional transition by removing the one note that characterizes any minor key from the melody and harmony, the minor third. The result is a sort of limbo feeling, not quite sad, but not yet happy. Newman also changes the musical texture by adding the marimba and removing the vibraphone. He delineates the moment of transition with a descending bass glissando.

Grabbing the dumbbells, Lester catches a glimpse of himself in the garage window and peels off his shirt to evaluate his physique. He reveals a side of himself that we have not yet seen in the film; an anxious, motivated Lester, focused and mission driven. His object of desire is to reclaim the energy and excitement of his lost self.

Meanwhile, the music disappears as Ricky's voyeurism is interrupted by his father politely knocking at his bedroom door before entering. He hands Ricky a covered jar and reveals to us for the first time that Ricky has had a drug problem and must be tested every six months. Ricky takes the jar, promising to fill it in the morning. After his father leaves, he replaces it with a previously filled jar from his in-room refrigerator. For the second time, we see Ricky deceiving his father, thus defining the nature of his relationship with his elder.

Chapters 11, 12: Choking the Bishop, "I Want to Look Good Naked"

[00:42:29]

A direct cut to Lester and Carolyn's bedroom finds Lester seemingly awake in his bed, staring at the ceiling. An upward glissando in the guitar hints at the alternative reality Lester is experiencing. As he rises and moves to the bathroom, it becomes clear that we are being drawn into another of his fantasies. The ethereal nature of the music, a series of musical gestures almost used as

[00:42:57]

sonic effects, eventually yields to a more sustained rhythmic idea with the entrance of detuned mandolins, as Lester enters an extremely steamy bathroom. Clearly the *fantasy* motif has returned. He spies Angela languorously lounging in the bathtub, the sunlight veiled by the window dressings. As

[00:43:20]

Lester approaches Angela in the bathtub, now filled with rose petals, musical tension is built by layering rhythmic ostinatos on top of each other until

[00:43:38]

a complex rhythm is established. The rhythmic momentum pauses briefly as Angela delivers her seductive lines.

This pause is crucial for two reasons. First, the complexity of the rhythmic layering and the nature of the timbres used would only obfuscate Angela's delivery, and the lines would be lost from an aural perspective. Secondly, the sudden suspension of the rhythm, only to be continued after Angela delivers her lines, serves to bracket and therefore highlight the lines, making them all the more dramatic and important.

The result is an intensely seductive moment. The bass and guitar continue their glissandos in both upward and downward directions, building in frequency as Lester reaches his hand downward, toward the bath of rose petals. Angela reclines while spreading her legs to allow Lester access. At the climactic moment, Lester's hand enters the water between Angela's long stems. **[00:44:06]** The layers of music peel away, leaving only a single rhythmic strand repeating as we cross an edit point. Returning to Lester's bedroom, we find him masturbating at precisely the same tempo as the remaining ostinato, which quickly fades away. We are left with just the rhythm of Lester and his hand.

His activity wakes Carolyn up. What is an embarrassingly awkward and humorous moment eventually ripens into an argument reflecting the barrenness of their relationship. Lester rediscovers his manliness and his self-esteem as he asserts his sexual needs and his own sense of self. He has the last word and turns away from her as he resettles into bed. We see a slight smile of satisfaction as he realizes his own power. A leitmotif Newman calls **[00:46:00]** the *real estate king* emerges, supporting Lester's self-knowing smile.

The *real estate king* leitmotif is an assertive theme, slightly quicker in tempo than other themes and in a decidedly major tonality. The opening **[00:46:14]** melodic fragment rockets upward, leaving us with a sense of optimism, assertion, and positive opportunism. The theme evokes confidence. Buddy, the Real Estate King, is the epitome of contemporary manliness. He is tall, quiet, yet confident, handsome, and a financial success. The motif's appearance at this point helps to define Lester's rebellion against his wife and the life she represents.

The leitmotif takes us across the edit as Lester continues to take control of his life by joining two of his neighbors in their morning jog for the first time. This is yet another assertion of Lester's newfound strength, and its link to this particular leitmotif is undeniable.

The music continues as we see Ricky emerge from his house holding the urine sample for his drug test. His father is outside as well, washing the car. As Lester detours from his run to greet Ricky, the music ends in a *hard out*, **[00:47:04]** having served its function by establishing its connection to a state of mind, while smoothing the transition to the new scene.

A somewhat flippant and energized Lester greets Ricky's father, Colonel Frank Fitts, USMC. After exchanging some very cold amenities with the colonel, Lester and Ricky adjourn to the teenager's bedroom, where the two establish their connection as dope dealer and user.

Chapter 13: Mom's Mad

In the ensuing garage scene, Carolyn, who has been fussing with the roses in **[00:50:08]** her garden, discovers Lester weight lifting in the garage and smoking a joint while listening to Bob Dylan's "All along the Watchtower."

"All along the Watchtower" is one of Dylan's more esoteric (if that is pos-sible) songs, a short and succinct affair that is all verse, no chorus, with only a guitar and harmonica interlude between the first and second sections. The opening lyric, burned into the soul of the 1960s generation, speaks to a sense of fear- or panic-invoked desperation:

"There must be some kind of way out of here," said the joker to the thief.
"There's too much confusion, I can't get no relief."

It is the timing of the next line that once again underscores the subtle but important role of the music editor:

"Businessmen, they drink my wine, plowmen dig my earth . . ."

[00:50:34]   We hear them a moment after a primly shocked Carolyn opens the garage door, confronts Lester, and asks, "What the hell do you think you're doing?" The placement of the beginning of the lyric allows Carolyn to verbalize her outrage first, leaving room for the lyric to be distinctly audible during the natural pause between spoken lines.

The implication of the lyric, when coupled with the visual element and the dialog, is that Carolyn (the archetypal businessman, a salesperson) has been using and abusing Lester, robbing him of the sweetness (wine is a *spirit*, of course) of his own life. But the next two lines look closer:

"None of them along the line
Know what any of it is worth."[4]

The lyric suggests that the businessman and the plowman (Carolyn and perhaps Lester's boss as well) do not understand the nature and value of Les-ter as a person. In short, they (and the banality of their own pastel existence and all it represents) are sucking the life out of him without understanding what they are doing.

Chapter 14: An Ordinary Guy with Nothing to Lose

Dylan's (and Lester's) song of defiance is abruptly terminated mid-lyric as the camera cuts directly to the image of Lester sitting in Brad Dupree's office as if he had been sent to the principal. The abruptness of both the musical and visual edits shocks Lester (and us) back into the reality of his daily life and the trouble brewing at work. Dylan has vanished. Lester seems to be lost again, as Brad begins to read Lester's self-evaluation of his responsibilities at work. The ominous setting and Brad's dry reading of the letter seems to spell doom for Lester's career. A dumbfounded Brad continues reading, as Lester's oeuvre reveals just how disgusted and bored he really is with his job. What transpires next is blackmail at its best, with Lester negotiating a year's salary as severance pay.

Rather than being shattered by his firing, Lester is elated, no doubt by his
new freedom but also by the success of his self-assertiveness in reclaiming
that which is valuable to him, his joy of life. We are treated to a return of the **[00:52:51]**
real estate king leitmotif as the scene closes on a confident and buoyant Lester marching out of his office with a single box of belongings after fourteen
years of work.

The *real estate king* theme crosses the edit, taking us to a lunch meeting
between Carolyn and Buddy, the *real* real estate king. The set for the plush and
elegant dining establishment is designed to conjure up the feeling of intimacy,
a familiarity both Carolyn and Buddy hope to capitalize on. Matter-of-factly, **[00:53:33]**
Buddy explains that his wife has left him because he is too focused on his career. The music, which has propelled the scene forward to this moment, pauses
as Buddy announces the reason for her leaving, only to continue as he hyper-
intellectualizes about the situation. In his own neurotic way, Buddy asserts
himself as did Lester, hence the continuation of the *real estate king* leitmotif.

The theme continues through the next cut, to a shot of Ricky towering above **[00:54:22]**
his camera, filming a dead bird on the ground. Ricky is a boy who has, throughout the film, been the symbol of self-assuredness and assertion. His filming of
the lifeless corpse requires a softening of the orchestration. This is important
because it lets us know that he is not a *mental boy* as Angela posits, but perhaps
has motivations other than sadistic ones for filming the lifeless carcass.

Ricky's camera moves to a close-up of Jane just after he explains to Angela
that he was filming the dead bird because it was beautiful. The significance of
the statement is lost on Angela, but Jane remains intrigued, even as she asks
him to stop filming her. He complies, and their gazes remain locked. The *real
estate king* leitmotif reflects Jane's new assertiveness and her momentous
decision to break away from her friend Angela and walk home with Ricky.

The theme continues into the next scene as Buddy and Carolyn consummate their flirtation with a rather vociferously vocalized bedroom assertion of
their own life-altering decisions. Therefore, this musical motif of optimism,
which has provided the sonic continuity for the three previous scenes, reflects
the newfound assertiveness and choices in life for all of the main characters in
the film. The theme serves to amplify the psychological revelations and transformations of Lester and his daughter, and on a more subtle level, his wife.

Chapter 15: The Royal Treatment

Lenny Kravitz's rendition of "American Woman" is an earthy tune that transitions us from Buddy and Carolyn's vocally evocative hotel tryst to Lester
smoking a joint while driving through the city to the local burger joint. The
windshield shot of Lester smoking while bouncing to the beat reflects the
"American Woman" on his car's radio.

While the song begins at the climax, so to speak, of the hotel tryst scene, **[00:55:51]**
the actual lyrical reference to "American Woman" does not emerge until a
few moments into the shot of Lester cruising down the road. The timing of the **[00:56:09]**

entrance of the lyric is important as Lester sings along with the opening line. The song as interpreted by Lester is an anthem about his freedom from the tyranny of his adult life, as represented by his all-controlling wife. After his argument with Carolyn in the previous bedroom sequence and their confrontation in the garage, Lester is rebelling and striking out on his own, reliving and rediscovering the happiness from his earlier life.

The importance of the lyric is reinforced by the amount of time and sonic prominence it is given in Lester's car as he speeds up to the drive-through window. The music ends with the scene and is replaced with the canned music one would expect to hear in a fast food restaurant.

[00:57:15]   On an impulse, Lester decides to apply for a job at the burger joint. The choice of source music blaring from the restaurant interior is a disco tune from the mid-1970s, when Lester was growing into manhood. It underscores the absurd image of Lester being interviewed for the job by a peach-and-pizza-faced teenaged manager. The source music reflects Lester's desire to flip burgers and regress to the carefree days of his youth.

After a brief *après sex* scene between Buddy and Carolyn, we find Jane and Ricky walking home from school together. They stroll down the center of a street with large, mature trees arching over them. The image is distinctly cathedrallike; man and woman walking down the church aisle or perhaps the path of life. It is an intimate moment, the two of them, comfortable with each other and themselves, a moment away from the adults and their own strangest family moments.

[00:58:33]   Surprisingly, the *weirdest home video* leitmotif accompanies them on their path. But Mendes uses the music as a sort of sarcastic foil, counterpointing the honesty of their moment together while emphasizing both the couple's alienation from their relations with others and their own mutual compatibility.

A funeral procession of cars approaches them, and they step aside to watch it pass. This leads to a discussion about the natures of death and beauty. Ricky delivers the climactic monologue of the film in which he explains that he sees beauty everywhere and that it can overwhelm him, which is why he uses the camera as a protection. He references God in his speech, lending further support to the confessional nature of their walk and talk. The music and scene fade out on Ricky's final line, leaving us to wonder in a contemplative reverie about his concept of beauty.

Chapter 16: The Most Beautiful Thing

Ricky brings Jane to his home and introduces him to his mother, who perfunctorily apologizes for the condition of her house. The camera pauses for a moment, framing the symmetry of the house with an emotionally flat Mrs. Fitts as the centerpiece. Jane surveys the immaculately kept interior, cleaned and ordered so perfectly that it seems devoid of any life, much like Mrs. Fitts's personality. She remains distant throughout the film, absent of any visible emotion, lost in some faraway world we can only imagine. Ricky's *beauty*, as he describes it, is noticeably absent from the scene, as is the music, highlighting the antiseptically cold environment that is Ricky's home.

Ricky takes Jane into his father's study to show her his collection of war memorabilia, including a plate with a swastika on the bottom. At first horrified, Jane comes to understand and trust what Ricky says after hearing the explanation about his father's collecting hobby.

Ricky invites Jane into his room, enticing her with a chance to see the most beautiful thing he has ever seen. In his room, Ricky and Jane are seated with their backs to the camera, watching a video shot by Ricky. In the video, we see a plastic grocery bag being aimlessly blown around by gusts of wind in an empty parking lot. The *American beauty* theme emerges, accompanying the image of the bag being tossed and turned by the unseen eddies and currents of the wind that blows through its environs.　　　　　　　　　　　　　　　　　　**[01:01:54]**

The film's parable is upon us, as Ricky explains the beauty of this random event to Jane. It is the most spiritual moment of the film as Ricky describes the force that he feels, telling him about the beauty all around. The lecture is for us as well, given our placement behind the couple as if in the row behind them in a movie theater. This moment is the key to understanding the creative vision and sociological commentary behind *American Beauty*.

The *American beauty* leitmotif is now presented in its simplest and clearest incarnation, forlornly tempoed and unembellished. The theme is played by an intimately microphoned piano, gently accompanied by a drone figure in the strings that carries no rhythmic pull and is voiced with open strings to give us a sense of timelessness and endless space. It is as if the visual image of the wandering bag and the open voicings of the strings invite us into the harmoniousness of the moment, a gentle tranquility in the sea of turbulence that surrounds the two youths. They have found beauty in each other. The harmony progresses, albeit slowly, driven by the visual close-up of Jane gazing at the screen, unafraid of what she is seeing. The music pauses as the camera　　　**[01:03:43]** switches to a close-up of an awestruck and reflective Ricky delivering the line, "Sometimes there's so much beauty in the world, I feel like I can't take it." The music resumes after the briefest of pauses as Ricky, choking back the only emotion he has revealed in the film so far, continues his discourse.

Jane now sees and understands what he sees and understands. She takes his hand as the orchestration develops a lushness and warmth not previously heard. Their gazes meet and she leans into him, giving him a gentle, knowing kiss. She momentarily reflects on his visage with a quiet, peaceful contemplation. The music resolves as they part lips and look into each　　　**[01:04:45]** other's eyes, unafraid. The *American beauty* motif softly fades out as she is drawn back into the world around them, remembering that she is late for dinner with her parents.

Chapter 17: Pass the Asparagus

We return to the Burnham dining room as Jane dashes in, accompanied by Carolyn's choice of dinner music, "Call Me Irresponsible." The carefree aspect of the song itself, its major key, fast pace, and mellifluous singing by Bobby Darin caricatures the plethora of irresponsible behaviors that envelops the evening's repast.

On the surface, the music reflects Jane's tardiness to the table, something not exactly unknown to families with teens:

Call me irresponsible
Call me unreliable
Throw in undependable, too.

But as the dialog develops, the lyrics reflect deeper, additional associations, first to Lester and the seemingly irresponsible act of quitting of his job:

Call me unpredictable
Tell me I'm impractical
Rainbows, I'm inclined to pursue.[5]

But as Carolyn begins her histrionics in response to Lester's unemployment, it becomes clear that the lyrics also reflect her irresponsible inattention to her husband's emotional and physical needs. In addition, her hysterical outburst would seem to be irresponsible in the presence of her daughter.

The choice of source music, from both a musical and lyrical perspective, renders the scene comical. As Lester alternates between rationality and anger, Carolyn goes hysterical. Jane watches with amazement as the adults behave like children. "Call Me Irresponsible" ends, concluding the dinner table discourse.

Chapter 18: "Don't Give Up on Me, Dad"

The after-dinner mother-daughter chat does not end so well. After her mother leaves the room, Jane looks in the mirror and reflects upon her freshly slapped face. We *hear* the silence. She then turns her gaze through her window to Ricky's window, where she sees him watching her through his camera.

[01:09:24] The *American beauty* theme enters as gently as before. She waves to him and moves toward her window. He responds, as the melody focuses in. She approaches the window and removes her blouse and bra, revealing herself to him. Though she has stripped away all adornments, all pretenses, he never looks up from the camera, though he does zoom in (*look closer*). His interest is in her inner beauty, not her sexuality. They lock eyes; neither of them ever blinks throughout the scene. Ricky exposes himself to her in his own way; he puts down his camera, his mask to the world. He, too, is now figuratively naked. The mutual disclosure is intimate and honest as they open themselves to each other, revealing their beauty to each other, accompanied by the *American beauty* motif. The shy and gentle waves they exchange are further confirmations of their understanding.

The tenderness of the moment is brutally interrupted as the colonel breaks into Ricky's room and violently assaults him while accusing him of breaking

[01:10:46] into his locked gun closet. A direct visual cut and truncated musical end-

[01:10:51] ing exacerbates the violent intrusion that is soon accompanied by ominous musical gestures, more underlying ambiences than actual musical cues. The gestures are more like the vocalizations of impending doom, often found in horror movies, except that the mayhem is already upon Ricky. The gestures fade away as the colonel comes to realize that Ricky has a girlfriend and was simply trying to impress her. The fading of the musically maniacal gesture may also reflect the colonel's psychological relief in discovering that his son is interested in girls, something that he has been unsure of until this moment.

Chapter 19: Mr. Smarty Man

While the scene fades out and concludes without music, reinforcing Ricky's aloneness, it provides contrast to the ensuing scene, set in a pistol firing range in which Carolyn appears to be thoroughly enjoying herself by popping off round after round. The accompanying music, "Don't Rain on My Parade," sung by Bobby Darin, is at first nondiegetic. It is the music that plays in **[01:13:21]** Carolyn's head, the music she plays at the family dinners. In this sense, this particular style of music is her perception of her life, carefree and surrealistically optimistic. It is her idea of a life worth living. She doesn't want any member of her family to ruin her show. She wants them to march to her beat and dance to her music.

After the short establishing scene at the firing range, the sequence jumps to a cheerfully satiated Carolyn driving home in her car, still accompanied by the same song, now source music emanating from the car radio. A quick shot of a handgun lying on the seat next to her confirms her sense of empowerment when she's *packing*, and it also serves as a visual cue that something unusual is at hand.

The form of the musical cue cleverly bridges the two scenes, a sonic glue that also peels back another layer of Carolyn's psychological makeup. In the shooting range scene, we hear a brassy introduction without any lyrics. This introduction is a musical vamp; the kind of thing that a band would keep repeating over and over until the singer seizes the melody. The phrasing is grouped in four-bar phrases, with modulations upward every phrase. The absence of any melody is significant, signaling that the firing range is simply a warm-up for the main event. The vocals begin just as we see Carolyn in the **[01:13:41]** subsequent scene, singing along in her car.

The final chorus of the song very much smacks of a Broadway kick line. The tempo and meter has been altered. The underlying triplet figures cre- **[01:14:13]** ate rhythmic propulsion that effectively pulls the audience toward the final cadence. While musically signaling that the end of the song is approaching, the final chorus also indicates that Carolyn is nearing home. The chorus accompanies the visual of Carolyn turning onto lesser-trafficked suburban side streets. The song's ending, a quintessential showstopper, coincides **[01:14:34]** with Carolyn's final turn into her driveway and a view of a parked, flaming-red Firebird.

The effect of the final lyric is ironically funny when paired with the visual element of the Firebird's audacious grill and crimson color confronting Carolyn's perfectly staid Mercedes SUV. We don't need Carolyn's acting (and Annette Bening wisely underplays the emotion) to wring the sarcasm out of the scene. The visuals and the music do that job admirably.

[01:15:39]

[01:16:55]

The car is, of course, another expression of Lester's new assertiveness and rediscovery, characteristics that threaten Carolyn's world according to Bobby Darin. Carolyn storms into the house, but her living room confrontation with Lester soon turns into a seduction. The *Mr. Smarty Man* cue sneaks in as Lester makes his moves and unnerves his wife. The sultriness of the music creates a dreamlike environment and helps to create an intimacy between the two characters. He disarms her, cunningly complementing her looks and reflecting back to their courting days as he begins to climb on top of her. The music disappears, however, precisely at the moment when Carolyn spies a beer can in Lester's hand and warns him about spilling it on their couch. The fantasy is over, reality has reemerged, and the music of the romance that used to be theirs has vanished. A distraught Carolyn runs upstairs to sulk.

Chapter 20: Massive Psychological Damage

[01:17:42]

A direct cut recounts the opening scene of the movie in which Jane and Ricky relax in a bedroom, presumably after sharing a physical moment. Once again, we see Jane through the lens of Ricky's camera.

The *American beauty* theme returns to support the honest conversation between them. It is clear that by using the signature motif at this point, the filmmakers are addressing one of the core themes of the movie: the issue of what constitutes true beauty.

The dialog between Jane and Ricky is sincere and caring. They each bare themselves, physically and emotionally, to each other. Ricky is naked, while Jane remains with a top and a blanket draped around her. She takes the video camera from Ricky, who has been filming her. She views him through the viewfinder, reversing the perspective. He is unfazed and unashamed. She takes this moment to ask him the most personal of questions, "So tell me about being in the [mental] hospital?" He does respond, unhesitatingly and deeply. For the first time, we see Ricky shift his gaze and become (relatively speaking) emotional.

[01:19:24]

While the music may seem static and unmoving at first, a careful listening finds subtle orchestrational and textural changes at significant moments in the dialog. Newman begins to add additional high-string sustained notes as Ricky's story reaches a climactic moment, reflecting his loss of control. But the strings subside as he regains his composure. The strings are replaced by lower-pitched horns and woodwinds, which thickens the musical texture. This reflects the complexity of Ricky's decision not to hate his dad for sending him to military school or the hospital. The thickening texture ameliorates some of the tension inherent in high-string notes.

[01:20:19]

As Jane begins to open herself up emotionally, she gets progressively angrier toward her father. We hear a series of faint rumblings in the music, undefined, dark, and cloudlike. They simmer below the musical surface, barely in the audible range. They are more felt than heard. We hear the anger within her brewing. As Jane's hostile thoughts toward her father intensify,

[01:21:36]

the texture again thickens. This time the dissonant harmonies and emerging lower strings cast a glaze of foreboding into the scene, especially when Jane half-jokingly suggests that Ricky should kill her father. The scene ends with a slow visual fade, the music following suit, uncadenced, unresolved. Ricky utters the final prefade line as the two tenderly lie together, "You know how lucky we are to have found each other?"

[01:23:12]

Chapter 21: The Day You Die

Chapter 21 begins with a sharp sonic contrast to the almost spiritual ambience created by the previous scene. We are treated to a loud rock tune, "The Seeker," as Lester emerges from his house to begin his daily run. The choice of song is again, no accident. The lyrics reflect Lester's search for his inner self:

[01:23:16]

I've looked under chairs
I've looked under tables
I've tried to find the key
To fifty million fables.

(Chorus)
They call me The Seeker
I've been searching low and high

The final lyric before the music fades out is prescient enough,

I won't get to get what I'm after
Till the day I die.[6]

Remember that the voiceover at the beginning of the scene has already announced that today is the day that Lester dies.

The following sequence finds Ricky having a brief conversation with his father. The *power of denial* motif seems to emerge for no immediately apparent reason. But a closer examination of the rhythmic and harmonic structure of the cue gives us an idea as to the role of the music at this particular moment. The music is in a triple feel, though more musically adept listeners will recognize that it is really 6/8 meter, technically a compound duple meter. But this is not the crux of the issue. The emphasis is on the beat, or the first of the three notes. This pulsing is matched by a move of a minor third in the bass line. It is an ostinato figure at a tempo that evokes the ticking of a clock—Lester's clock, the ticking of time until he dies.

[01:25:11]

The cue is not especially exciting from a musical perspective. The ostinato continues with insignificant gesturings by various instruments pitched above and below the ostinato, as Ricky leaves for school with Jane and her family. A naturally suspicious Colonel Fitts has become even more so, given the unusual friendliness between his son and his neighbor, Lester. The music continues as Frank searches his son's room for anything suspicious. A minimalist, rhythmically based melody from the *power of denial* theme begins to emerge as Frank places a videotape into his son's camera and watches what Ricky has recorded. In this case, it is a naked Lester working out in his garage.

[01:26:19]

Chapter 22: Smile, You're at Mr. Smiley's

[01:27:10] "As Long as You're Singing My Song" blares from the radio as Carolyn and Buddy (aptly named now) pull up to the drive-through of Mr. Smiley's. Lester, who has been working the grill, appears at the takeout window to confront them as he hands them their food. The scene is both humorous and painful.

The choice of source music supports the underlying psychological subtext of the scene. Carolyn, who has always demanded that Lester *sing her song*, attempts to control the situation but is cut short by Lester who announces to her that "you don't get to tell me what to do ever again." In this sense, the song reflects Carolyn's history of controlling her husband's existence, but it also acknowledges Lester's acquiescence to the family dynamic determined by Carolyn. In short, the song reflects the nature of their relationship up to this moment of confrontation when Lester announces that she no longer

[01:28:16] controls him. In perhaps the only unintentional cliché of the film, we hear thunder shortly after the drive-through confrontation, as the outed Carolyn and Buddy return to the Top Hat Motel, sullen and dethroned.

[01:29:25] As Buddy departs, Carolyn has another little talk with herself. Unable to control her emotions, she finally lets loose a frustrated, gut-wrenching scream that yields to the car radio blaring the Rolling Stones anthem, "All Right Now." The volume levels of her scream and the guitar lick are perfectly matched in the mix. She matches the pitch of her scream to the tonic note of the signature Stones song, allowing for a clever and skillful cross-fade between the two. Visually, we fade into the image of a contented and motivated Lester pumping iron in his garage, admiring his new physique in the window and reaching for another joint. The inimitable lyric convinces us that Lester has found himself, or at least for the moment, has regained elements of his youthful energy and commitment. He strains at the weights, yet never loses his smile. His body glistens with sweat and is cast in a light that indicates a healthy tan. The set behind him reveals lit candles, a poster of a marijuana leaf, and an old, 1970s-era stereo system. As he admires himself in the window, we see more candles and a decidedly retro lava lamp in all its 1970s glory. Note that we see the rain from the thunderstorm just outside Lester's window, presaging tragedy that is about to befall him.

[01:30:00] The music is abruptly cut off, accompanied by a direct cut to the Fittses' family dinner table as Ricky's beeper interrupts the meal. Ricky excuses himself from the dinner table, ostensibly to return Jane's geometry book, but in actuality, to roll a joint for Lester who has just beeped him.

The relatively curt sequences that follow quicken the pace of the film, raising the tension as we approach the film's climactic segment. We jump to a conversation between Jane and Angela as they drive home. Tired of Angela's intrusive behavior, Jane asserts herself and rebels against Angela's verbal onslaught.

An exterior shot reveals an agitated Colonel Fitts inside his house, the rain from the continuing thunderstorm pouring across the screen. By now, the colonel has become suspicious of his son's activities, though he by no means comprehends what is going on. The *power of denial* theme reemerges as he
[01:31:00]

peers through his own window into Lester's garage and sees his son and Lester engaging in what appears to be homosexual activity.

In actuality, Ricky is rolling a joint for Lester, but the staging and camera perspective are so deliberately ambiguous that the colonel misinterprets the scene. It is an ironic moment. The music reflects the colonel's denial of his son's drug-dealing activities while also subtexting his denial of his own latent homosexuality.

Support for this interpretation is found in the staging, lighting, and camera perspective. The interior shot places the colonel moving out of the shadows into the relative light of the window to observe the activities in Lester's garage. This movement, accompanied by the *power of denial* theme, is meant to subconsciously tap into the contemporary metaphor of the gay person coming out of the (shadowy) closet, no longer denying his or her true being.

The *power of denial* theme is a subtle affair, with no discernible melody. It consists of a rhythmic pad accompanied by the occasional bass glissando downward, no doubt used to subconsciously reinforce the colonel's fear of homosexuality. The occasional gestures of the nonpitched percussion, synthesizer, and strings contribute a kind of psychic whispering, ghostlike, as if the shadows were releasing or speaking to the colonel.

As the theme continues, the colonel spots Jane and Angela pulling into the driveway while Lester and Ricky both rush to hide the stash. Lester hurriedly puts on his shirt, while Ricky grabs his coat, presumably to flee out the back door. The leitmotif slithers away into silence, as the colonel quiet slips back into the shadow of his house and the denial of who he really is.   [01:32:28]

Chapter 23: "You Like Muscles?"

Ricky returns to his room and is confronted by his father, who again turns violent. The musical cue is ominously ambient at first, adding atmospheric   [01:33:27]
effects more suitable to the psychological horror genre. But the cue develops with the addition of the organumlike structure reminiscent of the *American*   [01:33:33]
beauty theme. It does, however, acquire its own identity, called *structure and discipline*, precisely at the moment Frank strikes his son, ironically reflecting the former marine's own loss of discipline. This bastardization (really a musical variation on the original *American beauty* theme) reflects the dysfunctional father-son relationship, one bound up both in loyalty and distrust, love and hate, acceptance and denial; dichotomous traits embodied in the respective personalities of the two characters involved.

After being smashed to the floor by his father, Ricky realizes that by accepting his father's accusations of homosexuality, though untrue, he will be banished from the house and finally free to leave. This realization is presaged   [01:34:16]
by a *tinkling* gesture in the strings and wind chimes, underscoring Ricky's epiphany. He goads his father, who does indeed exile him.

Ricky descends the stairs, where his distraught mother admonishes him as he leaves to "wear a raincoat." The term, *raincoat*, is a popular euphemism for a condom. Remember that the rain has continued throughout the scene. But coming after hearing her spouse label her son a homosexual, Mother's unintentional double entendre advisory adds a touch of black humor to the otherwise bleak moment. The entire sequence is accompanied by occasional low rumbles.

The *structure and discipline* theme carries over into a shot of Carolyn in her car as she listens to a motivational tape. Obviously in turmoil, she reaches for her gun in the glove compartment. The dysfunctional *structure and discipline/American beauty* motif underscores the dissolution of the structure and discipline of her life as it once was. The theme continues as Jane confronts Angela about her sexual intentions with her father. In this sense, the theme serves as a sonic glue, providing continuity for the visual elements of the three scenes while highlighting the turmoil of each of the characters as their personal crises reach their apex.

[01:36:58]   As Ricky knocks at Jane's door and asks her to leave town with him, the theme softens a bit by removing much of the dissonant overlay and replacing it with a gentler flute figure. The musical change throughout the scene is subtle but distinct. The dissonance of the lives of Jane, her mother, and Fitts yields to the softer, more honest harmony she feels with Ricky. We are closer to the original *American beauty* theme than we have ever been since this musical cue has started.

But the respite is momentary, as Angela interjects herself into the conversation, provoking Jane into a heated response. Voices are raised, although Ricky remains calm while he confronts Angela with the truth about her.
[01:37:39]   Perhaps the return to the dissonant overlay is reflecting the final dysfunctional relationship in the film, the relationship between Angela and Jane. The dissonance continues as Jane and Ricky hug each other, though with the
[01:38:20]   addition of a melismatic line from the bass clarinet, they symbolically reject Angela and her notion of beauty. A distraught and unnerved Angela retreats to the hallway steps.

Chapter 24: "Our Marriage Is Just for Show"

The ominous nature of the theme continues with more frequent bass rumblings and a more pronounced series of flute gestures, as Colonel Frank Fitts walks through the rain and approaches Lester in his garage. The scene is ripe with visual dissonance. A sweaty, shirtless Lester opens the garage door. A thoroughly soaked Frank emerges from the darkness into the relative light of the garage. Both men are breathing deeply, Lester because of his weight lifting and Frank because of the rain, the intensity of his confrontation with his son, and the dawning realization of the denial of his own homosexuality.

Their dialog is more openly suggestive, though unintentionally so on Lester's part. Frank misreads Lester's compassionate verbal cues as a sexual invitation and hugs a momentarily hesitant and confused Lester. A
[01:41:00]   subtle but strategically placed bass drum hit coincides with a close-up of Frank's hand, kneading Lester's back during the embrace. It articulates the precise psychological moment when Frank overcomes his own *power of*
[01:41:08]   *denial*. He kisses a startled Lester as the dissonant bed of sound disappears.

The long, underlying dissonance in his life has been resolved. He has confronted his demons and kissed a man.

A stunned Lester explains to Frank that he is mistaken. Frank leaves the garage, fading into the rain and the darkness of the night. The *Mr. Smarty Man* leitmotif, now clearly harmonically related to the *American Beauty* theme, sneaks in a moment before we cut to a shot of Carolyn returning home in her car, still listening to the motivational tape and staring at her gun, apparently summoning up her courage for some still unknown act. **[01:41:56]**

Chapter 25: "You Couldn't Be Ordinary If You Tried"

The music abruptly ends on an edit, taking us into Lester's kitchen as he raids **[01:42:19]** the refrigerator for another beer. He is drawn to living room by the stereo sys- **[01:42:30]** tem sounds of Neil Young's song, "Don't Let It Bring You Down," referring to the chaos that is swirling around him. It is important to recognize that Newman's own lightly orchestrated string accompaniment fleshes out Young's classic rock tune. It is this orchestration that forms the harmonic basis of the *structure and discipline* motif. Its deployment at this moment may indicate Lester's own upcoming loss of discipline.

He spots a distraught Angela cowering in the corner. Against the backdrop of Neil Young, and in a rare moment of honesty and frailty, Angela reveals that she and Jane had a fight. Both Angela and Lester exude neediness as they draw toward each other. The ever-present vase of American Beauty roses comes into frame, splitting the distance between the camera and the couple. It is a moment of simmering passion, or perhaps lust. But it is also a moment of honest intimacy. Angela's vulnerabilities are exposed, and Lester's lust is unleashed. The allegorical importance of their conversation reflects Lester's true understanding of his existential search. His line, "I want you," while overtly both lusty and seductive when whispered to Angela, is directed toward the ideals of youth and beauty, as embodied by his blonde, seductive muse.

Angela's vulnerability is exposed as she seeks his assurance that she is not *ordinary*, her worst fear. The excruciating intimacy of the moment is cut **[01:45:38]** short, interrupted by an abrupt sequencing to Carolyn ranting in her car, accompanied by the beginning of the *mental boy* motif.

The melodic figure for the *mental boy* motif enters as Lester seduces Angela. She reclines on the couch, Lester hovering above her, slowly removing her clothes. The deployment of the *mental boy* theme may at first seem related to Lester's seduction of his daughter's cheerleading friend. But from its previous uses, we have come to accept it not as a theme of abnormality or difference, but rather as a musical commentary, reflecting the irony of what is considered normal. Mendes and Newman have held a mirror up to our notions of normalcy through their sardonic use of the theme labeled *mental boy*.

As Lester undresses the excited but apprehensive Angela, the theme is **[01:46:16]** fleshed out with some delicately balanced high strings that soften the cue and add a level of intimacy and sweetness. The cadence of the initial section **[01:46:40]** of the theme is subtly extended by several beats, so that the B section of the music, defined by the movement to the minor IV chord, coincides with cut-away midshots of Jane and Ricky lying on a bed. They are dressed in their overcoats, staring at the ceiling while sharing their thoughts and anxieties

[01:46:41]   about leaving home and running away. The strings, now voiced in their lower ranges, reflect a warm sense of contentment and resolution for the two now-committed teens.

[01:46:49]   The low strings disappear as we return to the rapidly progressing coupling of Lester and Angela. The music simply disappears as Angela confesses that this is her first time. Lester is momentarily left speechless and breathless, the latter for obvious physical reasons. We are left with the silence of the moment, broken only by the sound of the rain that has been falling throughout the scene.

[01:47:17]   The musical image of the *mental boy* evaporates at the precise moment when Angela is the most honest and the most exposed. Newman and Mendes's sonic sarcasm has receded. Angela and Lester's craziness, our perception of their *mentalness*, has come to an end with the cue. Lester backs off, deciding not to deflower his muse, choosing to preserve her *beauty* in his thoughts. His *crazy* behavior is gone, the pressure dissipated, the tension gone. He has come to his senses.

Chapter 26: "I'm Great"

[01:48:37]   But the *mental boy* motif almost immediately returns as we see Carolyn in her car, now parked outside her front door. By using the *mental boy* theme to link these two scenes into a single sequence, Newman is counterpointing our ideas of normal and *mental behavior*. He is forcing us to confront what constitutes truly unacceptable action: whether it is Carolyn's blind ambition or Lester's beauty lust.

The musical cue continues through the sequence to Lester and Angela, who are now seated at the kitchen table. In a moment of honest reflection, Lester

[01:49:14]   asks Angela about Jane's well-being, as the midrange strings reenter to soften the cue. Lester's question is a general overarching, fatherly one, hence the softened aural image.

[01:49:56]   The theme fades as Angela tells Lester that Jane is happy and in love. He is overcome with quiet joy, resolution, and inner satisfaction. The fade itself also serves to link Lester's happiness with his daughter's. Just after the fade is complete, leaving us with a silence we have not heard in some time, Angela asks Lester how he is, and he responds, "I'm great." The *mental boy* theme is never heard again.

Left alone in the kitchen, Lester picks up a portrait of his family. He tears

[01:50:53]   up as he gazes at the picture, appreciating the beauty that it reflects. Even the music seems complete, with a return to the major-key *blood red* theme. But then the gun appears . . . and the camera pans past Lester, past the picture of

[01:51:36]   his family, past the bouquet of American Beauty roses on the table. . . . The music simply fades out, unresolved, its final punctuation, a gunshot.

Chapter 27: "My Stupid Little Life"

The violence of Lester's death is matched by the silence that follows. The **[01:51:45]**
American beauty theme slowly emerges as Jane and Ricky respond to the
sound of the gun by moving down the stairs and entering the kitchen. The
incongruous use of the *American beauty* motif at this moment seems contrary
to the notion that it represents the qualities of honesty and beauty. But the
melody blossoms precisely as Ricky bends down to see Lester's body. Ricky
is unafraid, almost emotionless, as he gazes at the corpse. He cocks his head
slightly, like an inquisitive dog. He is again seeing the beauty that surrounds
him, just as he investigated and filmed the dead bird earlier in the film. He
finds beauty even in Lester's death.

The musical cue segues back into the *blood red* theme, as a voiceover by **[01:52:53]**
the now dead Lester philosophizes on the process of death and recalls the
exquisite moments of his now lost life. He is, after all, dead, and the *blood
red* theme has one of the clearest associations in the film. The ruminating
voiceover and combination cue of *blood red* and *American beauty* provide
the aural glue for the sequence of shots as Mendes manipulates time and
perspective, allowing us to relive the moment when Jane and Ricky, Angela,
and Carolyn hear the gunshot. The *blood red* theme is in triple; waltzlike,
flighty, fleeting, and floating, like the plastic bag in the parking lot. It turns to **[01:54:30]**
a major key, a more positive sound, as Carolyn rejects murder by frantically
abandoning her gun. The voiceover ends on a positive note as well, reflecting
on the beauty in the world.

Chapter 28: End Cues

The choice of end music is deliberately incongruous. The initial song, "Be- **[01:55:50]**
cause," written by John Lennon and Paul McCartney, emerges from the black
screen. It may be in response to our own existential question, "Why," with
the obvious response in the opening lyric. It is the closest statement yet to
Ricky's perspective about the world that surrounds him, a view Lester finally
recognizes in the moments before he dies.

SUMMARY

American Beauty uses music in a very subtle way to propel the story forward. Leitmotifs are
not as easily defined as the other films discussed here. Additionally, virtually all of the musical
cues are related to each other. Tempos, pitch materials, rhythms, and orchestration do not vary
very much from cue to cue. This gives the film an almost organic aural space, an overarching
mood that overlays the daily activities of the characters, leaving us with a feeling as to just how
engulfed they are in their "silly little lives," to quote Kevin Spacey's character.

Thomas Newman's score is not as orchestral as some others, though he is clearly capable
of writing such massive works. He takes a thoroughly contemporary approach, using a semi-
minimalist structure while orchestrating unusual acoustic instrumental sounds to catch important
moments in a cue. At the same time, he sticks close to the concept of leitmotif, in most cases

choosing to underscore the emotions and moral dilemmas that surface, rather than the narrative itself. All this may not be initially apparent, but as Lester's desktop sign says, "Look closer."

NOTES

1. "Color, Melody and . . . Perfume: An Interview with Composer Thomas Newman," *Motion Picture Editors Guild Newsletter* 17, no. 1 (January–February 1996). http://www.editorsguild.com/v2/magazine/Newsletter/newman.html (accessed May 28, 2009).

2. "ScoreKeeper Chats with Composer Thomas Newman!!," interview by ScoreKeeper. Ain'tItCoolNews.com. www.aintitcool.com/node/38356 (accessed May 28, 2009).

3. "ScoreKeeper Chats with Composer Thomas Newman!!"

4. Bob Dylan, "Track: 'All along the Watchtower,'" ReasontoRock.com. http://www.reasontorock.com/tracks/watchtower.html (accessed September 12, 2006).

5. Sammy Cahn and Jimmy Van Heusen, "Bobby Darin Lyrics—Call Me Irresponsible," Oldie Lyrics.com. http://www.oldielyrics.com/lyrics/bobby_darin/call_me_irresponsible.html (accessed November 19, 2006).

6. Pete Townshend, "The Seeker," Sing365.com. http://www.sing365.com/music/lyric.nsf/The-Seeker-lyrics-The-Who/972EC09BD0844A204825697A001256EF (accessed August 23, 2008).

Altered States

HISTORICAL CONTEXT AND ARTISTIC CONFLICT

Altered States is a curious amalgam of opposites. An existential quest for the meaning of life is manifested in a Harvard scientist's search for the physiological key to our past, and in the process, he undergoes a mystical and spiritual transformation in addition to a physical one.

Paddy Chayefsky wrote the original novel and screenplay. The book and screenplay is dialog driven, but in director Ken Russell's hands, the film becomes a visual orgy of hallucinogenic experiences, the imagery all referencing the protagonist's inner struggles and Russell's own personal impression of drug-induced visions. In the book, the characters all remain aloof, Chayefsky referring to his creations by their last names. Onscreen, first names are the order of the day, removing at least one layer of detachment. According to Chayefsky, "This is a modern version of the old Jekyll and Hyde story updated to the Harvard Medical School in the Sixties to give it added credibility."[1]

But, reflecting a conceptual difference that would rupture their personal and working relationship and cause Chayefsky to remove his name from the screen credit (and substitute his natural rather than pen name), Russell describes their film as "all sci-fi stuff based on the experiments and out-of-body experiences of [Aldous] Huxley, [John C.] Lily and [Carlos] Castaneda."[2]

Paddy Chayefsky, a Bronx Jew, was already a well-respected and established Hollywood powerhouse, having written numerous live television scripts during the golden age of television in the 1950s. He already owned three Academy Awards for his writing, for *Marty*, *The Hospital*, and *Network*.

Ken Russell, a London Catholic convert, had his own Oscar for Best Director for *Women in Love*, and he was known as the director of a series of controversial composer biographies, including *Lisztomania*, *The Music Lovers*, and numerous television biopics, including *Prokofiev*, *Elgar*, *Bartok*, and *The Debussy Film*. Unlike veteran Chayefsky, *Altered States* was Russell's first Hollywood experience.

John Corigliano, son of the New York Philharmonic Orchestra's former concertmaster, was already successful as a classical music composer, but he was a newcomer to film music and its special requirements and techniques. While his score for *Altered States* was nominated for an Academy Award, it was his score for *The Red Violin*, a magnificently coherent score, that eventually did win him the Oscar. He later won a Pulitzer Prize for his *Symphony No. 2*.

A musically knowledgeable Russell tapped Corigliano for the score to *Altered States* after hearing one of his classical orchestral works in a concert format. As a classical composer, Corigliano is experienced with long musical forms, orchestral works that derive their sonic organization from the careful control and development of musical ideas. Film music, while amenable to classical music structural forms, uses the visual element as its primary organizational skeleton upon which musical motifs and ideas are hung. According to Corigliano, "Film music is not developmental, it's a minute and twenty seconds of this, thirty seconds of that. And what happens at the very end of that road is often the product of the director censoring and changing and making you change things you wrote. It is not your vision at all. It can't be. It's not about you. You are a service to a film."[3]

Nonetheless, Corigliano approached the score as an organic whole, complete with themes and their developments. Russell, in turn, used the music as he liked, cutting and editing it to fit his own vision and editorial needs, often indistinguishably melding it with the considerable sound effects in service of the larger film experience. Much of Corigliano's form and conception is therefore lost, though he preserved the essence of his original vision and form, rescuing his wounded music from the edited film score and resurrecting it in his work, *Three Hallucinations for Orchestra*.

If in his book, and to a lesser extent his screenplay, Chayefsky emphasized dialog, Russell emphasized visual image. If Chayefsky's vision raised scientific and philosophical questions, Russell's concept emphasized religious and mystical experiences and the questions they raised. If Corigliano's composition underscored organic cohesiveness and growth, Russell's deployment of edited sections of music deliberately fragmented that cohesiveness, reflecting the disjointedness of the key hallucination scenes, as well as the disparate creative voices that formed the film.

Ken Russell's visual rendition of Paddy Chayefsky's novel and screenplay *Altered States* elucidates the quintessential existential search for the meaning of life. Dr. Eddie Jessup, a brilliant researcher and academic physiologist, is convinced that the answer to the question of why man exists is tied up in the limbic system of the human body. The limbic system is the part of the brain that seems to harbor ancestral and primal instincts and actions. His experiments with a sensory deprivation tank, also known as a flotation tank, leads him to begin experimenting with hallucinogenic drugs along with episodes in the tank in the hope of liberating that primal part of his being.

Jessup is consumed by his work. He is remote, detached from the world around him, and only becomes engaged when it is related to his researches. He is in love with his work, not the equally brilliant but more grounded Emily, whom he eventually marries. Early in their relationship, she explains to him that love and existence are the only meanings to life, but it will take him until the end of the movie and the near destruction of all that is meaningful to him to finally grasp this obvious concept.

Russell's interpretation relies heavily on allegorical signifiers and imagery as manifested in the hallucinatory scenes that Jessup experiences. These scenes invite frame-by-frame analysis with deep references to religion, myth, and psychology.

John Corigliano's music encourages microscopic inspection with a similar degree of intensity, as well. But while Russell's phantasmagoric imagery is limited to the hallucinations, Corigliano's score fills out the rest of the movie, in addition to exploiting the *trips* for all their auditory allusion.

Corigliano establishes a few central themes, alternative leitmotifs if you will, that signal Jessup's descent into the primitivism he is attempting to explore. But Corigliano's music also crops up at times when no hallucination is imminent or immediately apparent. His leitmotifs essentially become that alter ego, that primal ur-man that is Jessup.

CORIGLIANO'S COMPOSITIONAL METHOD

For this film, Corigliano needed to write a significant amount of music in a relatively short amount of time. To accomplish this, he used what is called an *aleatoric process* for much of the music. He created a series of what he calls *motion sonorities*, a series of notes or rhythmic figures that when played by the ensemble give a sense of vibrancy to the sound.[4] Corigliano will specify a series of notes or rhythmic figures that are to be played within a short amount of time. The exact timing and location of the figures within the specified time frame is up to the individual performers. This approach allows Corigliano to deal with larger shapes and textures, leaving the individual performance decisions to the skilled players.

For example, Corigliano will specify in the score that the violins should glissando between two pitches over a period of five seconds. Necessarily, not all of the violins will glissando at the same rate, thus causing a *wall* of violin sound to generally move en masse between the two boundary notes of the glissando.

The result of these well-known aleatoric processes is that Corigliano can create broad textures that occupy significant amounts of time while retaining a sense of vibrancy or movement within the structure. This avoids any sense of stasis in the music. When we see the craggy mountains and the camera pans, we are left with a sense of desolateness, loneliness, and mystery, while having the feeling that the mountains are not dead, but secretly alive, pulsing with an inner energy.

This pulsing is exactly what Corigliano was going for. His musical features are filled with *breathing motif* figures that ebb and flow, proceed into and recede out of our consciousness. He creates an audible space that is large, endless, and unbounded, while making us aware of the potency and vibrancy that lies within.

Corigliano does not solely use these aleatoric techniques, but rather integrates them with more traditionally notated figures, noticeably the *love theme*. Additionally, we hear this integration of tonal and atonal sonorities when he embeds the "Rock of Ages" hymn into the body of larger aleatoric sections.

Chapter 1: Trying the Tank

The film opens with no music, just the low rumbling of the sensory deprivation tank, a close-up of Jessup's glass-globe-enclosed head from within the tank, and the gentle clicking of the various machines recording data. A voiceover dispassionately describes the scientific basis of the experiment and reveals none of the obsessive drive behind the exploration.

Chapters 2, 3: Credits, "Where Will We Be Going?"

A piano enters with a low-pitched sustained note, followed by another one, **[00:02:21]** seemingly of the same pitch, but slightly out of tune. In fact, the second **[00:02:24]** piano strike is the same note, deliberately tuned one quarter-step lower than the first. To our Western ears, it may sound out of tune, or perhaps of a different timbre. Other, non-Western cultures would immediately recognize it as a separate and distinct pitch.

Regardless of the cultural implications and perceptions, the second note is clearly lower in pitch than the first. This leitmotif, a *descending* or lowering figure, will become an aural indicator for Jessup's regression into a more primitive state in which he hopes to find the meaning of life. This idea

[00:02:41] of *descending* finds musical reinforcement in the trombones, which enter and begin glissandoing downward, effectively pulling us down with them.

[00:02:46] We also hear what sounds almost like a synthesized filtered sound opening up. It is, in fact, trombones controlling their mutes in a specifically designed manner to evoke the unnerving sound. No electronics are involved. This opening (and later closing) figure can be considered a *breathing leitmotif* and connects us to the primal figure (and psychological implications) of the primal man that is Jessup (and by extension all humans). Corigliano continues to weave these two motifs together through some truly brilliant orchestration, underneath the titling and credit sequences. When coupled with the repeated images of Jessup floating in the tank, and the way the film title seems to languidly float across our view, we are left with a sense that we, too, are floating, being drawn into some ethereal, weightless space, devoid of time and effort. The music continues, unrelentingly dense, highly reverberated, and designed to leave us with a sense of texture rather than the more usual melodic motif material.

Jessup emerges from the tank, carefully debriefing his technician-colleague, Arthur, about the religious allegories and imagery he has experienced. This reference to religious experiences permeates the film and reflects Jessup's obsession with altered states of experience and consciousness. We later find out that his academic research is in the field of schizophrenia, in which religious inspiration and imagery often manifest itself. During the debriefing process, Arthur asks him, "What are we looking for?" Jessup responds, "I don't know," an innocent, yet existentially revealing, response. The rest of the film reacts to this brief encounter.

Chapter 4: Two Whiz Kids

After establishing the basis of these bootleg experiments, the film cuts to an apartment-based party of academics, slightly sophisticated, as we would

[00:06:36] expect from young, upcoming professors in the 1960s. A party needs source music, and this one presents us with the Doors singing "Light My Fire" in the background. The choice of bands (and song) is a natural. The Doors named themselves after *The Doors of Perception, and Heaven and Hell*, Aldous Huxley's book about drugs, hallucination, and the search for self that became the raison d'etre for the counterculture of the times. What is more subtle and nuanced is the specific section of the music we hear underscoring the dialog. It is the extended jam from "Light My Fire," the improvisatory nature of the selection, perhaps reflecting the bootlegging science that Jessup and Arthur are engaging in.

The fact that Emily and a colleague are toking up during this scene is amusing, but the artwork in the hallway behind Emily is of relevance to the story line. Behind her we see a picture of a volcano, a cauldron of raw, primal [00:07:10] energy belching smoke from a deep, primordial interior. The volcano speaks on many levels, especially when coupled with the background music: the unbridled passion that is about to be uncorked between Jessup and Emily, his inner driven-ness, the primordial eruption that will eventually consume Jessup.

As Emily waits in the foyer for Jessup's entrance, we see a stained glass [00:07:16] window behind her and then next to her, coloring the light into the room, giving us the first visual glimpse into the spiritual nature of their encounter.

It is the appearance of Jessup at the door as Emily looks on that makes us realize that the song "Light My Fire" is about them. Jessup appears as a [00:07:25] god, emerging from a white light at the end of a long entrance hallway. He is bathed in the white light; nothing else is in the frame. She is immediately taken with him.

A rather abrupt jump cut leads us into the kitchen where Jessup is preparing a sandwich while Emily attempts to engage him in conversation. The [00:07:33] music jumps as well, to an Indian raga. Improvisation is an integral component in many ragas. In this sense, the Indian music is simply an extension of the jam from "Light My Fire," and in fact, it is edited as such. Emily attempts to draw a reticent and inwardly focused Jessup out, only to meet with resistance. Their conversation is stilted and one sided. She is remarkably assertive for a young woman in the 1960s. Jessup is unimpressed and attempts to intellectually intimidate her with a rapidly cadenced explanation of his research. She does not wither, however, and parries with her own pronouncements of intellectual achievement. As the conversation begins to come to life, Jessup begins to hunt around the kitchen for a condiment for his sandwich. He is lost, not knowing where he is going. He is unfamiliar with earthly banalities. Emily supplies Jessup with the exact condiment he is looking for as she pronounces, "I'm a whiz kid, too."

The importance of this moment cannot be overstated. Without her, Jessup is lost, unable to find his way through even the most mundane of everyday tasks. She provides him with what he needs, grounding him by providing nurturing. The allegory of the female providing the male with food has obvious biblical significance, and as we shall see later in the film, she does provide him with the knowledge he needs, though he is oblivious to it at first.

Only now does Jessup acknowledge his manly interest in her. Their intellectual repartee continues, foreplay between academics. Jessup is smiling. It is clear now that the way to Jessup's heart is through his brain. Intellectual exercise is the only thing that truly excites him.

As Emily and Jessup walk across the academic yard at Columbia University, Jessup's religious/sexual passion for his work reflects itself in his speech patterns and his relations with Emily. He professes nonstop to her about his [00:09:05] work, his research with schizophrenics, and their perceptions of religiosity. Without pausing to breathe, he asks Emily if he can sleep with her. The link between Jessup's aliveness, sexual drive, and intellectual rapture is secured.

Chapter 5: Fascinating Bastard

[00:10:02]
As they adjourn to her bedroom, Corigliano's music takes on a decidedly unromantic air. It is primal, full of writhing musical figures devoid of any obvious rhythmic content. It's not immediately clear if the couple is enjoying their libidinous behavior. Do their faces and contortions reflect rapture, animal instinct, or pain? Jessup interrupts his thrusting to gaze at a glowing heater shaped much like the stained glass window seen in the apartment in which he first met Emily. He pauses and becomes distracted to the point that she recognizes that he has momentarily left her.

Though the music has no overtly discernible pulse at the initiation of the coitus, it nonetheless maintains vibrancy through the aleatoric process described earlier by Corigliano. The strings are actively vibrating, and glissandos abound. Jessup and Emily's lovemaking is hardly portrayed in a romantic light. While the lower string section races chromatically up and down the fingerboard, the upper strings are perfecting a series of glissandos, a primal movement of sound designed to reflect the ebbs and flows of the sex act. Jessup maintains the superior position to Emily, and it is unclear as to whether either partner is in ecstasy or pain. They are bathed in sweat and red light. Jessup is momentarily distracted by an electric heater that could easily double as a stained glass window, not unlike the one in the apartment where he first
[00:10:11]
met Emily. Only when Jessup gazes at the heater and loses his own thrusting rhythm do the strings come to a point of stasis, holding high, shrill notes as they disappear. The torridness of the lower strings momentarily abates, disappearing in a flurry of glissandos as Jessup forgets what he is doing and mentally wanders off. Emily, of course, notices his diversion, and asks what he is thinking about. His response, curious as it is, reflects the underlying religious strain of the film. In the middle of sexual intercourse, he is thinking of God, thus inextricably intertwining the two.

The result of all this is that we see that Jessup's scientific work is metaphysical in nature and bound up in his sexual energy and personal relationship with Emily. This in turn brings out the religious questioning which, as we shall see in a moment, is related to his personal development as he reflects on his father's death and his ensuing existentialist quagmire.

As Emily questions Jessup about his fixation with Christ and crucifixions during sex, Jessup lays his head on Emily's naked breast and reveals a conversation he had with his father as his father lay dying. As a properly raised child, Jessup was dutifully religious. But as he watched his father die a slow and painful death, he asked him what "it" was all about. His father simply replied, "Terrible." Jessup reveals to Emily that with the death of his father, "by dinnertime, I had dispensed with God altogether. I never saw another vision." The pronouncement also explains what is subconsciously driving Jessup's obsessive interest in studying schizophrenia: its tantalizing religious connections and altered states of consciousness.

[00:10:32]
Musically, this scene takes on many meanings for both Jessup and John Corigliano himself. Moments before Jessup confesses, we hear a somewhat altered rendition of the traditional hymn "Rock of Ages." Its pitch and rhythm is warped, distorted, almost stretched beyond recognition. But it is there, and

intentionally so. Just as Jessup's perception of the religious experience was profoundly changed, so has the music.

Orchestrationally, Corigliano brings the violas in a moment before Jessup [00:12:00] utters the word he heard from his father. The prominence given to the viola at this moment heightens the presence of the father and intensifies the meaning of the word he is about to speak. Texturally, the father's voice is frail and thin, but higher pitched, as one would expect from a very sick man. The pitch range of the voice lies in the heart of the viola sound. Scoring the passage for a violin instead of a viola would have been sexually ambiguous. In short, the viola figure is struggling to speak, as would a man dying.

For John Corigliano, the significance of the psalm is of equal importance. It was during the writing of the music for this film that Corigliano's own father passed. Corigliano's relationship with his father was deep and intense. As concertmaster for the New York Philharmonic for thirty years under Arturo Toscanini and Leonard Bernstein, John Sr. served as a sort of mentor for John Jr. Corigliano embeds the "Rock of Ages" theme into the body of the score as much an homage to his father as to Jessup's.[5] To this day, the son's writing for strings reveals an intimate knowledge of the instrument's capabilities often lacking in today's lesser composers.

"Rock of Ages," in its various musical manipulations, fades out as Jessup concludes his reminisces and returns to the psychological present with Emily. Their nakedness is revealing in more ways than one. It is one of the few times Jessup truly bears his inner self. This will not occur again until the very end of the film, when they are again naked as Jessup finally comprehends the meaning of his life.

The descending piano figure from the opening scene in the film returns, [00:13:04] taking us across the scene change to another session in the isolation tank. Psychologists would maintain that Jessup's revelations to Emily would enable him to connect with her on a more intimate level. In this sense, the descending piano figure would take on added significance as Jessup and Emily kiss and he relaxes into her arms, relaxing into his more primal urges, moments before the cut. Even more so, the music cue links Jessup's personal searching for love and meaning with his scientific explorations.

Chapter 6: Dream on Fire

The isolation tank scene presents the first of three major hallucinations that occur within the film. The music for this scene becomes almost note-for-note the source for the first of the three movements in Corigliano's orchestral suite, aptly named *Three Hallucinations for Orchestra*.[6]

Painted in broad strokes, the music reflects Jessup's sliding into the primal experience in his attempts to access the limbic system in his body and mind. At first glance and hearing, the visual and aural imagery seems to be without significant form, or at least a series of random, free associations. But a measure-by-measure and frame-by-frame analysis reveals some decidedly deliberate sonic and visual imagery, designed to reveal Jessup's subconscious dilemma and to embellish and embroider our view of his psychological makeup and what is driving him.

[00:13:27]

Visually, we see Jessup in the tank, wired and floating freely. He is serene, his assistant dozing in the control room. The two descending piano notes from the film's opening sequence reappear, signifying his regression into a primal experience. He begins to see flashes of light and to hear voices, undecipherable at first. He seems to smile in recognition. He begins innocently enough to float in the clouds and later in a sea surrounded by exotic fish. It

[00:13:38]

is a thoroughly predictable *trip*, if there is such a thing. Sliding motifs in the strings emerge as the fish and clouds combine. Jessup's face loses the smile.

[00:13:49]

The woodwinds give us the first clear rendition of "Rock of Ages" harmonized in a dissonant fashion. We see the image of an elderly man, bedridden in a simple, white room, his arms outstretched in recognition, with three bay windows behind him, revealing a fiery red sky. "Rock of Ages" continues as we momentarily cut to a younger, preppily dressed Jessup, dutifully smiling at his father with innocent admiration. A quick cut shows the father caving inward with pain, followed by a fiery yellow and red collision of ocean waves.

[00:13:52]

The music erupts into violence, disrupting the hymn, leaving it incomplete, unresolved. Jessup lurches violently in the tank as he experiences the violence of his father's pain.

In the hallucination, the younger Jessup looks concerned and apprehensive as he offers his father a Bible. The Bible falls from Jessup's hand, however, never reaching his father. A quick edit shows a cloth with the image of Jesus, complete with a crown of thorns, falling and then covering the father's face. The father grabs the cloth, tossing it to the ground, where it bursts into

[00:14:03]

flames. A series of guttural blasts from the trombones speak for the father, a cry of outrage either against the religion imposed upon him or perhaps at the pain he must endure. In either case, the intense violence and conflict of the moment manifests itself in the brass fanfare figures that clearly announce the beginning of the end.

The religious imagery that ensues reflects more of Jessup's turmoil upon seeing his father die and his epiphany regarding his own religious experience than his father's death itself.

[00:14:06]

The turmoil engendered by the contrapuntal brass figures, supported by the woodwinds and to a lesser extent the strings, becomes even more dissonant and violent as we experience rapid-fire images of a seven-eyed ram, a flaming cross superimposed upon an agonizing old man screaming in pain and heat, a writhing Jessup in the isolation tank, and the image of Christ with the ram's head crucified on a cross floating in space. The seeming cacophony that consumes the music is really a densely packed series of motifs contrapuntally treated by Corigliano. It is more texture than melody and harmony.

[00:14:33]

A pronounced and recognizable rendition of "Rock of Ages" emerges from this chaos of rapid-fire images and oscillating musical figures, traditionally harmonized in chorale fashion and performed by a traditional brass orchestration. Visually, we see a Salvadore Dalíesque image of the remains of a medieval cathedral, with wooden telephone poles running to the vanishing point. An oversized silver-plated Bible, resting on a rock within the columns of the church, remains. Still, the hymn is not complete. In a close-up shot, we see a hand reaching across the Bible, attempting to open it. We see a shadow cross the path of the hand, and it suddenly retreats from the book, leaving it unopened. The musical chaos of a few moments earlier returns as we seen the seven-eyed ram and the Bible set upon the rock. A knife is raised in obvious reference to a ritual slaughtering of the ram, though we do not see the actual slaughtering. We see a downward stroke of the blade, then blood dripping onto and defacing the Bible. Confirming shots reveal the slaughtered ram and blood on the knife. The "Rock of Ages" hymn returns, rising above the contrapuntal chaos. A female voice reinforces the brass theme: the only time [00:14:47] we actually hear an unaltered, solo human voice in the music for the film.

The counterpoint is abruptly interrupted, as is the visual image by a series [00:14:49] of bursting images that seem to have an organic quality to them. Is it an embryo taking shape? Is it the birth of mankind that Jessup is attempting to experience? We see light from the distance, as if we are looking outward. We see flashes of Jessup and Emily in coitus, with Emily seeming to fight against his penetration. Is this rape? Is this primal man fulfilling his most basic of biological needs? We see what seems to be an iconized ram's head zooming in toward the camera, against the image of a sun. Yet, is this the sacrificial ram or the ultimate fertility image, the vision of a woman's fallopian tubes? The music certainly gives us no clue, leaving us unresolved. It simply disappears in a wash of noise and reverberation as we close with a shot of Jessup thrashing in the tank followed by the image of a female medical patient, nervously looking around a laboratory room while seemingly disembodied hands attach electrodes to her head.

Chapter 7: Hearts Touched and Untouched

Sonically, all we are left with is the repetitive, steady beeping of medical [00:15:03] equipment monitoring the female patient's life signs. She is anxious and confused by the science that surrounds her. She does not comprehend, even though a retreating camera shot reveals Jessup watching her on a television monitor while dispassionately explaining to Emily what the schizophrenic woman is and will be experiencing. The sonic and visual intensity of the previous sequence is gone, vanished as if it had never happened. Jessup is again emotionally flat, consumed by his experiments and only remotely responsive to Emily's proposals regarding their future together.

Emily proposes marriage to Jessup and is met with only a minimal response. She tells him that he is a "Faust freak, Eddie. You'd sell your soul to find the great truth." This provokes an existential diatribe on her part, lecturing Jessup that the only true meaning for existence is to love one another. It will take him until the end of the film to discover the truism that his future wife has just revealed to him.

Her sermon is met with no response from Jessup. He returns his focus to his schizophrenic patient and ignores Emily. She removes herself to the sterile and vacuous hallway outside his laboratory, where he eventually joins her, sitting on the generic plastic seats on the opposite side of the hallway from her. His scientific jabbering is met with a brooding silence on her part. A momentary pause allows a clarinet to sneak in with the first clearly [00:18:00] definable new melody of the film, the *love* leitmotif. It is an odd melody, a symmetric yet dissonant one, faintly reminiscent of the *Maria* theme in *West Side Story*. Indeed, the two have in common the same crucial musical intervals that define each theme, a half step and a tritone.

[00:18:06]

Nonetheless, the clarity with which the theme is stated reflects a momentary stripping away of all of the clutter that permeates Jessup's life. He declares that he is willing to get married, if it's that important to her, and that he will never find anyone as devoted and loving as her. Emily recognizes the extent of Jessup's feeling, declaring that "I suppose that's the closest thing to a declaration of love I will ever get out you." The clarinet theme has blossomed underneath this dialog, supported by a gentle, high-string countermelody that eventually replaces the clarinet as our primary focus, a soft orchestration of harp, woodwinds, and horns, and with a highly tonal harmonic structure. This dissonant, obtuse melody line in the upper strings yields to the oboe line, which then is passed among the upper woodwinds and strings in a florid, orchestrationally lush, tonal treatment suited to more conventional love stories. The scene is resolved; their love declared.

Chapter 8: Unafraid of Solitary Pain

As the scene changes to a long shot of a lonely Emily staring out the window of a toney Boston apartment building, it becomes clear that some time has passed. The *love* leitmotif, which carries us across the cut, is passed to the lower strings that emerge in a minor key and with a decidedly darker repetition of the *love* theme. The more traditionally harmonic treatment is gone. As the cue fades out, the melody remains tonally unresolved, devoid of any semblance of a final cadence. This leaves us hanging, questioning the viability of this seemingly ideal academic marriage.

[00:19:00]

[00:19:27]

The chapter continues without music as Jessup and Emily are met at their apartment by Eduardo Echeverria, an old colleague from Columbia, and their colleague/friend, Mason. From a plot development perspective, the remainder of the scene establishes that Jessup and Emily have become estranged and are going their separate ways for a year, and that Jessup is still interested in exploring the use of psychotropic drugs in combination with an isolation tank he has just discovered at the medical school where he teaches.

Chapter 9: Ourselves and Nothing But

After having had a few drinks with his colleagues and friends at the local eatery, Jessup is better able to articulate the nature of his searching and his desire to explore the human soul. He enunciates his search for the meaning of life and declares his intention to discover the "original self." A short reaction shot reveals the concern Emily has as she realizes the all-consuming nature of his search and his insatiable appetite for the meaning of life.

[00:23:37]

The flute/guitar duet in the background is just that—the source music one would expect to find in this slightly offbeat, upscale, hipster sit-down delicatessen. A drunk yet intense Jessup declares that the answer to his search for meaning lies in the human limbic system, tied up in energy and molecules millions of years old, and he intends to find this *original self.*

Chapter 10: His Unborn Soul

As the camera zooms into Jessup at the climax of his declaration, he looks up toward the sky as the scene cuts to a breathtakingly panoramic shot of sharp, jaggedly foreboding mountains and blue sky. Jessup is in Mexico, where, as part of his search, he intends to participate in an ancient Toltec psychedelic mushroom ritual under the guidance of his Mexican colleague, Eduardo. Corigliano's music is just as jagged as the mountain peaks. The brass instruments perform a series of crescendoing and decrescendoing chord clusters that serve as *breathing* motifs. The lower brasses create a timbral variation of the *breathing* motif by playing long tones while opening and closing their mutes. The sonic result is a synthesizerlike filtered sound, even though no electronics are involved. The result is that we hear a sort of static soundscape that pulsates from within, evoking a sense of mystery. Yet at the same time, it retains the aliveness of the mountain range that Jessup and his Mexican colleague are hiking through. [00:25:12] [00:25:39]

Jessup and Eduardo eventually meet up with members of the Hinchi Indians, who describe the ritual that Jessup is interested in. He asks their permission to join the ritual, and they are agreeable.

Chapters 11, 12: The Ritual, Straight for the Brain

Chapter 11 blasts into our ears with a series of rapidly pulsing trombone figures, the *breathing* motif highly animated and alive. We see Jessup, Eduardo, and the Hinchi elder silhouetted against the entrance to a cave. It is the same cave entrance Jessup witnessed during his first hallucination in the isolation tank. We hear primitive drums and a tuba announcing the arrival of the three visitors to the cave. It is a primal fanfare of natural-sounding horns; the horns used before today's sophisticated brass instruments, before the valves and metal alloys that make the instruments contemporary. [00:28:09] [00:28:48]

This, in fact, is the primitive orchestra of the Hinchi Indians. We see them with skinhead drums and a collection of wind instruments that remotely resemble vertical flutes and alphorns. They are not, of course, European, but native instruments, reflecting the ritual that is about to transpire. In this sense, this primitive music sets the time and place. The music is as old as the ritual. It is timeless. The paintings on the cave wall are as they have been for centuries.

As the hallucinogenic brew simmers, we hear what can only be described as a gaggle of oboes being played in what is called the *rhietta* style. In this performance technique, the oboist takes the entire reed into his/her mouth and basically honks out the notes. There is no refinement of sound here. It is coarse and shrieking. We hear ritual chanting by men entering the aural landscape and then fade out as the trombones enter, presaging the bloodletting of Jessup as he makes his own personal, physical contribution to the psychedelic brew. [00:29:07] [00:29:40]

[00:29:48] The musical counterpoint associated with the chaotic and unknown aspect of the ritual yields to the repetition and rhythmic nature of the voices and drums. The chaos coalesces as the ritual participants begin to drink the potion. It is as if the chaos of the real world, as well as the participants' existence, evaporates into the clarity induced by the drug.

[00:30:42] The vibrating trombones that initiate the scene return as the Hinchi shaman gestures to Jessup that it is his turn to drink. Here we find clear support for the notion that the *breathing* motif can be linked to a heartlike fluttering, the kind of palpitations that one would experience as one begins down an unknown and potentially dangerous path, especially a path that involves drugs, an alien culture, and an existential search for meaning.

Jessup drinks the potion and is almost immediately interrupted by what at first sounds like a thunderstorm but turns out to be the beginning of his hallucination. It begins with fireworks.

Jessup's psychedelic flashes focus around images reflecting his own angst, his relationship to his wife, and the staid existence of his professorial life as well as his search for meaning. Author Paddy Chayefsky was not explicit in his book (from which the screenplay was adapted) regarding the actual imagery of any of the hallucinations. This allowed Russell the creative freedom to express his own visions during the three major hallucinatory scenes. In this sense, we are seeing and experiencing what Jessup is seeing and experiencing through the filter of Ken Russell's interpretation of Paddy Chayefsky's vision.

[00:31:50] The initial graphic images are of a skeletal-looking man and woman either offering or receiving a mushroom from a lizard, underneath a giant mushroom. Both humans are covering their genitals, an obvious reference to the **[00:31:52]** Garden of Eden parable. We are presented with a momentary glimpse of Jessup and Emily dressed in Victorian attire, sitting at a patio set in an idyllic world, a sun-filled world filled with flowers. We return to the fireworks as **[00:32:08]** Jessup staggers outside. A few glimpses of Emily looking skyward are interjected, and we see a lizard (chameleon?) hanging from the patio umbrella, accompanied by xylophone glissandos in both directions, clearly implying the *breathing* motif.

The fireworks may well represent the random firing neurons in Jessup's brain as the drug takes effect. He is, of course, trying to discover the original self through bodily manifestation, and as he becomes more aware of his physical self, he no doubt experiences the sensory overload we see. It is important to note that Corigliano makes no attempt to create musical links to every experience that Jessup undergoes in the sequence. Rather, the intensely atonal and contrapuntal nature of his writing, coupled with a densely woven orchestral texture, gives us a sense of the intensity of Jessup's trip, with its overwhelming speed and seemingly random, fragmentary archetypal images.

[00:32:49] Corigliano does, however, manage to catch the primitive dance of the Hinchi Indians with a carefully mixed blend of rhythmically coherent drums and blaring brass rips that momentarily, at least, bring some sense of coordination **[00:32:56]** and order to the scene. A recognizable melody even emerges from the oboes, played in the previously described rhietta style.

Intercut with the ritual dance are flashes of Jessup and Emily sitting at a   **[00:33:02]**
decidedly proper garden table, alternating with images of a snake descending
from the garden table's umbrella. Emily elegantly dips a spoon into a dish   **[00:33:14]**
of sherbet and begins to enjoy the delicate flavor, perhaps the symbol of
genteel, refined existence, the very existence that Jessup questions. She feeds
him a spoonful, and we see his resentment reach the boiling point. The rate
of the edits accelerates, reflecting Jessup's increasing level of disturbance.
He lies gasping on the ground, peering up as the snake uncurls itself from
the umbrella. A momentary cut to the snake curled around Jessup's neck and   **[00:33:45]**
face is the clearest imagery of the emotional and psychological asphyxiation
Jessup is experiencing in his daily life. The snake, the biblical representation
of temptation and knowledge, is suffocating him. What becomes intriguing is
the ambiguity of the image. The juxtaposition of the images of civility in the
form of the umbrella, and primal existence, manifested as the snake, pose a
dilemma for our analysis. Is it the temptation of the knowledge of his primitive existence that is stifling him, or the refined civility of his current life? We
find clues to this analytic dilemma earlier in the film, when Jessup confesses
to his technical assistant, Arthur, that "I sit around the living rooms of other
young married faculty members talking infantile masturbation, sucking up to
the head of the department whose tenure is hanging by a thread," and "if I
don't strip myself of all this clatter and clutter and ridiculous ritual, I shall go
out of my fucking mind."

Taken as a whole, the visual imagery shows Jessup's psychic restlessness
in several allegorical ways, all related to the issue of temptation and knowledge. The Hinchi cave drawings pictorially represent the story of Adam and
Eve. Jessup's image of the snake curling around the umbrella and ultimately
strangling him, followed by images of a refined and well-dressed Emily
feeding him sherbet, and their kisses, all reflect his ambiguity regarding the
relationship between knowledge, love, and religion.

In the midst of the hallucination, Jessup begins to remove the dressing from
his injured hand. He sees tiny points of light emerging from the wound. The   **[00:34:10]**
sequence immediately crosscuts to the image of Emily and Jessup walking
away from the camera toward a mushroom cloud, bathed in a filtered red
light, a burst of climactic energy that can only symbolize the birth of existence, at least in this context. It is as if his blood and the light from his wound
are the molecules and energy of life.

The climax of the polyphony abruptly yields to a series of pulsing figures,   **[00:34:17]**
a return to the *breathing* motif as Jessup is able to halt the flurry of images.
He focuses on a baby lizard, which is now languishing in his wounded hand.
As he draws his hand away from his face, his view and the camera focus on a
much larger monitor lizard, its tongue occasionally lashing outward, sensing
its environment. The lull in the hallucination is only momentary, however,
as the large lizard soon morphs into the image of his wife, naked, sprawled
across the sand. She assumes a very lizardlike pose and lizardlike movements:
abrupt head turnings, a beguiling look on her face. The biblical temptress is
still here. Jessup is also lying on the sand, and he watches as a sandstorm soon
transforms Emily into a sphinx. Jessup gazes longingly upon her, though she

[00:34:36]

does not recognize him. Her look becomes enigmatic, sphinxlike, with all the mythology that accompanies it. A first glance seems to indicate that Emily has become an Egyptian version of an archetypal sphinx.

A strong solo violin line has emerged to accompany the transformation, intervallically related to the *love* theme. It consists of minor seconds and perfect fifths, the defining musical intervals of the *love* theme. The music fades out as the sandstorm consumes both Sphinx-Emily and a now-reclining Jessup. They both sleep (or at least lose consciousness) as the sands of time swirl around them. When the sands have all but consumed them, an abrupt edit terminates the hallucination, with the grotesque image of a disemboweled Gila monster surrounded by silence. Eduardo views the eviscerated carcass with disgust, while Jessup walks away, sick to his stomach. The scene lingers for a moment, planting the image in our mind.

Chapter 13: New Tank for Dumb Experiments

A direct cut shows Eduardo and Jessup hiking along a dirt trail, indicating that they have left the mountains in the distance along with the Hinchi Indians and their rituals. An anxious and animated Jessup denies that he killed the Gila monster. The discussion ends abruptly, with a reoccurrence of hallucinogenic images.

Jessup's new hallucination contains much of the same collagelike imagery as his original hallucination. The music throughout the sequence is a collage as well, with densely mixed elements from previous cues playing a secondary role to the sound effects accompanying the visual cacophony. Jessup's voice, reverberated and electronically echoed, is rendered almost indecipherable as he describes the grotesque and random images he experiences.

[00:37:34]

The hallucination ignites with flashes of lightning and appropriately accompanying sound effects. This time we see additional footage: of a hell complete with fire and naked bodies writhing in pain, images of his schizophrenic patient, his coitus with Emily, frenzied horses, mass crucifixions, lizards, and his own electrode-wired head. Torment and agony permeate the imagery. Oceans and reptiles coalesce into one confusing image as we fade to the back of Jessup's head, wired for encephalographic data. The camera pulls back, revealing his entire hallucination experience has occurred within an isolation booth, this time being observed by Arthur as well as his medical professor friend, Mason.

As a scientist and medical doctor, Mason is horrified to find two of his colleagues involved in drug experimentation with an untested substance and no proper scientific controls. Mason, Arthur, and Jessup continue their heated ethical discussion as they cross the campus to look at an unused sensory-deprivation tank Jessup has just discovered in the basement of a campus building.

Chapter 14: No Longer Observing

Jessup enters the newly reclaimed isolation tank to experience the waterborne effects of the tank after having ingested the psychotropic mushroom mixture he brought back from Mexico. Arthur coordinates the experiment, though Mason joins them after abandoning his own research for the day. Jessup begins his hallucination by relaying his observations of the African savannahs, elegantly and cognitively describing the rock formations and landscape that surrounds him. He is euphoric. Even Mason begins to smile. But as Jessup begins to include himself into the hallucination, by exclaiming that "I'm becoming one of them," Mason becomes concerned.

The music sneaks in as Jessup descends further and further into his delu- **[00:44:51]** sion of becoming primitive man. The cue begins with a high-pitched string ostinato, followed by some low, *breathing* motif figures in the brass. This **[00:44:54]** cue is a bit of what is called a *red herring*. The music crescendos, apparently headed toward a climactic moment, raising our expectation that something cataclysmic is about to transpire. That moment occurs when an apprehensive Mason opens the door to the tank to check on Jessup. But rather than some consummate expression, the music simply stops—a false climax, a false **[00:45:20]** alarm—as Jessup indicates that he is fine, and the experiment continues. Mason closes the door; the music does not return.

Only after Jessup utters what sounds like a choking sound does the **[00:45:50]** *breathing* motif return, clearly and urgently defined by the trombone. The *breathing figure*, however, is unidirectional, as if gasping for air, sans exhalation. While the trombones gradually open their mutes as on previous expressions of the *breathing* motif, there is no opposite movement, just as there is none in Jessup's gasp. The trombone figure does not complete the closing of the mute, leaving us with an open-ended, incomplete feeling. As Jessup relaxes, the resolution of the *breathing figure* finally manifests itself. In this sense, all seems to have returned to normal, or at least as normal as the bizarre experiment can produce.

Chapter 15: "Before I Reconstitute"

Several hours pass, as indicated by Mason's returning from the bathroom just as Arthur begins to remove Jessup from the tank. The shrieking strings return **[00:46:27]** as he and Mason approach the tank.

Unlike the previous *red herring* cue, the crescendo is prescient this time, leading to an alarming image of a terrified Jessup, with blood running from his mouth as he stares up from the tank. The use of low, undefined brass and **[00:46:34]** percussion understates the intensity of the visual image, leaving us to absorb the terror of the three scientists. The music is borderline sound effect. It remains restrained, with occasional low-intensity outbursts, mostly of the *breathing* motif. We do not know what has happened to Jessup, neither does Arthur or Mason. The upward glissando figures in the strings do indicate that he is rising **[00:46:49]** or emerging upward in some sense. A logical analysis would indicate that if downward glissando figures are a leitmotif for regression to a more primitive state of consciousness, then upward figures would reveal a return from a lower state of being or consciousness toward a more cognitive state.

As Mason and Arthur lay Jessup on the ground and begin to tend to his medical needs, they recognize that he is unable to verbally communicate. Jessup gestures for a pad and pen and indicates that his blood should be drawn and x-rays of his neck should be taken immediately, before he *reconstitutes*. The ever-flappable Mason refuses to believe that Jessup has physiologically regressed millions of years. Nonetheless, he takes Jessup to the hospital for a workup.

Chapters 16, 17: X-Rays—of a Gorilla, Transformation!

[00:52:58]

The radiologist confirms Jessup's self-diagnosis that he has, in fact, physically regressed. At the moment of validation, the strings return and continue, bringing us across the ensuing cut to a sleeping Jessup and his girl du jour. While the imagery indicates a fitful sleep, with Jessup contentedly resting on his girl's breast, the strings indicate otherwise. Contrary to the imagery presented, they are Jessup's subconscious, the restless primordial self, bubbling

[00:53:07]

up from within. Downward and upward glissandos reflect his confusion upon waking and indicate his subconscious ambiguity about regressing. While he regains his cognitive self by awakening, his forearms begin to spasmodically

[00:53:27]

bulge, simian muscles making their presence felt. A series of tremolo and trill figures present the sense of restlessness and confusion that Jessup experiences, reflecting the conflict between the state of his mind and the condition of his body. On one hand, the tremolos and trills are a series of rapid alterations between notes and thus a manifestation of the *breathing* motif. Even the glissandos alternate directions, supporting the notion of quickened breathing. Yet at the same time, they may also represent Jessup's battle between the cognitive and physical manifestations he is experiencing. In this sense, the concept of vacillating musical notes and gestures, in the forms of tremolo, trill, and glissando, plays out not just the *breathing* motif, but also Jessup's inner superego versus id conflict.

[00:54:18]

Jessup retires to the bathroom to examine himself in the mirror. The strings begin a pyramidlike thickening of the texture. A single viola begins an upward and downward glissando motif that is taken up with more and more strings, each at its own pace. This contrapuntalization of the texture

[00:54:44]

intensifies as Jessup undergoes an increasing physical regression. The first musically climactic moment occurs as the lower brass enter when Jessup sees his feet, now transformed with a sixth toe on each foot, accompanied by an abnormally thick amount of hair. The image quickly disappears, as does this second musical red herring, implying that Jessup was simply experiencing an hallucinogenic flashback, and all would return to normal

[00:54:57]

as he returns to the bed with his student. The glissando figures continue, though within a diminished pitch range, symbolically indicating that the regression, while not gone, is either receding or under control. The music

[00:55:00]
[00:55:15]

implies so with a momentary tonal resolution, albeit in a minor key. As Jessup approaches the bathroom door to return to bed, however, a prominently placed upward glissando in the strings foreshadows the dangers awaiting him as he turns the doorknob.

His hallucination returns with more intensity as he crosses the bathroom threshold. The hellish images he experiences as he lingers on the precipice are

[00:55:17]

accompanied by a sudden burst of brassiness from the orchestra. The blurring

of sound effects and the music is intentional. The flashback is interrupted by the girl turning on the light and innocently inquiring as to whether Dr. Jessup is all right. The hallucination is repressed, though not completely gone, as we see and hear. The disquieting *motion sonority* figures in the strings continue   **[00:55:36]**
as Jessup returns to his bed and the girl. Another prominent upward glissando   **[00:55:45]**
in the strings implies that Jessup has returned from his experience. He announces that "I'm fine, I just want to make a few notes."

The issue of Jessup's physical regression and flashback seems to be momentarily resolved, but the two pulsing trombone and low string figures that   **[00:56:06]**
emerge as Jessup exits the frame and the girl turns off the light imply that there is more lurking underneath. Indeed, as Jessup begins to jot a few notes, his bulging biceps return, as does the flurry of string activity.   **[00:56:22]**

Chapters 18, 19: A Small Quantum Jump, Out of the Tank

The next scene finds a buoyant Jessup meeting Emily and their children at the airport. Emily has just returned from a year of observing primates in Africa. While unpacking at home, Emily confronts Jessup about his experiments. He becomes agitated and very aggressive as he explains his frustration at not being able to repeat his experiments. He verbally strong-arms Emily into looking at his data and supporting another experiment to confirm his data.

Not content with waiting for her blessing, Jessup leaves Emily and returns to the tank to repeat his experiment, this time alone. A cutaway shot shows Emily discussing her concerns with Mason on the phone.

We are soon visually directed toward Jessup, who is preparing himself in   **[01:02:48]**
the tank. We hear the solo piano note from the film's very first cue. Instead of treating us to the second piano note from the first cue, however, we see a gnarled and hairy arm emerge from the tank. Unlike the first cue in which it is the music that signifies the terrible descent into primitivism, we *see* the next note of the cue rather than hear it.

A series of machinelike rumbles or drones fill out the beginning of the cue. They serve the same function as a more traditional low-pitched sustained note would under the same circumstances. They give us the sense of impending drama, a precursor to something bad happening. This becomes one of the few cases in the film in which sound effects serve in the role traditionally reserved for music. In fact, the rumble intensifies as music would, as we approach a dramatic point.

The building's night custodian opens the door to the tank room and is surprised by Jessup with his newly evolved physiognomy, that of an apelike creature. This provides the opportunity for shrieking string figures to enter,   **[01:04:06]**
though they dissipate quickly, as does the simian formerly known as Dr. Jessup. In this sense, the real role of the shrieking strings becomes clarified. They serve as a leitmotif for the mixture of fear and confusion. In this case, the leitmotif serves to reflect the fear and confusion of both man and ape—the custodian and Jessup—as the hunt/chase begins.

As unusual as his harmonic, motivic, and orchestral vocabulary is, Corigliano's music in the ensuing scene follows many of the norms of a typical

Hollywood chase sequence. There are moments of suspense and surprise, and moments when the hunted becomes the hunter.

[01:04:40] In the current scene, the string figures never really disappear, lurking in the background as the custodian examines the electrodes discarded by the simian-Jessup. The strings return more intensely as he hears a series of thumping sounds, indicating that the threat is real and not his imagination. Sensing that he is in danger, the custodian runs down a hall and shuts a fire door, providing a degree of safety between him and the simian-Jessup. The strings abruptly stop. A first reading would indicate that the string leitmotif must be associated with the fear and confusion of the simian, since it disappears once he is removed from the frame. But another perspective could be that once the door is closed, the fear and confusion of the custodian dissipates as he regains his breath and composure and develops a plan to contact security. He has recovered from his own primal fears, even as simian-Jessup discovers his.

Chapter 20: Animal Loose

[01:04:55]
[01:05:00] Motivated by the distress of the custodian who comes running to his office and an unusual noise from the hallway, the building security officer grabs his nightstick from the wall as the contrabassoon begins a meandering solo line, soon to be imitated and counterpointed by other low instruments. The first stage of the chase sequence begins with the investigation of a strange, unexplained phenomenon or circumstance. The accompanying contrabassoon and low wind figures continue the Hollywood tradition of stalking
[01:05:11] motifs. The high string line is another cliché used in the service of provoking trepidation in the audience.

Both Corigliano and Russell were aware of the humorous aspects of the chase and ensuing zoo sequences. Although Corigliano closely synchronized his music to the original footage given to him, Russell made extensive edits and borrowings from other cues. Corigliano was less than satisfied with the result, but he was not present for the editing sessions and so could not make his voice heard. The result is a reflection of Russell's sensibilities (and ironic sense of humor) and not Corigliano's filmic perspective.

Nonetheless, Russell delays the entrance of the chase music past the moment when the security officer first sights the ape. This prevents the music from obscuring the officer's radio communications. In addition, the custodian and security officer are still investigating the disturbance, and no one is yet physically chasing the animal.

We are treated to a series of shots of the simian examining his surroundings, looking for an escape or a place to hide. Corigliano's music during
[01:05:36] these moments is a series of high pedal-notes in the upper strings and a contrapuntal morass of meandering lines in the low strings and woodwinds. The remaining strings, brass, and woodwinds create a texture consisting of seemingly randomly spaced gestures, intensely performed as if they were in a roiling hot bouillabaisse, occasionally popping to the surface. The analogy is appropriate. The musical result is a sonic metaphor for the bubbling cauldron of fear, anxiety, and scheming. We are visually treated to a series of short

vignettes as the ape tries to hide, while the security officer and janitor explore the subterranean surroundings in search of the creature.

The musical gestures are short, abrupt, and clearly defined: a densely packed sonic image, full of musical nooks and crannies befitting the setting in the boiler/machine room of the building. A series of miniature red herrings decorate the sonic landscape. The security officer raps his nightstick on an oil drum, alarming the night watchman as a blaring brass note underscores his **[01:06:20]** fright. Squirrelly figures in the high strings form a sonic onomatopoeia for the labyrinthine pipes and conduits that fill the boiler room.

The security officer trips or falls downward as the simian screams. This is followed in short order by a low brass exclamation that ignites a series of **[01:07:00]** string and high woodwind *scream* figures. Drums and low brass soon follow as we witness the ape beating the security officer with his own nightstick. The imagery is as blaring as the brass, as naked as the ape. He turns toward the night watchman, a close-up of his grimacing face accompanied by a trumpet **[01:07:12]** section *same-note trill* (actually a timbre-derived trill), designed to heighten the ape's declaration of intent toward the human.

An ostinato, characteristic of true chase music, is never established until after the officer has been surprised and beaten by the ape and the ape turns to chase the custodian. A series of rhythmic percussion figures emerge as the **[01:07:17]** hunted becomes the hunter and the chase truly begins. The ape catches the custodian just as he reaches a door and the potential safety of two waiting security officers. The ape completes his attack on the custodian and begins to flee, the two backup officers in pursuit.

At this point, the chase music is used in the most traditional of ways: a **[01:07:24]** bed of continuously running rhythms designed to evoke images of running feet, accompanied by fast-paced musical gestures or evocations seemingly randomly placed, designed to evoke a sense of impromptu decisions and unexpected actions that are the essence of any chase sequence.

The contour and texture of the music now begins to follow the little dramas within the larger one. The music crescendos and climaxes as the ape, **[01:07:56]** now outdoors, encounters moving and abandoned cars, finally pausing as he encounters some street dogs rummaging through garbage, looking for food. The music and the ape rest for a moment as the simian contemplates his next move.

The seething music bed reenters as the simian steals away from the dogs **[01:08:16]** and the garbage. No longer feeling chased (the chase music has given way to a string *motion sonority* figure), the ape bounds down the street and discovers another set of garbage cans. His rummaging is quickly disrupted by another set of dogs that bound after him, perhaps protective of their own garbage-can dinners. The rhythmically pulsed chase music begins anew as the ape climbs **[01:08:34]** a standpipe to avoid the dogs.

The dogs continue to give chase as the music increases in density, volume, and complexity, culminating in the hand-to-paw combat between the two predators on the roof of a car. The ape gains the upper hand and flees the scene. The music's rhythmic drive continues, however, until the ape leaps a fence and lands in the Boston Zoo.

Chapter 21: Visiting the Zoo

[01:09:24]   The immediacy of the chase has momentarily dissipated. Nonetheless, the ape is not out of the woods. He drops in on a rather placid rhinoceros, onomato-poetically accompanied by a meandering contrabassoon line that serves as an abstract form of mickeymousing. Russell's use of Corigliano's music under-scores the humorous aspects of an ape visiting a zoo with both real animals and man-made replicas.

The musical line is deliberately slow and plodding, confirming our stereo-type of the rhinoceros as a gentle yet lumbering beast, ignoring the fact that it can charge short distances at up to forty miles per hour, very much faster than the ape could run or scale a tree. Sensing the rhino's displeasure, the ape scrambles up the fence, escaping the rhinoceros's pen. Ken Russell gives us a momentary image of a concrete rhinoceros, the kind of gargoylelike archi-tectural flourish one would expect to see above the entrance to a zoo exhibit.

[01:09:36]   Careful listening will reveal a short collage of birdlike screams, very much in the background at the moment we perceive the fixture. One can only surmise that their subtle placement at this moment is to underscore the inner scream the ape must be experiencing. A further conjecture might lead us to the con-clusion that the scream can also reflect Jessup's inner consciousness (or what is left of it at the moment), as he continues to wrestle with his primordial self (the ape) and his more advanced being, represented by the man-made rhi-noceros icon. This reasoning may lead us to conclude that the psychological battle between Jessup's cognitive and primal selves is reflected by the duality of the concrete and live rhinoceros juxtaposed in such visual proximity.

[01:09:40]   The contrabassoon, accompanied by a few high string and woodwind ges-tures, gives the ape and us a psychological respite as he finds some welcomed
[01:09:44]   water in the elephant pen. We continue to hear *breathing* motif gestures,
[01:09:49]   noticeably in the clarinet tremolos. The oriental-tinged oboe line conjures up faint images of India. The oboe, piccolo, clarinet, and flute gestures, layered on top of the still-plodding contrabassoon line, are noticeably more animated than the *beast of the orchestra*, as the contrabassoon is known. The somewhat perturbed elephants begin to aggressively investigate the intruder.

The density of the musical gestures, now including short, bright, brass figures, reflect the increasing unease of the ape as he makes his way through the zoo. We are given short glimpses of two concrete statues of lions looming ominously over his shoulder. A cutaway gives us a medium-long shot of the two lions towering above the camera's perspective. The ape backs into frame,
[01:10:09]   momentarily replacing the image of one of the lions. He is accompanied by a series of *breathing* motifs, densely packed chords crescendoing and decre-scendoing in the lower brass. A trumpet figure mirrors the *breathing* motif, shifting its timbre in a series of pulses.

The *breathing* motif is useful in adding a human element to the image of the simian. Jessup is still in the ape's body, reacting to his unfamiliar feelings and surroundings. The musical breathing emphasizes both Jessup's sense of primitive aliveness and disorientation. The simian-Jessup sniffs the air and senses food nearby. He leaps another fence and attempts to steal some raw meat from a tiger cage, an act that infuriates the local residents. The scene

is accompanied by a series of rapidly paced rhythmic interjections that are **[01:10:20]**
passed from English horn to trombone to clarinet to trumpet, finally culminating in rapidly tremoloing horns, high in their range, evoking yet another
breathing motif figure. The tiger, acting on instinct, attacks the simian's hand
as it reaches through the cage toward the raw meat.

The simian quickly withdraws as trumpets and trombones blare his anger **[01:10:32]**
and fear. The pulsing piano and low brass figure that has accompanied the
simian as he runs from zoological station to zoological station momentarily
returns, at least until simian-Jessup encounters the souvenir shop. The driving chase rhythms are momentarily paused, replaced by a surreal, childlike **[01:10:41]**
melody, albeit an atonal one, played by the piano accompanied by a single
clarinet trill figure. The trill figure, yet another variation of the *breathing*
motif, encourages the sense of aliveness to continue as the simian pauses,
trying to understand the incongruous imagery of the inanimate stuffed
elephants, tigers, and monkeys lining the shelves. The childlike melody
reflects the simplicity of his thought process. The moment confirms the earlier premise that the use of man-made objects such as the concrete statues
and stuffed elephants juxtaposed with the real creatures reveals the duality
of simian-Jessup's being.

The gesture-laden musical figures return as the ape continues to roam
throughout the zoo, finally discovering a potential food source in the gazelle
pen. The wind and brass gestures give way to extended string mutterings as **[01:11:10]**
the shock from an electrified fence gives the ape pause. The brass interjections temporarily disappear as the ape begins to plan his attack, using a tree
to mount the electrified fence unscathed and a well-thrown rock as a tool to
fell his prey.

The simian's use of hierarchical activities and tools in the execution of
a plan to accomplish a goal (dinner) are signs of more advanced thinking.
Had the brass figures continued through this moment, we would have been
under the assumption that the chase was still afoot and that the ape was
instinctually responding to threats, rather than exhibiting thought and el-
emental forms of logic.

At the moment that he launches his attack, the horns return with a grandiose **[01:11:45]**
rip that signals a primitive call to battle. The chase is again afoot, although
it is the gazelles that must now respond instinctually. As they scatter, we are
treated to perhaps the most obviously mickeymoused moment in the film.
A gazelle leaps across a rock as the xylophone performs a measured glissando **[01:11:58]**
up and down the length and range of the instrument. It is a clichéd moment,
one worthy of the early film cartoons such as *Popeye the Sailor* and *Betty
Boop*. The scurrying strings continue as the gazelles flee, giving way to a
series of blatting bass trombone figures, hinting at the *breathing* motif. The
music fades as the ape satiates himself by devouring his meal.

Additional musical clichés support the notion that Corigliano is adhering to
one of the tried-and-true uses of music in films, albeit with a novel and unique
musical vocabulary and syntax. As the zoo's security guard approaches the
gazelle cage to investigate, he shines his flashlight into the cage. The moment
that the light shines directly into the camera is the moment that he realizes

[01:12:44]   that something is clearly amiss. It is supported by a sforzando entrance lead
by the horns, and then shared with trumpets, emitting a strongly articulated
[01:12:58]   pedal-note, moderately high in their range. A contrasting low pedal tone,
enunciated most clearly by the bass trombone and other low brass, focuses
our attention on the sight of an eviscerated gazelle. The camera pans to the
image of a naked Jessup sprawled across the rocks by the watering hole,
[01:13:03]   contentedly sleeping off his dinner. At the moment we sight Jessup, we
hear the opening quarter-step piano figure, bouncing off the previous brass
low note, thus reinforcing the descending quarter-step motif as a signal for
Jessup's regression. The resulting high-note/low-note contrast figure is a
bit melodramatic, film noirish in its styling, but nonetheless evocative in
the current context.

As a side note, it is not clear that Corigliano had editorial control over the
use of his music in this scene. As we already know, much of the music was
[01:13:10]   recut and used for scenes different than originally intended.[7] The edit between
this scene and the ensuing jail scene abruptly truncates the end of the piano
note. It is a small point, a careless inattention to audio detail, but one that nev-
ertheless confirms Corigliano's unease with how his music was implemented
in the editing stage of the film.

Chapters 22, 23: Supremely Satisfying, "What the Hell Was That?"

A now clean-shaven, reconstituted Jessup is released from jail and taken
home by Emily and Mason. At home, an intellectually animated Jessup joins
Emily with a bottle of champagne and virtually explodes with concern for
Emily's well-being. His display of emotion is disturbingly pronounced, with
hugs and kisses for Emily and signs of remorse for all she has suffered because of him. Emily is worn out; her reaction is one of enduring stress mixed
with a sense of hopeless resignation. Just as Jessup builds up her hopes by
announcing that "my God, Emily, I don't know how to tell you this, I really
don't . . . ," he sidesteps a pronouncement of love to convey an intellectual
analysis of his experience.

[01:16:22]   A series of machinelike low rumblings emerge as Mason enters the apartment and questions Jessup about an ape that almost killed a man in the vicin-
ity of the isolation tank room. We see Jessup in the long, dark hallway in his
apartment, a dark negative image of the man at the end of the tunnel when he
first enters Emily's life at the faculty party earlier in the film.

We next see Emily reading Jessup's notes and transcripts from his earlier
[01:17:17]   tank experiments. The low, machinelike rumble returns, for the first time
indicating her own emerging existential crisis, caused by her realization that
Jessup may have indeed tapped into a primal state of being, thus challeng-
ing her core beliefs as both a wife and scientist. A final close-up reveals her
profound anxiousness regarding Jessup and her own assumptions regarding
the nature of existence.

[01:18:01]   A sudden exterior shot of Emily's house looming in front of the camera,
hauntedlike in its framing, is accompanied by the densely packed hallucination music from earlier scenes, driven by percussion instruments and filled

with *breathing* motif crescendos and decrescendos. The imagery is strikingly allegorical. Emily's house now appears haunted, as are her dreams. We see Emily sleeping. In her dream we see uncannily accurate imagery of simian-Jessup being chased by dogs. The scurrying string figures from Jessup's **[01:18:17]** transformation return only to ascend and wisp away as Emily awakes to the wind aggressively blowing through her curtains. She closes the windows and goes to check on her children, accompanied by the plodding bass figures from **[01:18:26]** the rhinoceros and elephant pens at the zoo.

As Emily gazes on the children in their room, we hear the child/piano **[01:18:39]** figure from simian-Jessup's scrutiny of the zoo's souvenir shop. The use of these series of motifs, especially the child/piano figure and the plodding bass line, seems to reinforce the common experience that Emily has just shared with Jessup and further underscore her own emerging doubts.

Emily phones Jessup, asking him to come over. She explodes with anxiety, declaring her terror at realizing that Jessup may in fact be undergoing some genetic, physiological transformation. This poses a direct challenge to all that she believes in regarding the natural world, an especially hard concept for a scientist rooted in logic and the laws of nature and physics. She becomes frantic, pacing the room, ranting, trying to convince Jessup not to repeat the experiment as planned. She explains that she loves him, which he acknowledges even as he continues to justify his intentions. An elegiac **[01:20:02]** string melody quietly wends its way into the scene, supported by other string lines as they enter and meander in an eerily complex polyphony, reflecting her sense of powerlessness.

Emily's conflict between her irrational love and belief in Jessup and her training in rational scientific thought drives her anxiety and her increasing loss of faith in both. Support for this is found in the telling exchange between the two. Jessup exclaims, "For God's sake, Emily, you're a scientist. You must know how I feel." Emily confides that "yes, I know how you feel." Just as his experiments are opening Jessup to the world of emotion and love, they are carving a path through Emily's belief in love as the supreme guiding force.

Emily hesitatingly asks Jessup to stay the night as the *love* theme returns **[01:20:25]** in the oboe. It is a tender moment; each has grown toward the other, accepting their weaknesses, needs, and passions. She curls into his lap as he gently caresses her hair, two lovers growing toward one.

Chapters 24, 25: Altered State Observed, Through the Primordial Void

The use of music as sound effect has been steadily growing in the field of general release film, especially so in sci-fi, horror, and war films. In *Altered States*, we find manifestation of this role of music in chapter 24, as Jessup prepares to undergo another tank/drug experiment designed to confirm his previous metamorphic experience. Across the cut into the current chapter, the *love* theme yields to a lugubrious, low bassoon line that meanders back and forth, **[01:20:50]** accompanying the camera as it wends it way through the bowels of the academic building where the tank resides. Light filters in from the institutionally functional overhead bulbs and grating above the hallway, lending a hazy, underworldly air to the basement in which we find cadavers being bussed around by anonymous scientists and orderlies in white coats. The camera is handheld, putting us into this netherworld, where we meet a nervous and harried Emily knocking on the locked door to the tank room.

The bassoon wanderings fade out as we are left staring at Emily, anxious and alone. Arthur lets her into the lab where Jessup is submitting to Mason's preexperiment medical checkup.

Jessup's closest friends and colleagues have now all gathered to both support him and themselves emotionally, as well as to assist in the science involved. As a wife as well as a scientist, Emily's own inner conflict between emotion and intellect is being brought to the forefront. The apprehension of all involved manifests itself in Emily's reactions to the preparations for the experiment, acknowledged by her pressured speech and the increased machine noise that underscores her delivery. She gazes at Jessup in the tank,

[01:21:56] his face inverted on the screen. The accompanying dronelike machine noises glissando up and down in a decidedly musical fashion, mimicking what has become the regression motif.

Emily's panic attack two hours into the experiment presages what is about to happen. The machine drone sound subtly underscores her concerns. Is it music or sound effect? Ultimately the question is irrelevant, except for the postproduction creators and editors and those who study the

[01:23:23] history of sound in film. Without warning, the soundtrack explodes with a series of sonic flashes closely followed by brass outbursts, string flourishes, and percussion rampages. There are no clearly defined musical motifs, just a series of short-lived riffs, scattered about the soundscape. The densely packed sonic events and their contrapuntal nature match the disconcerting images on the screen: a series of surreal and terrifying visual flashes, fragmented, distorted, and closely cropped.

The percussion figures continue underneath a cacophony of sound effects. The total visual and sonic effect is a frightening chaos with ill-defined form or function. We are experiencing what is happening to Jessup, as his genetic and molecular structure undergoes the transformation he has been hoping for. As Mason opens the tank door, sound effects induce the climax of the scene,

[01:23:59] a role traditionally reserved for music. Music and sound effects merge into a single sonic force as a whirring effect intensifies in loudness spiraling up-

[01:24:04] ward, climaxing at the moment Mason slams the tank door shut. A Ligeti-like mass of sound swirls as Mason wrestles Emily out of the lab. The spiral ends in a deafening silence as Mason returns to the room and closes the tank door.

[01:24:25] Emily recovers and approaches the lab door as a series of insectlike high harmonics emanate from the strings. She surveys the destruction and checks the pulses of her two now unconscious friends.

[01:25:13] A *breathing* motif in its most object form, a bulging, amorphous low sound that crescendos and decrescendos in a circadianlike pattern draws Emily

[01:25:19] toward the tank. It is followed by the *descending* motif, now more clearly defined as a full half-step downward movement. The *descending* motif accompanies Emily as she moves closer to the tank, the source of the sound.

In another context, the musical gesture might seem clichéd, but given the framework already developed around it, the gesture is organically appropriate. The tank itself remains intact. Emily observes the image of Jessup glowing through its walls, fluoroscopelike in its imagery, his heart rhythmically pulsing, rocking his body. A steady pulse from the tympani is the only clearly orchestral sound we hear.   **[01:25:33]**

Music and sound effects continue to overwhelm us sonically as the tank room begins to implode; water pipes beginning to buckle as steam bursts into the room under an almost supernatural blue-and-white light that shines like a sun from the tank that is central to the visual framing.

Jessup unleashes a primal scream unlike anything we have ever heard as we see his body transformed into an unfathomable shape, like a writhing co-coon in appearance. His screams literally shake the foundations of the room (and our notions of science), shattering windows and gauges, collapsing water pipes, bursting others. In the sequences that follow, the music continues in its primary role as sound effect, supporting the humminglike electrical sounds and rushing waters.

A low string pedal tone materializes as Emily attempts to enter the tank   **[01:27:03]**
room. Horn figures and other gestures grow in support as Emily enters the   **[01:27:18]**
vortex of water that has engulfed Jessup. In this moment, the music under-scores the dangers that Emily experiences as she risks her own life and jumps into the whirlpool to save Jessup. The gestures themselves pulse, the *breathing* motif resurfaced, while conveying a sonic equivalence of the vortex that is consuming Jessup.

We assume Jessup's perspective; he experiences no music, just sound effect. We are treated to a hallucinogenic series of images of cells dividing, red-tinged images traveling at high speed down darkened holes (are these his veins and arteries?). We see what appear to be undersea algae, followed by an egg with a noticeably beating heart within it.

Corigliano clearly states that he used no electronic instruments in his composing of the score, though score notations do indicate minor electronic manipulations of the acoustic sound, such as adding noticeable, unreal levels of reverberation at certain points. He makes no reference to the soundscape that we hear during this sequence. Nor does the score indicate a musical cue for this sequence. We must assume that it became one of the juicier moments for the sound designers to create.

We do hear the undeniable inklings of tonality centered around the pitch of E (the opening note of the piano as the film begins) at the moment that the cells burst toward the camera. As Emily's hands reach for and embrace   **[01:27:44]**
Jessup's granulated head, providing a steady and supportive force as he re-constitutes, a fully unadulterated tonal center emerges in the music.

The implications are clear. As the representative of existential love in the film, it is Emily who rescues Jessup, bringing him back from his primordial self. The music is that of a single female vocal holding a sustained note. In   **[01:29:25]**
short order, it is accompanied by another line, an octave below: Eddie and Emily have become totally and harmoniously one with each other. We are   **[01:29:30]**
treated to the most tonal and harmonious moment in the score to this point.

[01:29:33]   The pitch center is again E, but it is now supported with a series of fifths used to confirm the key.

A drenched Emily clutches the unconscious Jessup to her breast as a mother would clutch her child, the other universal symbol of love and life. We even

[01:29:45]   hear a momentary glimpse of a suspended fourth-scale degree resolving to a major third, one of the most reverential melodic and harmonic movements and a defining characteristic of Christian church music (the "Amen" heard at the end of most Christian psalm and prayer music).

Chapter 26: Ravished by Truth

[01:30:03]   Mason and Arthur have regained consciousness, and a strongly orchestrated *love* theme accompanies the sight of the unconscious Jessup, slung across Mason's shoulder, being carried into Emily's house. Russell may well be encouraging us to recognize that both Arthur and Mason share Jessup's love of science and commitment to finding the truth. In addition, we should not neglect the strength of the personal feelings between the three men. The scene change fills the screen with love and caring. Once Jessup is in the house, Emily removes his coat as Mason pulls his stethoscope from his medical bag.

[01:30:37]   The *love* theme is treated quite contrapuntally, cueing us to examine the range of Emily's conflicted emotions. In fact, the camera leaves Jessup and follows Emily as she moves from room to room, ruminating about the events of the evening and their consequences. The camera follows Emily from outside the building, spying on her private moments and thoughts through the passing windows. The underlying *love* theme serves as a sonic glue and revealer of emotions. The visual sequence gives Emily time to process the events. The distance afforded by the window view also allows us, as the viewer, a moment to more fully appreciate and absorb what has transpired. The gentle pacing of the sequence and the music also serves as a welcomed counterpoint to the intensity of the previous tank scene.

Chapter 27: Afterglow of a Breakthrough

Emily's delayed response to the events unfolds in a hysterical manner. She is overwhelmed by the immediate events, her foundation of rational thought having been shaken as well. Her speech, while rambling and slurred, is nonetheless a string of coherent thoughts reflecting her own loosening grip on

[01:32:52]   what is real and what is the meaning of love. In this case, the contrapuntal nature of the *love* theme reflects her inner conflict and is confirmed by her ranting monologue.

As Emily goes into shock and stares out the window, the *love* theme continues as we look down upon a now-awake Jessup, also gazing upward, out the window. Their visages are unworldly. Their eyes focus out beyond the camera, beyond the room that contains them, through the window toward the infinite. As Jessup stares, we hear Arthur offscreen, excitedly exclaiming that "we may have reached the point tonight where physical science breaks just down. We're in blue skies. Tonight is history and what are we going to do about it?" Both Emily and Jessup stare off into those same skies, presumably asking themselves that question. The scene continues as we see Arthur pouring himself a cup of coffee. The ever even-keeled technician begins to come apart, revealing that "I'm on fucking fire."

Chapter 28: Now Real to Eddie

A tenderly orchestrated variation on the *love* theme, played by the wood-winds, reemerges as we see a sleeping Emily and a now fully awake Jessup. Both of them are naked and exposed to a new world in which they will awake, absent any adornment. It is if their souls have been bared, all pretext shorn away.   [01:35:09]

Corigliano is wise in the subtlety of his variation. The *love* theme, in its own unembellished form, has appeared twice in the two previous scenes. A third rendition, while narratively appropriate, would have rendered it banal. The variation brings the psychological association of the theme to the scene, but with a fresh perspective. The melody is varied, as are elements of the counterpoint. But the orchestration and tonal sense, the two most recognizable aspects of the *love* theme, remain close to the original, surrounding us with the aura of the love between Emily and Jessup.

A ringing phone interrupts a sleeping Emily and brings a now-robed Jessup into her room. He proclaims to her how much he needs her and acknowledges with awe the fact that she saved him. It is apparent that he finally accepts that no ultimate truth exists, professing that "truth is what is transitory. It is human life that is real." It is perhaps Jessup's most emotionally honest moment to this point.

He confesses that he is being consumed by all that has transpired. Emily implores him to try to fight it, but as he leaves the room, he suggests that it may be too late.

Chapters 29, 30, 31: The Final Fight Back, "I Love You, Emily," End Credits

Jessup's final regression begins as soon as he leaves the room, declaring, "It's too late. I don't think I can get out of it anymore. I can't live with it. The pain is too great."

Though Jessup moves offscreen, we recognize that as the music begins, he is spontaneously undergoing yet another metamorphosis. The synergy of the   [01:37:27]
sliding musical motifs, polyphonic densities, and thick orchestration conjures up all the discordant and blisteringly paced images we have experienced from his previous regressions. Emily implores him to "defy it, Eddie." Accompanied   [01:37:36]
by wildly raging glissandos in all directions, she reaches out to him, determined to bring him back from the abyss into which he is again being pulled. Emily travels down the hall toward Jessup, down the tunnel he has traveled. We see her as Jessup sees her. As she reaches toward Jessup, she is also reaching toward us, furthering our association with Jessup, drawing us into his existential hell. He reaches for her, even as he is consumed by his transformation.

[01:37:45]   At the moment they touch, the glissandos climax and morph into a series of trills, mimicking their screams as they connect. Low brass blattings emphasize their excruciating agony. She is electrified, consumed by his horrible transformation. Jessup's existential crisis is now hers, though we have seen it welling up inside her for some time. Emily's previous dream, experiencing Jessup's transformation into the ape and his escape from the predatory dogs, reveals her increasing empathy and understanding of Jessup's search for meaning, even as she has begun to question her own scientific and rational response to what is essentially an irrational question and experience.

                   Music and sound effect once again merge as Jessup fights to regain rational control. Emily, meanwhile, is overwhelmed by the transformation she is
[01:38:02]   experiencing. Brass figures are generally submerged by the sound effects, but a crescendoing trumpet sustained note does emerge, accompanying Jessup as he pounds his fists against the walls and floors in attempts to force his reconstitution.

[01:38:27]   Rising string figures support his attempts to pull himself up, as do ascend-
[01:38:40]   ing clarinet gestures that increase in rapidity as Jessup accelerates his flailing. Jessup is eventually successful in his reconstitution, and the half-step clarinet figure yields to a solo violin repeating the figure. The upward-moving half-step figure can be considered as an inverse and slight expansion of the descending quarter-step dual piano figure that opens the film. The symmetry of this interpretation is quite facile, in that Jessup's initial submersion into the primordial unconscious life has been resolved by his now intentional assertion of his conscious life.

                   While Jessup has successfully reconstituted, Emily, unable to help herself, is
[01:38:58]   being consumed. The *love* theme emerges in the clarinet as we see a close-up shot of a determined and emotional Jessup moving down the hallway toward Emily (and the camera), reaching down to embrace her, pulling her back into the rational world. They momentarily dissolve into a display of pure energy as a blast of white light reveals the two lovers, now back in their original forms, nakedly embracing on the floor. The *love* theme blossoms with the most consonantly harmonized and lushly orchestrated music of the entire film. The violins
[01:39:16]   build the initial *love* theme into a B section, soaring up to their higher notes as the horns begin a gently supporting counterline, very much a traditional orchestration for a scene consumed with love realized and accepted. Jessup's search, discovery, and realization are complete. The violins momentarily pause their
[01:39:30]   melody, allowing Jessup to finally announce, "I love you, Emily." The film fades to black as they embrace and the lower strings accept the melody and its repetition. The credit music flows from this lush enunciation of love, confirming the answer to the film's question.

SUMMARY

Although John Corigliano's score to *Altered States* suffered many of the inevitable edits and rearrangements that are an inherent aspect of the film-scoring process, his underlying structural components survive intact. The *breathing* motif finds manifestation in many musical forms, vibratos, tremolos, trills, and paired crescendos and decrescendos. He defines the notion of reversion or descending to a more primal existence through a series of figures that move from high to low, in the form of downward glissandos, quarter-step piano motifs, and half-step motifs. His *love* theme, though unusual and dissonant in its contour, nonetheless contains the warmth and lyricism we have come to expect from a romantic love story. But despite his unusual compositional and orchestrational palettes, Corigliano does, in fact, support the drama and story in traditional ways, using his own language within the syntax established by the film composer greats who have come before him.

NOTES

1. Ken Russell, *A British Picture: An Autobiography* (London: Heinemann, 1989), 170.

2. Russell, *A British Picture: An Autobiography*, 171.

3. "The Gospel According to John Corigliano," NewMusicBox.org. http://www.newmusicbox.org/articles/the-gospel-according-to-john-at-home-with-john-corigliano-john-corigliano/ (accessed May 26, 2009).

4. John Corigliano, guest lecture to music composition students, School of Music, Ithaca College, Ithaca, New York, 1989.

5. Corigliano, Ithaca College guest lecture.

6. Peter Rothbart, "John Corigliano's Film Score for *Altered States*: An Analysis of Selected Cues," DMA dissertation, Cleveland Institute of Music, 1991, 2.

7. Corigliano, Ithaca College guest lecture.

Conclusions and Final Words

In *West Side Story*, we see how a well-conceived and crafted leitmotif can reflect the archetypal conflict in a film. We also experience the aural and visual realms in their most synergistic relationship as the music closely coordinates and synchronizes with all of the visual elements. In *Psycho*, we experience a series of recognizable leitmotifs that help define and illuminate the psychological and allegorical story that is being told. In *Empire of the Sun*, music is only one element in the total context of sound design, serving as one of several aural components that support and emphasize both the plot and the psychological engines that drive Jamie/Jim and enable him to survive. In *American Beauty*, the aural focus is on setting the tone of the film. We experience the leitmotif as it comes to symbolize more ephemeral ideas such as abstract personality traits and moral statements rather than being associated with any one person or situation. At the same time, we see how source music and lyric can integrate into the film's sonic texture and reflect the drama and various underlying emotions and psychologies at work. Finally, in *Altered States*, we hear leitmotif manifested musically in a nontraditional manner, with more emphasis on musical color, texture, and the use of dissonance rather than melody. We hear a kind of musical onomatopoeia that reflects the characters' emotional and physiological transformation.

Along the way, we've seen and heard how music can play a vital role in moving the plot forward while underscoring unseen motifs, actions, and psychological conditions. We now understand how a composer can use our own society-influenced preconceived constructs to put the drama in a temporal and physical context. At the same time, we experience how the careful and constructive placement of music by a creative composer and skilled director can soften the edges of edits and intensify drama.

All this is not to say that music cannot be used in other ways. Experimental films and videos, multimedia and intermedia productions swell the potential uses of music with visual materials, expanding the boundaries that have developed over the years in the more traditional and commercial Hollywood movie. Cartoons, documentaries, television, radio, and Internet commercials and both professional and amateur online videos, while relying to some extent on conventional uses of music, are no longer limited by the historical trail blazed by the first Hollywood film composers. Whether people are forging these new directions with little more than a well-tamed computer and a passing knowledge of musical syntax and structure or a trained and skilled musical intellect married to an understanding of drama, psychology, historical precedence, and a knowledgeable musical palette is a matter for philosophical, sociological, and economic discussion, one beyond the scope of this book. If these new pioneers can use this book to further their knowledge and appreciation for the role of music in film while developing their craft and new forms of expression, then I have made my contribution toward an appreciation of our aural world.

FINAL WORDS

Let me reiterate that observation is of paramount importance in raising one's awareness, understanding, and appreciation of a work of art. As you become more consciously aware of the music, sound, dialog, editing, lighting, costuming, set design, and all of the other elements that go into making a film, you can begin to understand the personal expression, intent, and message of those who created it.

By describing what is happening aurally and revealing its relationship to the visual image and all of its elements, as well as the screenplay, I hope to raise an awareness of all of these elements so that filmgoing becomes a profoundly insightful event even as it retains its value as entertainment. Only after the act of observation, accomplished through the process of cognitively describing all of the elements brought to the creative table, can one then begin to fully appreciate the art of film. I do hope that what I have written deepens not only your filmgoing experiences but also your perspective and approach to your *own* life's endeavors, long after the final credits have rolled.

This is what I hope to accomplish with this book.

Glossary

This glossary is designed to facilitate the fundamental understanding of musical and filmic terms found in this book. It is not intended to be a comprehensive glossary.

A cappella   Sung without any musical instruments.

Aleatoric process   A method of composing in which the composer sets up processes or limitations for the performers to follow. The performer is then free to improvise within those processes or limitations. The results are sonic textures that are not usually available to the more traditional composer.

American Beauty rose   A type of deep pink hybrid rose most popular in the United States in the 1920s.

Arpeggio   A chord whose individual note entrances are rhythmically staggered. Usually played lowest to highest or vice versa.

Atonal   The opposite of tonal; a method of organizing the notes of a melody and harmony such that they have no "pull" or gravity or sense of movement toward the tonic or *root* note.

Bach, Johann Sebastian   Famous eighteenth-century composer known for his mastery of contrapuntal writing in both secular and religious works. His works are considered the culmination of the Baroque era in music.

Bebop   A style of jazz (embodied in the music of Charlie Parker and Dizzy Gillespie), characterized by an emphasis on virtuosic soloing, nonregular phrasing (especially in the drums), jagged melodic lines, breakneck tempos, and the use of extended and alternative harmonies.

Berlioz, Hector   Mid-nineteenth-century composer known for his innovative orchestration and development of the idée fixe.

Block chords   A progression of chords in which all of the notes of each chord sound simultaneously.

Bossa nova   A Brazilian popular music style, derived from the samba, but with less emphasis on percussion and influenced by the cool jazz of the 1950s.

Cadence   A musical resting point, a kind of period at the end of a musical sentence or phrase. Composers control cadences through changes in harmony, melody, texture, and rhythm.

Canon   A polyphonic form of music in which each entering musical line is an exact or almost exact copy of the original line. "Row, Row, Row Your Boat" is an example of a canon.

Cha-cha   A form of popular Latin-Cuban dance developed in the 1950s.

Charm song   A genre of song in musical theater that serves to describe a character's personality or state of mind, rather than move the drama along.

Chopin, Frederic   Polish composer from the Romantic era, primarily known for his piano writing, which was characterized by its romantic expressiveness, technical agility, and subtle nuance of style.

Chorale   A style of German Protestant hymn characterized by straightforward rhythms, a mixture of homophony and polyphony, a vernacular text, and strophic form.

Chromatic   A scale or passage that includes many pitches outside of the tonal key. In most cases, the greater the chromaticism (the more nontonal scale notes included), the greater the dissonance of the music.

Church chorale   A religious hymn characterized by block chords and a homophonic texture.

Cinematography   The art of controlling lighting, camera movements, lens and camera choices, and the actual image capture in film. The director of cinematography is often considered to be as important as the director.

Close-up shot   A camera perspective that closely frames an object, face, or other part of the body.

Composite score   A film score consisting of individual music cues that are not related to each other in any close way. The result is an eclectic mix of music that can serve to clearly delineate each scene. Often contains contemporary popular songs.

Compound duple meter   A repeating musical beat pattern consisting of two strong beats, each subdivided by three weaker beats.

Consonant   Having a relatively stable harmonic or melodic sound. Often considered to be the opposite of dissonant, but actually they exist on a continuum in relation to each other.

Contrapuntal   Characterized by counterpoint; polyphonic in nature.

Cool jazz   A style of jazz characterized by more lyrical and longer melodic lines than its predecessor bebop, medium tempos, use of nontraditional jazz instruments such as flute, electric guitar, muted brass, vibraphones, and a generally softer-edged sound than bebop.

Countermelody   A secondary melody that is subordinate to a primary melody, but within a homophonic texture.

Counterpoint   Two or more melodies sounding simultaneously, but of equal importance.

Counterpointing the drama   Using music that at first glance seems to be the opposite of the image onscreen. Counterpointing the drama is often an effective way to elicit a stronger emotion from the audience than if the composer had written music that accompanies the drama. Example: slow, orchestral music underscoring a battle sequence can elicit the sense of futility and loss in the audience.

Crescendo   A gradual increase in volume.

Cutaway shot   A film editing technique that disrupts the flow of time by inserting another image, often a reaction shot, before returning to the original, continuous image.

Debussy, Claude   French composer from the late nineteenth and early twentieth century, credited with being one of the founders of Impressionism, a musical movement characterized by the use of nontraditional (at the time) scales such as the whole-tone and diminished scales, static harmonies and melodies that did not move toward traditional cadences, and a reliance on orchestration to achieve unusual musical colors. The movement is philosophically related to the Impressionism art movement of the same time period.

Decrescendo   A gradual decrease in volume.

Diegetic music   Music that onscreen characters can hear. Music that is part of the scene. Example: a band playing in a nightclub or bar onscreen.

Diminished chord   A chord consisting of three stacked minor thirds that can be used to evoke a sense of tense expectation.

Dissonant   Having a relatively unstable harmonic or melodic sound. Often considered to be the opposite of consonant, but actually they exist on a continuum in relation to each other.

Dolly shot   Also called a tracking shot, it is a moving sequence in which the camera is placed on tracks and smoothly follows a subject.

Drone note   A steadily held, long note, usually heard underneath or above a musical texture.

Duple   A repeating musical beat pattern consisting of one strong beat followed by one weaker beat.

Eroica Symphony   Beethoven's Third Symphony, originally dedicated to Napoleon, but subsequently rescinded and retitled when Napoleon became emperor.

Establishing shot   A camera perspective designed to establish the place and perhaps time of a sequence or entire film.

Film score   A series of musical cues written especially for a film. The term excludes pre-existing music. This differs from the term *soundtrack*, which usually indicates a selection of significant cues from a film, which have been recorded and released in an audio format, such as CD, MP3, etc.

Freedom from Fear   One of Norman Rockwell's most famous oil paintings, it was part of a series called Four Freedoms, based on a State of the Union speech by President Franklin D. Roosevelt, and used as a war poster during World War II.

Fugue   A compositional structure in which the melodic theme is subsequently stated in all of the parts and separated by episodes of freely composed counterpoint. All fugues are contrapuntal in nature due to the constant repetition and entrances of the melody by the different parts.

Gilbert and Sullivan   English libretto and composer team known for creating lighthearted comic opera in the late nineteenth century.

Glissando   A smooth, steady slide in pitch up or down.

Gregorian chant   Roman Catholic Church religious vocal chant from the Middle Ages. Melodies were uncomplicated and usually contained within a small range.

"Gretchen am Spinnrade"   A German song called *lied*, composed by Franz Schubert in which the piano accompaniment mimics a spinning wheel. The wheel momentarily stops as Gretchen's breath is taken away by the memory of a kiss.

Half-step   The smallest distance in pitch in most Western music. An example would be moving from a black note on a keyboard to the nearest adjacent white note.

Hitchcock chord   A minor chord with an added major third interval on top. Often called a minor-major seventh chord. In general, the chord will sound slightly dissonant and unsettling.

Homophony   Melody with accompaniment.

Idée fixe   A musical idea with extramusical significance that returns, usually intact and only minimally altered, throughout a larger work.

Imitative counterpoint   Many melodies or musical lines played simultaneously with each line being independent and equal to the others. Certain recognizable musical motifs will be repeated by each of the parts in imitation of the other parts.

Indian raga   A form of subcontinent Indian music characterized by the use of specific musical modes or scales. Indian music was briefly popular in American culture in the 1960s.

Integrated musical   A term used to describe a musical show in which all of the elements contribute seamlessly to the natural flow of time in the narrative.

International Settlement (also called European Settlement), Shanghai   A geographic area and administrative organization in Shanghai from the late 1800s to the end of World

War II, which was administered by the English and Americans, to look after their Chinese business interests.

Interval   The relationship or "distance" between two pitches. In Western music, intervals are constructed on the basis of what is called a half-step. For example, two adjacent notes on a piano is the interval of a half-step, a minor third consists of three half steps, a major third contains four half-steps.

Jump cut   A film editing technique in which the continuous flow of the image is disrupted by the removal of some frames, causing the image to appear to jump. Its purpose is to deliberately interfere with the film's continuity with the intention of startling the audience.

Legato   A style of music playing in which all of the notes are played as if they were attached, with no space or silence between them.

Leitmotif, also leitmotiv   A recognizable musical gesture, usually a melody associated with a person, place, object, action, or psychological state.

Ligeti, György   Twentieth-century Romanian-Austrian composer known for his avant-garde composing. Many of his most famous works were exploited in films such as *2001: A Space Odyssey*, *Eyes Wide Shut*, and *The Shining*.

Locked picture or film   A term used to describe a film in which all of the elements have been edited and synchronized together into its final form.

Long shot   A camera perspective designed to capture the whole image of a person or object as well as its surroundings to give context.

Mambo   A popular Afro-Cuban dance form developed in the 1940s.

Match cut   A film editing technique in which each actor's perspective is visually aligned to the other across the edit point to give a sense of continuity and communication.

Mazurka   Polish folk dance form. Many composers such as Chopin adapted the form for classical music.

Measured glissando   A steady, steplike rise or descent in pitch using the scales of Western music.

Medium shot   A camera perspective that yields an image farther away than a close-up, yet closer than a long shot. There is no clear demarcation point between a long and medium shot.

Melismatic   A form of singing in which many notes are sung using just one syllable.

Melodic gesture   A short musical idea that is complete by itself. It does not need development or explanation.

Mickeymousing   A process of music rhythmically or melodically matching some onscreen action, usually in a comedic way. A musical analog to a visual action, often used in cartoons. Example: a glissando downward as a character falls down a flight of steps.

Minimalism   A musical genre that evolved in the mid to late twentieth century, characterized by relatively simple repeating melodic and/or harmonic patterns that slowly evolve over a period of time. Minimalism is based upon the idea that maximum effect can be brought about by minimal change.

Mise-en-scène   In film and theater, an amalgamation of all the visual elements that appear within the frame, including set design, costuming, lighting, camera perspective, props, and the actors, and anything that is visually noticed. It is a type of visual gestalt.

Mode/Modal   A collection of pitches or notes related to each other by their sense of gravitation toward a final home or root note.

Modulation   The process of changing from one key to another in tonal music.

Monophony   One single melody with no accompaniment.

Monothematic score   A musical score that uses a single melody as its primary building block for the entire duration of the work.

Motion sonority   Process defined by John Corigliano in which blocks of sound retain a sense of vibrancy within themselves. This is a stochastic process in which rhythmic, melodic, or harmonic boundaries are established by the composer. The performer is free to create within those boundaries.

Musical pyramid   Musical process by which instruments build a chord by staggering their entrances. The result is a sense of musical *piling on*.

Nondiegetic music   Music that characters in a film cannot hear; music designed for the audience only.

Octave   The musical interval between one note and either half or double its frequency. One of the two most consonant intervals in music and nature.

Orchestration   A compositional process by which combinations of instrumental sounds are organized to yield different musical colors.

Organum   A medieval form of polyphony.

Ostinato   A rhythmically and melodically repeating figure that gives a sense of movement forward.

Overture   A musical composition used as an introduction to a dramatic work. In musical theater, the overture usually encapsulates the major musical themes or songs to be heard later.

Patter song   A quick-paced song, characterized by rapidly elicited humorous lyrics. Made popular by Gilbert and Sullivan.

Pedal tone or note   A low- or high-pitched extensively sustained note, usually under or above a moving harmony and melody. In film music, often used to create a sense of building tension or anticipation.

Phrase   A musical structure roughly equivalent to a phrase in language. A musical unit, which makes up a larger form when grouped with other phrases. A phrase can be thought of as a self-contained musical unit consisting of a series of notes, harmonies, and rhythms that sound logical and relatively complete by themselves. We tend to hear phrases in groups or multiples of two. An irregular phrase is one that does not follow the pattern of phrases established within a piece of music. Composers will often use irregular phrases to heighten expectation and to create a sense of tension.

Pierrot   Famous European clown character in drama and opera who is characterized by a sad but innocent look. Often portrayed as being unaware of the world surrounding him.

Pizzicato   Plucked string sound.

Polyphony   Two or more independent melodic or rhythmic lines sounding simultaneously and of equal importance. Same as counterpoint.

Reaction shot   An editing technique that quickly cuts away from one image to another of someone reacting to the action or dialog.

Recitative   A style of singing or performing music that mimics the rhythmic and pitch patterns of speech, avoiding the repetition of text or syllables and extreme leaps in melodic line. Often used in dramatic musical works such as opera.

Red herring   Compositional technique of building tension toward a climax, but the climax deceptively never occurs. Creates a false sense of expectation.

Rhietta style   A style of double-reed instrument playing in which the performer takes both blades of the reed entirely into their mouth to play. The result is a nasally, primal sound.

"Ride of the Valkyries"   Orchestral work from Richard Wagner's opera, *Die Walküre*. Made famous in film in the helicopter scene from the movie *Apocalypse Now*.

Rockwell, Norman   Twentieth-century American painter and illustrator known for his illustrations of typical American people in uniquely American settings. He provided the cover artwork for the *Saturday Evening Post* for decades.

Rubato   A temporary slowing or accelerating of the tempo, used to give more expression to the music.

Rumba   An Afro-Cuban musical form.

Screenplay   The written book used to make a film, which includes all dialog, descriptions of action, and sometimes camera instructions.

Sforzando   Musical notation telling the performer to play one note suddenly loud then immediately soft.

Shakuhachi flute   A traditional Japanese bamboo flute. Very melodic but primal sound, incorporating some of the performer's breath sounds into the overall timbre.

Shout chorus   In jazz, the final chorus of a song in which either singers shout rather than sing the lyrics, or in instrumental forms, all the instruments play together one last time.

Soundtrack   Usually used to describe the commercially released LP, CD, or download compilation of the major musical cues (including preexisting songs) from a film. Also used to describe the complete audio from a film, including dialog, effects, and music.

Source music   Term used by most people in the film industry to describe music that the on-screen characters can hear. See diegetic music.

Speech-rhythm   A deliberately rhythmic pattern built into the dialog or delivery between several characters. Accelerating the speech-rhythm in a scene will heighten tension.

Spotting session   A film preproduction meeting in which the specific audio cues for the film are discussed and determined by contributors, such as the director, music, sound effects, and dialog editors. Others may be included in the meeting as well.

Staccato   A style of performance in which all the notes are played short, leaving space between each note.

Tabla   A pair of drums from North India, part of the defining sound of North Indian music.

Timbre   The specific quality or nature of a sound, made up of its unique components of fundamental tones, overtones, volume envelopes, and resonance.

Tonality   A hierarchical musical system in which all notes relate to a center, home, or tonic note as the point of repose. The result is a sense of musical gravity, with all combinations of notes leading to the feeling of resolution on the tonic.

Tone   The psychological mood or atmosphere of a film or piece of music.

Tone cluster   A densely packed group of pitches played simultaneously that defy traditional chord characterization.

Tracking shot   In film, a shot in which the camera is mounted on a wheeled device, often on railroadlike tracks, to give a smooth flow to the action.

Tremolo   Musical technique consisting of one rapid and rhythmically repeating pitch. Also refers to a trill using a musical interval larger than a major second.

Trill   Musical technique consisting of a rapid and rhythmic alternation between two pitches of a major second or less.

Triple   A repeating musical beat pattern consisting of one strong beat followed by two weaker beats.

Tritone   A specific musical interval consisting of six half-steps. It is unique in that it has an extremely dissonant, unresolved, and ambiguous sound to it.

Vamp   A musical figure that continually repeats until a cue to continue with the rest of the music is given by the leader.

Wagner, Richard   Mid-nineteenth-century German composer most known for his grandiose operas based upon myths and legends. His works are characterized by contrapuntal writing, the use of leitmotifs, innovative orchestration for large ensembles, and an extreme use of dissonance. In many ways, his composing and use of leitmotifs in his operas served as the model for early and even contemporary film music composers.

Bibliography

Altman, Rick, ed. *Sound Theory Sound Practice*. New York: Routledge, 1992.

Arms, Gary, and Thomas Riley. "The 'Big-Little' Film and Philosophy: Two Takes on Spielbergian Innocence." In *Steven Spielberg and Philosophy: We're Gonna Need a Bigger Book*, edited by Dean A. Kowalski, 7–37. Lexington, KY: University Press of Kentucky, 2008.

Ball, Alan. *American Beauty: The Shooting Script*. New York: Newmarket Press, 1999.

Ballard, J. G. *Empire of the Sun*. New York: Simon & Schuster, 1984.

Banfield, Stephen. *Sondheim's Broadway Musicals*. Ann Arbor: University of Michigan Press, 1993.

Bartholomew, David. "The Filming of *Altered States*." *Cinefantastique* 11, no. 2 (1981): 16–36.

Bazelon, Irwin. *Knowing the Score: Notes on Film Music*. New York: Van Nostrand Reinhold, 1975.

Beck, Jay, and Tony Grajeda, eds. *Lowering the Boom, Critical Studies in Film Sound*. Champaign, IL: University of Illinois Press, 2008.

Bellour, Raymond. "The Unattainable Text." *Screen* 16, no. 3 (1975): 19–28.

Bernstein, Leonard. *Findings*. New York: Anchor Books, 1982.

———. composer. *West Side Story*, lyricist Stephen Sondheim, director Robert Wise, choreographer Jerome Robbins. 1961. Special Edition, MGM. DVD 4004282.

———. *West Side Story*. Milwaukee, WI: G. Schirmer, Inc., 1959.

———. *West Side Story*. Original Broadway Score. Leonard Bernstein Folio. Library of Congress, Washington, DC.

———. *West Side Story*. Original Movie Score. Columbia University Rare Books and Manuscripts, New York.

———. *West Side Story* Folio. Unpublished notes. Library of Congress, Washington, DC.

Block, Geoffrey. *Enchanted Evenings: The Broadway Musical from* Show Boat *to Sondheim*. New York: Oxford University Press, 1997.

Bordwell, David. *Narration in the Fiction Film*. Madison, WI: University of Wisconsin Press, 1985.

Brown, Royal S. *Overtones and Undertones: Reading Film Music*. Berkeley: University of California Press, 1994.

Bruce, Graham. *Bernard Herrmann: Film Music and Film Narrative*. Ann Arbor, MI: UMI Research Press, 1985.

Burton, Humphrey. *Leonard Bernstein*. London: Faber and Faber, 1994.

Burton, William Westbrook. *Conversations about Bernstein*. New York: Oxford University Press, 1995.

Cahn, Sammy, and Jimmy Van Heusen. "Bobby Darin Lyrics—Call Me Irresponsible." Oldie Lyrics .com. http://www.oldielyrics.com/lyrics/bobby_darin/call_me_irresponsible.html (accessed November 19, 2006).

Chachere, Richard. *Jungian Reflections on Literary and Film Classics: Opus I* American Beauty. Lafayette, LA: Cypremort Point Press, 2003.

Chayefsky, Paddy. *Altered States.* New York: Harper & Row, 1978.

Clarke, James. *The Pocket Essential Steven Spielberg.* Harpenden, UK: Pocket Essentials, 2004.

"Color, Melody and . . . Perfume: An Interview with Composer Thomas Newman." *Motion Picture Editors Guild Newsletter* 17, no. 1 (January–February 1996): n.p. http://www.editorsguild.com/v2/magazine/Newsletter/newman.html (accessed May 28, 2009).

Corigliano, John, composer. *Altered States*, director Ken Russell. 1980. Warner Brothers. DVD 11076.

———. *Altered States.* RCA Victor, 1981. CD 3983-2-RG.

———. *Altered States.* Personal Manuscript Copy. Original Musical Score.

———. "The Gospel according to John Corigliano." NewMusicBox.org. http://www.newmusicbox.org/articles/the-gospel-according-to-john-at-home-with-john-corigliano-john-corigliano/ (accessed May 26, 2009).

———. Guest lecture to composition students. Ithaca College School of Music, 1989.

———. *Three Hallucinations for Orchestra.* New York: G. Schirmer, 1986.

"Cue Sheet: *Psycho*." Bernard Herrmann Society. http://www.uib.no/herrmann/db/cuesheets/film_psycho.html (accessed April 15, 2004).

Darby, William, and Jack Du Bois. *American Film Music.* Jefferson, NC: McFarland & Company, Inc., 1990.

Dramatists Guild. "Landmark Symposium: *West Side Story*." *Dramatists Guild Quarterly* 7, no. 3 (Autumn 1985): 11–25.

Dylan, Bob. "Track: 'All along the Watchtower.'" Reason to Rock.com. www.reasontorock.com/tracks/watchtower.html (accessed September 12, 2006).

Eisler, Hanns. *Composing for the Films.* New York: Oxford University Press, 1947.

Eugene, Jean-Pierre. *La Musique dans les Films d'Alfred Hitchcock.* Paris: Dreamland, 2000.

Evans, Mark. *Soundtrack: The Music of the Movies.* New York: Da Capo Press, Inc., 1979.

Flinn, Caryl. *Strains of Utopia: Gender, Nostalgia, and Hollywood Film Music.* Princeton, NJ: Princeton University Press, 1992.

Friedman, Lester D. *Citizen Spielberg.* Urbana, IL: University of Illinois Press, 2006.

Garebian, Keith. *The Making of* West Side Story. Oakville, Ontario, Canada: Mosaic Press, 1998.

Gorbman, Claudia. *Unheard Melodies: Narrative Film Music.* Bloomington, IN: Indiana University Press, 1987.

Gradenwitz, Peter. *Leonard Bernstein: The Infinite Variety of a Musician.* Leamington Spa, UK: Oswald Wolff Books, 1987.

Grant, Mark N. *The Rise and Fall of the Broadway Musical.* Boston: Northeastern University Press, 2004.

Hanke, Ken. *Ken Russell's Films.* Metuchen, NJ: Scarecrow Press, 1984.

Herrmann, Bernard, composer. *Psycho*, director Alfred Hitchcock. 1960. Universal. DVD 20251.

Hitchcock, Alfred. Folder 589. Unpublished notes. Alfred Hitchcock Collection. Margaret Herrick Library, Academy of Motion Picture Arts and Sciences, Los Angeles. 1959.

———.Folder 576. Unpublished notes. Alfred Hitchcock Collection. Margaret Herrick Library, Academy of Motion Picture Arts and Sciences, Los Angeles. 1959.

Horowitz, Mark Eden. *Sondheim on Music: Minor Details and Major Decisions.* Lanham, MD: The Scarecrow Press, 2003.

Jowitt, Deborah. *Jerome Robbins: His Life, His Theater, His Dance.* New York: Simon and Schuster, 2004.

Kalinak, Kathryn. *Settling the Score: Music and the Classical Hollywood Film.* Madison, WI: University of Wisconsin Press, 1992.

Kassabian, Anahid. *Hearing Film: Tracking Identifications in Contemporary Hollywood Film Music.* New York: Routledge, 2001.

———. Personal correspondence with author.

Katsiavriades, Kryss, and Talaat Qureshi. "Cliches and Expressions Origins." BusinessBalls.com. http://www.businessballs.com/clichesorigins.htm (accessed July 2, 2006).

Kislan, Richard. *The Musical: A Look at the American Musical Theater*. Englewood Cliffs, NJ: Prentice Hall, 1980.

Kolker, Robert Phillip. *Alfred Hitchcock's* Psycho*: A Casebook*. Oxford: Oxford University Press, 2004.

Kravitz, Lenny. "American Woman." Sing365.com. http://www.sing365.com/music/lyric.nsf/American-Woman-lyrics-Lenny-Kravitz/E3CA7440B256682F482568C800325C70 (accessed August 2, 2006).

Larson, Randall D. *Musique Fantastique: A Survey of Film Music in the Fantastic Cinema*. Metuchen, NJ: Scarecrow Press, 1985.

Laurents, Arthur. *Original Story: A Memoir of Broadway and Hollywood*. New York: Knopf, 2000.

Lawrence, Greg. *Dance with Demons: The Life of Jerome Robbins*. New York: G. P. Putnam, 2001.

Lennon, John, and Paul McCartney. "Because." SongLyrics.com. http://www.songlyrics.com/the-beatles/because-lennonmccartney-lyrics/ (accessed August 23, 2012).

Levitin, Daniel J. *This Is Your Brain on Music: The Science of a Human Obsession*. New York: Penguin Group, 2006.

LoBrutto, Vincent. *Sound-on-Film, Interviews with Creators of Film Sound*. Westport, CT: Praeger Publishers, 1994.

McBride, Joseph. *Steven Spielberg: A Biography*. New York: Simon & Schuster, 1997.

Morris, Nigel. *The Cinema of Steven Spielberg*. London: Wallflower Press, 2007.

Newman, Thomas, composer. *American Beauty*, director Sam Mendes. 1999. DreamWorks. DVD 85382.

———. *American Beauty*. DreamWorks, 1999. CD.

———. *American Beauty*. Original Score. DreamWorks, LLC, Los Angeles. 1999.

———. "ScoreKeeper Chats with Composer Thomas Newman!!" Interview by ScoreKeeper. Ain'tItCoolNews.com. Harry Knowles, 2008. http://www.aintitcool.com/node/38356 (accessed May 28, 2009).

Palmer, Christopher. *The Composer in Hollywood*. London: Marion Boyars, 1990.

Peyser, Joan. *Bernstein: A Biography*. New York: Beech Tree Books, 1987.

Prendergast, Roy M. *Film Music: A Neglected Art*. New York: W. W. Norton & Co., 1992.

Reay, Pauline. *Music in Film: Soundtrack and Synergy*. London: Wallflower, 2004.

Rebello, Stephen. *Alfred Hitchcock and the Making of* Psycho. New York: Harper Perennial, 1990.

Rothbart, Peter. "John Corigliano's Film Score for *Altered States*: An Analysis of Selected Cues." Dissertation, Cleveland Institute of Music, 1991.

Rucas, Derek P. "An Analysis of How *American Beauty* Relates to the Melodramatic Genre." Angelfire.com. http://www.angelfire.com/film/articles/american_beauty.htm (accessed August 21, 2008).

Russell, Ken. *A British Picture: An Autobiography*. London: Heinemann, 1989.

Sabaneev, Leonid. *Music for the Films*. Translated by S. W. Spring. New York: Arno Press, 1978.

Sanello, Frank. *Spielberg: The Man, the Movies, the Mythology*. Dallas: Taylor Publishing Company, 1996.

Schelle, Michael. *The Score: Interviews with Film Composers*. Los Angeles: Silman-James Press, 1999.

Secrest, Meryle. *Stephen Sondheim: A Life*. New York: Alfred A. Knopf, 1998.

Silet, Charles L. P. *The Films of Steven Spielberg: Critical Essays*. Lanham, MD: Scarecrow Press, 2002.

Smith, Steven C. *A Heart at Fire's Center: The Life and Music of Bernard Herrmann*. Berkeley: University of California Press, 1991.

Spoto, Donald. *The Art of Alfred Hitchcock: Fifty Years of His Motion Pictures*. New York: Hopkinson and Blake, 1976.

———. *The Dark Side of Genius: The Life of Alfred Hitchcock*. Boston: Little, Brown, 1983.

Steiner, Fred. "Herrmann's 'Black-and-White' Music for Hitchcock's *Psycho*: Part I." *Film Music Notebook* 1, no. 1 (1974): 68–88. Reprinted in *Film Music Notebooks*, edited by Elmer Bernstein. Sherman Oaks, CA: The Film Music Society, 2004.

———. "Herrmann's 'Black-and-White' Music for Hitchcock's *Psycho*: Part II." *Film Music Notebook* 1, no. 2 (1974): 30–38. Reprinted in *Film Music Notebooks*, edited by Elmer Bernstein. Sherman Oaks, CA: The Film Music Society, 2004.

Steiner, Max. "Music Director." In *The Real Tinsel*, edited by Bernard Rosenberg and Harry Silverstein. London: Macmillan, 1970, 387–98.

Sullivan, Jack. *Hitchcock's Music*. New Haven: Yale University Press, 2006.

Swayne, Steve. *How Sondheim Found His Sound*. Ann Arbor, MI: University of Michigan Press, 2005.

"Thomas Newman (I)." IMDB.com. http://www.imdb.com/name/nm0002353/ (accessed August 23, 2012).

Thomas, Tony. *Film Score: The Art and Craft of Movie Music*. Burbank, CA: Riverwood Press, 1991.

Townshend, Pete. "The Seeker." Sing365.com. http://www.sing365.com/music/lyric.nsf/The-Seeker-lyrics-The-Who/972EC09BD0844A204825697A001256EF (accessed August 23, 2008).

Traditional. "Suo Gan." Musical composition.

Truffaut, Francois. *Hitchcock: The Definitive Study of Alfred Hitchcock by Francois Truffaut*. With the Collaboration of Helen G. Scott. New York: Simon and Schuster, 1967.

———. *Hitchcock/Truffaut*. New York: Simon & Schuster, 1995.

Williams, John. *Empire of the Sun*. Warner Bros., 1987. CD.

———. composer. *Empire of the Sun*, director Steven Spielberg. 1987. Warner Bros. DVD.

———. *Empire of the Sun*. Original Score. JoAnn Kane Music, Los Angeles.

Wood, Robin. *Hitchcock's Films Revisited*. New York: Columbia University Press, 1989.

Young, Neil. "Don't Let It Bring You Down." AZLyrics.com. http://www.azlyrics.com/lyrics/neilyoung/dontletitbringyoudown.html (accessed July 27, 2008).

Zador, Leslie T., and Gregory Rose. "A Conversation with Bernard Herrmann." In *Film Music I*, edited by Clifford McCarty, 209–53. New York: Garland Publishing, Inc., 1989.

Index

About the Author

Peter Rothbart maintains an inhumanely active schedule as a composer, performer, writer, artist, and teacher. He is a professor of music and director of the Electroacoustic Music Studios at the Ithaca College School of Music in Ithaca, New York.

With undergraduate music performance degrees from both the Eastman School of Music and University of Massachusetts, a master of music degree in woodwinds from Ithaca College, and a doctorate in composition from the Cleveland Institute of Music, he is active as a composer in both the acoustic and electroacoustic worlds. He has three Carnegie Hall premieres to his credit and has written numerous film scores as well as music for theater. His classical works have been published by the Lorenz Corporation, Brixton Publications, Seesaw Music Publishers, and the International Trumpet Guild.

Working as a music columnist for ten years, he has authored over three hundred published articles for *DownBeat*, the *Cleveland Plain Dealer*, the *Ithaca Journal*, and other magazines. His artwork, based upon the magnetic patterns of sound on analog and digital media, has been featured on magazine covers as well as in new media art shows in Europe and the United States. He plays a mean but stylish bassoon and contrabassoon with the Binghamton Philharmonic and other orchestras and is in demand as a rhythm-and-blues sax player. In his spare time he sleeps, kisses his wife, Linda, scratches the dog, Zeke, and desperately tries to convince his parrots, Annie and Sigmund Freud, to speak (English).